RICHARD A. McCORMICK AND THE
RENEWAL OF MORAL THEOLOGY

Richard A. McCormick and the Renewal of Moral Theology

by

Paulinus Ikechukwu Odozor, C.S.Sp.

UNIVERSITY OF NOTRE DAME PRESS
Notre Dame and London

Library of Congress Cataloging-in-Publication Data

Odozor, Paulinus Ikechukwu.
  Richard A. McCormick and the renewal of moral theology
/ by Paulinus Ikechukwu Odozor.
    p.   cm.
  Originally presented as the author's thesis (doctoral)—
Toronto School of Theology.
  Includes bibliographical references and index.
  ISBN 0-268-01648-8 (alk. paper)
  1. McCormick, Richard A., 1922-   . 2. Christian
ethics--History—20th century.   3. Catholic Church—
Doctrines--History—20th century.   I. Title.
BJ1249.O36 1994
241'.042—dc20   *94-15941*
                                                              CIP

∞ *The paper used in this publication meets the minimum requirements of the*
American Standard for Information Sciences—Permanence of Paper for
Printed Library Materials, ANSI Z39.48-1984.

*To the Reverend Thaddeus Nwagha Ihejiofor, Ph.D. (1941–1991),
exemplary priest, teacher, social critic and mentor,
in cherished but tearful memory*

CONTENTS

ACKNOWLEDGMENTS

Every publishing endeavor is a collaborative effort. This is true especially in theology, where one has to draw on the tradition and upon authors past and present in order to make the faith intelligible to one's self as well as to one's readers. I wish therefore to express appreciation to all those who shared in this project. My debts to published authors are acknowledged as best I can in the notes and in the bibliography. I also want to express sincere thanks to Professor Béla Somfai, S.J., my teacher, for his direction while I was in Toronto and for his continued friendship.

My gratitude to the Spiritan Province of Nigeria, who provided me the opportunity for graduate studies, and to the Trans-Canadian Province, who supported me financially and otherwise. Eugene E. Uzukwu, my friend and colleague at the Spiritan International School of Theology and my teacher during my seminary days, awakened my interest in the entire renewal movement in theology in post–Vatican II theology. I thank the following friends in the Nigerian Spiritan family for their support: Jude Ogbenna, Alex Ekechukwu, Gabriel Ezewudo, Francis Akwue, Remy Onyewuenyi, and Oliver Iwuchukwu. I am immensely grateful to Séan Byron, Barney Kelly, Joseph Kelly, Gary McCarthy, George Webster, Gerald Fitzpatrick and Rose Ann Hart from the Trans-Canadian Spiritan family for their kindness and generosity. Thanks too, to Mike Obi Onwuemelie, Spiritan Provincial of Nigeria, for his support and his continued effort to build a strong academic and research community at the Spiritan International School of Theology, Attakwu, Enugu.

Special gratitude goes to my brother and best friend Livy, to his wife, Ekwutosi Odozor, to my niece and nephew Ezinwanne and Uzodinmma for their familial support in Toronto. My father, T. N.

Odozor, my other brothers and sisters and their families: Cajetan and Helen, Anna and Frank, Eunice and Evaristus, Justina and Michael, Leo, Hyginus, Oluchi; my uncles B. F. and Philo Akor, Cletus and Christina; my cousins Elizabeth Agwu, Kelechi Akor, Chika Akor, Ebere, Ogechi, and my entire extended family never ceased to pray for me. This work is a tribute to their love.

I thank the following friends for their loyalty and care: M. Bernadette Anwuluorah, I.H.M.; Mary and Kevin Kelly; Titus and Paula Owolabi; Ida and Al De Souza; Mary Anne, Chris, Steph, and Nick Chambers; Chiedu and Ifeyinwa Onyiuke; Emeka and Ngozi Okongwu; Sabina Abiaga; Jude Igwemezie; 'Diche and David Ofordile; Patsy and Gordon Dalgano. May God bless you all. Thanks to my friend Cate McBurney for support during my research in Toronto. Cate challenged many of my assumptions and therefore provided me the opportunity to clarify my thoughts. She generously read and critiqued this entire work, as did Cora Twohig-Moengangongo and Meg Lavin, fellow doctoral students at Regis College, Toronto. I thank them immensely.

To my colleagues on the faculty of the Spiritan International School of Theology, Attakwu, Enugu, Nigeria: Innocent Anyanwu, Titus Chilaka, Augustine Ejike, Ernest Ezeogu, Myles Fay, Joe Gross, Cora Twohig-Moengangongo, Breifne Walker, Anthony Ekwunife, and Raymond C. Arazu, I am indebted beyond measure for the very challenging and stimulating context in which we labor together.

I offer my gratitude to the community of St. Augustine's Seminary of Toronto for a congenial teaching and writing environment: to John Boisseneau, rector; to the library staff—Jean Harris, C.S.M., Maryam Rezai-Atrie, and Theresa Vicioso—who patiently handled my requests for books and articles. Chigozie Okeke, my student at the Spiritan International School of Theology, helped to prepare the index for this book as did M. E. Okafor, research librarian at the Nnamdi Azikiwe Library, University of Nigeria, Nsukka. My thanks to them.

Finally, I want to thank Richard McCormick, S.J., for his interest in this work. The more I come to know this genuine Christian scholar, the more I appreciate the importance of his contribution to the renewal of moral theology.

INTRODUCTION

It is impossible to live outside every human tradition or, as one author puts it, to speak "from nowhere."[1] In other words, "there is no standing ground, no place for enquiry, no way to engage in the practices of advancing, evaluating, accepting, and rejecting reasoned arguments apart from that which is provided by some particular tradition or other."[2] To be steeped in a tradition therefore gives one the opportunity to be versed in some particular categories of thought and to acquire a context from which one can make sense of existence and of all reality in general.

Traditions sometimes share some beliefs, images, and texts with one another. However, a particular tradition may also employ its own standards to evaluate even commonly shared data. Consequently, it may, with time, come up with a distinct set of criteria for what constitutes rational discourse, and a distinct list of topics about which a rational discourse may be conducted. Therefore, anyone who works in the context of a particular tradition becomes affected by the 'categories' it employs for its argumentation and by its definition of rationality and rational discourse. One finds oneself caught up, as it were, in the concerns and interests of the tradition. For example, whereas moral theologians living and working in the latter half of the twentieth century would likely engage in discussions about third-world debt, abortion, the environment, the arms race, and so on, their predecessors in the thirteenth century would have been concerned with the morality of usury or of the revenge by "the insulted gentleman," and their counterparts in the first half of this century would have spent their time arguing over the morality of obliteration bombing or prize fighting. Whereas theologians in Latin America in the twentieth century may be concerned with the gospel as a message of liberation from oppression for the poor, their counterparts in Africa could be concerned with issues related to inculturation, the wider ecumenism and neo-colonialism, while theologians in North America wrestle with questions raised by gender inequality, new technologies, and consumerism.[3] As Richard McCormick says, all of us do indeed bear "the restricting marks of the cultural contexts in which we work."[4]

The inquiring subject may reach a point where the marks of the cultural context become too restricting and very inadequate for the evaluation of reality. This can result in an 'epistemological crisis', that is, a realization that the paradigms hitherto employed for the interpretation of reality have become a source of error or deception. This sense of inadequacy may be heightened by the subject's discovery of a set of paradigms that are recognized to be superior to the ones provided by the previous tradition.[5]

People react to an epistemological crisis either by capitulating to the new paradigms or by skillfully coopting elements of the new tradition which are thought to give it an edge over the old one. The first case is akin to conversion, "a change of course and direction."[6] The second example reflects a platonic confidence in the process of dialectic, that is, in the movement from a lesser to a greater knowledge of truth. In either case, what is involved is the construction of a new narrative whose principal aim is to help the agent to understand better the previously held beliefs and their binding force in the past. In the words of MacIntyre,

> The narrative in terms of which he or she at first understood and ordered experience is itself made into the subject of an enlarged narrative. The agent has come to understand how the criteria of truth must be reformulated. He has tried to become epistemologically self-conscious and at a certain point he may have to acknowledge two conclusions: the first is that his new forms of understanding may themselves be put into question at any time; the second is that, because in such crises the criteria of truth may always be put to question . . . we are never in a position to claim that now we possess the truth or now we are fully rational.[7]

Therefore, epistemological crises can lead to the dissolution of any propositionalist notion of truth and is an acute awareness of the limit, not only of one's scheme of reference, but of one's ability to grasp reality as well.

Roman Catholic moral theology is currently beset by an epistemological crisis. What began as mere dissatisfaction with some aspects of the method employed by most moral theologians has turned into a major debate over every aspect of the discipline. Since the Second Vatican Council, every aspect of the method, content, and goal of Catholic moral theology has come into question and become the subject of long and sometimes acrimonious debate. The issues involved have ranged from the nature of moral obligation to the manner of determining it. They include specific questions such as birth control, moral norms, abortion, the place of women in the Church, the role of authority (that is, scriptural, magisterial, or natural law), and so forth. For a discipline which, until recently, was very sure of its methods, content, and goals,[8] the current crisis is most intriguing.

While some regard the state of contemporary moral theology as chaotic,[9] others, McCormick included, do not appear to be that negative in their assessment. For McCormick, the crisis in moral theology is indicative of a transition from a classicist worldview to a historical consciousness within the discipline.[10] Some measure of 'chaos', he believes, is the price every human society pays for reform; "it can be no less so in the *ecclesia semper reformanda.*"[11] Moreover, the crisis in moral theology points to a tradition which is truly alive. As one author puts it, a living tradition is a "historically extended, socially embodied argument, an argument precisely about the goods which constitute that tradition." In such a tradition, the search for the human good is not settled or sealed.[12] For McCormick, what is required concerning the argument over the nature of the good in morality in the contemporary Church is faith in the ability of the Holy Spirit to ensure that "we moral theologians, in our honest if stumbling efforts to recover the freshness of a very old morality, will not, indeed *cannot* scuttle the Bark of Peter."[13]

Vatican II and the Call to Renewal

Long before the Second Vatican Council many people in the Church believed that moral theology could no longer adequately

confront the problems of modern society. The two world wars, the
great scientific and technological developments in the modern era,
the rise of new nations, and the emergent pluralism among these
nations and in the world at large were only some of the factors which
posed new questions for Christian living. Moral theology between
the two Vatican Councils was aware of many of these problems and
tried to resolve some of them, for example, those pertaining to
sexuality and the use of medical technology. However, the tools that
were employed proved to be inadequate. Consequently, the resultant solutions were, for the most part, out of touch with authentic
Christian and human values. By the time of the Second Vatican
Council, the dissatisfaction with this theology had become quite
palpable and led to the Council's call for the renewal of moral
theology.[14] As Josef Fuchs points out, this injunction had nothing to
do with the preeminence of moral theology over other theological
disciplines. The Council considered that the content and presentation of moral theology left much to be desired.[15]

Although several efforts to renew moral theology were already
afoot in the 1920s, the response which followed the call of the
Second Vatican Council was phenomenal. One of the theologians
who have been at the forefront in the renewal of moral theology is
Richard A. McCormick, S.J., the John A. O'Brien Professor of
Christian Ethics at the University of Notre Dame in Indiana. His
life as a theologian spans the period before, during, and after
Vatican II. For the past thirty-five years he has been an author,
critic, commentator, teacher, and consultant. His "Notes on Moral
Theology," which appeared on a regular basis in *Theological Studies*
from 1965 to 1987, have made him a well-known commentator on
and participant in the renewal movement. McCormick speaks of his
life and work as a theologian this way:

> I was trained in and for some years taught a moral theology with deep
> roots in what is now called a "classicist mentality.". . . The eccle-
> siological and moral theological perspectives introduced by Vatican
> II have led to a consciousness that is much more historically oriented.
> That has meant a new willingness to re-examine some traditional
> formulations that are authoritatively proposed to the Catholic com-
> munity. That task of doing this is far from easy and, obviously, not
> always successful. Nonetheless, I believe there is a real value in

our time in opening the shutters to allow others to see attempts at this re-examination. There are some who have resisted such a re-examination and have remained comfortable in a relatively traditional outlook and vocabulary. There are others who have felt the need to do so because they have never been thoroughly trained in the "traditional Catholic Categories." The present author fits somewhere in between. Trained in the classicist mentality, he has become conscious of both its strengths and its weaknesses–and the need to correct or modify the latter.[16]

Martin Marty notes that McCormick's whole career "has been given over to opening up the Catholic treasury, trying out its artifacts and achievements in the contemporary world, risking its values in a world that might need them more than it knows."[17] Such positive assessment of McCormick's contribution to moral theology abounds. There is another view, however, albeit a minority one, that he is no more than a popularizer of other people's thought. It is my intention in this volume (a) to establish the contribution of Richard A. McCormick to the renewal of moral theology, (b) to show whether and to what extent he has been consistent and coherent in his moral theological discourse, and (c) to critique his contribution to the renewal in moral theology.

Although he has written extensively, McCormick has not written an all-encompassing work in ethics. Systematization of his work is therefore an important objective in this study. The aim is to see whether his interests in ethics are wide-ranging enough to merit the adulation his admirers lavish on him and whether there are key hubs around which his work rotates.

To effectively pursue my aims I have divided the work itself into seven chapters. The first chapter situates McCormick; defines the historical, social, and ecclesial contexts of his formation; and delineates the parameters of pre-Vatican II moral theology. The next five chapters take up the themes I believe to be central to understanding McCormick's work: the nature of Christian ethics, the Church as moral teacher, anthropology, proportionate reasoning, and casuistry. The seventh chapter evaluates McCormick's contribution to the renewal of moral theology.

I have tried in the work to show the connection among these various chapters. The overall logic is simple: chapter one provides a context for understanding McCormick's work. The second and third chapters examine his theology. The fourth chapter reconstructs his view of the moral agent as being and moral actor. The fifth and sixth chapters consider the agency of the agent; that is, how and on what basis the agent should act in the world.

Another important element of method in this work is the attention it pays to history. To the extent that it is possible, I have tried to show how McCormick's thought on some of the issues evolved. I have also tried to find the reason behind his change from one position to another within the larger ecclesial, intellectual, and social world with which he has had to interact or to which he has had to respond. In short, I have tried to read McCormick in context—ecclesial and American. Attention to historical details has its price, though. An important 'cost' is the occasional repetition of previous information in order to explain a new insight or phenomenon in the author's work. Another is the occasional projection of a narrative voice over the analytical and the critical. I have consciously tried to minimize these shortcomings. Where they occur, they reflect a deliberate decision to narrate rather than critique or analyze as a way to treat the subject matter as fairly as possible.

The volume relies on three principal sources. McCormick's published works constitute the primary source. I have also relied on a number of secondary sources, which include authors with whom McCormick has been in dialogue and who have had an appreciable impact on him in regard to the topics treated herein; authors who have written about McCormick or about his work; and authors whose works shed light on the issues discussed.

The third source for this work consists of oral interviews which were granted to me by Edward Sheridan, S.J., in Toronto; Walter Farrell, S.J., and Howard Grey, S.J., in Detroit; and Richard McCormick himself at Notre Dame, Indiana. These interviews are available on tape. They provide information not available anywhere else.

1

BACKGROUND AND CONTEXT

In the introduction I alluded to the importance of context and to the role it plays in defining rationality and rationally acceptable discourse, because every theology is contextual and "a product not only of the religion it investigates and expounds but also of the cultural ideals and norms that set its problems and direct its solutions."[1] McCormick's cultural context is American. He was born in the United States and received all but two years of his theological training there. He is also a devout member of the Roman Catholic Church. This chapter collects the various 'memories' out of which McCormick speaks, with the intent of showing their impact on his theological formation and tracing their early influence on his theology.[2]

BIOGRAPHICAL SKETCH

Richard A. McCormick was born October 3, 1922, in Toledo, Ohio. He entered the novitiate of the Society of Jesus at the age of eighteen. After four years of spiritual formation and undergraduate studies, he went to study classics at West Baden College, a Jesuit seminary affiliated with Loyola University in Chicago. He received a B.A. degree in classics in 1945. For the next three years he studied philosophy at the same school. In 1947 he was sent to St. Ignatius High School in Cleveland, Ohio, to teach Greek and English. One of his students there remembers him as a good teacher who took "justifiable pride in being a pedagogue."[3] During this same time, he also received a Master's degree in English from Loyola University.

In 1950 McCormick returned to West Baden College to study theology and was ordained a priest in 1953. During these years his most influential teachers were John L. McKenzie in Old Testament studies, and John Connery and Edwin Healy in moral theology.[4] In 1955 McCormick went to the Pontifical Gregorian University in Rome to pursue doctoral studies. Two years later he obtained a doctorate in moral theology by defending a dissertation which dealt with the morality of removing a fetus probably dead to save the life of the mother.

West Baden was a town of five hundred people in southern Indiana, sixty miles from Louisville and one hundred and twenty miles from Indianapolis. The college was located in a former health spa with a golf course, swimming pool, and race stables. The building itself was doughnut shaped, with some rooms facing outwards and some facing the inner circle, which was covered with a glass dome. The outside rooms served as residences, while the inner ones were used as library, meeting rooms, and classrooms. Like the dome, the rest of the building was made of glass. At night the moon would shine through the glass dome on the potted palm trees and the terrazzo floors. Many former students of West Baden College have very pleasant memories of its idyllic surroundings. However, they also point out that it had notable problems. First, because of the shape of the building, the place was often very hot in the summer. Consequently, the community had to move to Ormena in northern Michigan for six to ten weeks of holiday and summer school. Also, as a consequence of the rural setting of the college, students and faculty were academically and socially isolated from the rest of the world.[5]

Rome was the most important intellectual center of the Catholic Church when McCormick arrived there. During the pontificates of Pius XI and Pius XII, Jesuit professors at the Gregorian University were particularly influential consultors of the Vatican. In questions of morality, Francis Hürth supposedly was responsible for major writings of Pope Pius XII on sexual and medical questions. Similarly, Arthur Vermeersch had done a lot of work on marriage for Pope Pius XI.[6] In Rome, McCormick came in contact with theologians who were to exercise considerable influence on his thought. These included Lucio Rodrigo, S.J., whose unpublished manual provided McCormick with the framework for the resolution of the question he studied in his thesis, and Josef Fuchs, S.J., with whom he has retained a close friendship.[7]

After his return from Rome in 1957, McCormick went to West Baden College to teach moral theology.[8] In 1965 the college moved to

Aurora, Illinois, on the outskirts of Chicago. There it became the Bellarmine School of Theology of Loyola University and a member of the South Side Theological Consortium, a loose affiliation of theological schools belonging to various Christian denominations. This setting provided McCormick with an ecumenical context for doing theology and an opportunity to consolidate some useful and lasting relationships with theologians from other Christian traditions. McCormick left the Bellarmine School of Theology in 1974 to become the Rose Kennedy Professor of Ethics at the Kennedy Institute at Georgetown University. In 1986 he became the John A. O'Brien Professor of Christian Ethics at the University of Notre Dame.

During these years McCormick also served on the ethics committees and on the boards of many associations, task forces, and learned societies, including the American Hospital Association, American Fertility Society, National Hospice Organization, Catholic Health Association, the Ethics Advisory Board of the Department of Health, Education and Welfare, and others. He is a past president of the Catholic Theological Society of America. In 1969 he received the society's Cardinal Spellman award as outstanding theologian of the year. At last count, McCormick has been conferred with honorary doctorates by thirteen universities. From 1965 to 1987 he was the author of the semi-annual (later annual) "Notes on Moral Theology" for *Theological Studies*. Here is how McCormick sums up his life and activities during this period.

> During those more than three decades it has been my privilege to be involved in thousands of difficult cases, in many committees and advisory boards and in the lives of many individuals and families. . . . Since 1965 I have composed "Notes on Moral Theology" for *Theological Studies*, a task that has brought me enlightenment, humility (I hope), and the friendship of colleagues around the world.[9]

AMERICAN CATHOLIC EXPERIENCE PRIOR TO VATICAN II

From the second half of the nineteenth century until the eve of the Second Vatican Council, three different trends of American

Catholic thought could be identified in the response to the American intellectual and cultural milieu: congregational Catholicism; cultural Catholicism; and "a form of neo-Thomism which attempted to present its conception of Catholicism as an alternative to the theological and philosophical strains of American culture."[10]

Congregational Catholicism was characterized by a desire to "establish an independent national Church with separation of Church and State."[11] Although it was not a theology but a political approach through which some individuals sought to identify and organize Catholicism in the United States in the Republican era, still it left in the American Church a lingering feeling of independence from all outside control and a desire for "ecclesiastical liberty, which the temper of the age and of our people requires."[12]

The next phase of American Catholicism was that of cultural Catholicism, which coincided with the arrival in the second half of the nineteenth century and in the early part of the twentieth century of large numbers of Catholics from Germany, Italy, Ireland, and Poland. This new wave of immigrations occasioned three major problems to which the American Catholic hierarchy tried to find solutions. The first problem was whether and to what extent American immigrant Catholics should be allowed to assimilate into the mainstream of American culture. The second question was whether or not the Catholic Church should be organized along the lines of the various nationalities which were becoming numerically prominent in the Church. The third problem pertained to the many secret Masonic organizations, which were tolerated by Protestants but already condemned as unchristian, atheistic, and anti-Catholic by European Catholicism. The labor movement, at that time beginning to take shape in many parts of the country, was suspect to many Catholic bishops because unions were considered clandestine and part of the society of Freemasons. The question also arose whether Catholics should join the labor movement, which was known at this time as the Knights of Labor. Although Rome preferred that Catholics form their own labor movements, since affiliation with already existing groups would make them cooperators in the sin of others, cultural Catholicism saw in a unified labor movement a potential instrument "which might alleviate the poverty experienced by so many of the immigrants."[13]

Cultural Catholicism generated a very bitter debate between conservatives and liberals in the American Church and the general public. Jay P. Dolan states that "what was at issue was not just fraternalization with Protestants, membership of secret societies, or support for the parochial school. These were but singular manifestations of a larger issue, namely the attitude of the Church toward the modern age."[14]

In 1899 Pope Leo XIII addressed a letter to Cardinal Gibbons of Baltimore and, through him, to the rest of the American hierarchy, condemning what he described as 'Americanism.' According to the pope, the principles of Americanism were forcefully expressed in a book whose French edition had just appeared with an introduction by a French priest, Felix Klein.[15] In the aforementioned letter, the pope said:

> The principles on which the new opinions we have mentioned are based may be reduced to this: that, in order the more easily to bring over to Catholic doctrine those who dissent from it, the Church ought to adapt herself somewhat to our advanced civilization, and, relaxing her ancient rigor, show some indulgence to modern popular theories and methods. Many think that this is to be understood not only with regard to the rule of life, but also to the doctrines in which the *deposit* of faith is contained. For they contend that it is opportune, in order to work in a more attractive way upon the wills of those who are not in accord with us, to pass certain heads of doctrines, as if of lesser moment, or to so soften them that they may not have the same meaning which the Church has invariably held.[16]

The pope further stated that "the rule of life which is laid down for Catholics is not of such a nature as to admit modifications, according to the diversity of time and place."[17] Dolan notes that the pope was fighting "a cluster of liberal ideas," which espoused active virtues, "an active, energetic laity, the dwelling of the divine Spirit in individuals, a more tolerant attitude toward Protestants, the need for the Church to adapt itself to the age, and the superiority of the American version of Catholicism to that of the Old World."[18] Also, the pope viewed 'Americanism' with antipathy because it was in fundamental opposition to the prevalent neo-scholasticism, which he had espoused a few years earlier in his encyclical on the revival of Thomism.

Compounding the problem was a difference of perspectives. The liberals manifested sensitivity to the idea of historical development in the area of religion, whereas in Rome the neo-scholastics were of the classical frame of mind, which viewed religion as absolutely immune to change. Thus, the crisis over Americanism represented a clash not only between opposing cultures but also between conflicting worldviews.[19]

Leo's XIII's letter brought the 'Americanism' debate to an end. However, what the letter could never suppress was the debate concerning the relationship between religion and culture and, more precisely, the attitude of the Christian Church to the world around it.[20] With Richard McCormick, as with some other American theologians, this debate surfaces again in the attempt to re-read the Christian story in light of modern scientific and technological advances, and in the effort to initiate dialogue between the gospel and society. In a way, the spirit of cultural Catholicism lives on in spite of *Testem Benevolentiae*. In McCormick's work one gets a feeling for the urgent need for the faith to be in dialogue with its host culture and perhaps the most sustained effort to construct a moral theology which is truly Catholic and truly American. This is so, not just because he is American, but because the questions he raises and the issues he deals with arise from his American cultural context. The solutions he proffers also reflect his experience as an American Christian.

The 'Americanism' debate was a forerunner of the much more widespread debate over modernism that engulfed the Church from the time of Pope Pius X until the Second Vatican Council.[21] Pius X's campaign against modernism contrasts sharply with Leo XIII's earlier effort to promote Thomism. The aim and spirit of the encyclical of Pius X against modernism was very different from that of *Aeterni Patris*.[22] While the former blocked some avenues, marking them 'off limits' for Catholic scholarship, the latter pointed decisively to a path along which all Catholic philosophy and theology worthy of that name ought to travel. In America and most other places the Thomism Leo's encyclical promoted "strengthened the case of Catholic unity and was seen as a strong defense against the violent extremes of modern life."[23] The same cannot be said of *Pascendi*, the letter on modernism. It brought bitterness, mistrust, and frustration throughout the Catholic community.

Leo XIII's letter against 'Americanism' and Pius X's directive against modernism had a devastating effect on many aspects of American Catholicism. For example, they isolated many American Catholics from their compatriots. By establishing and running its own hospitals, grade and high schools, as well as universities, the American Catholic Church protected Catholics from the cradle to the grave and made sure that Catholics had as little contact as possible with the 'corrupting' influences and ideas of the world around them. The result was a ghetto in which an entire Church, as one author states, "lapsed into an intellectual slumber from which it did not waken until the 1940s."[24] Another author summarizes the effects of these papal directives in this way:

> The condemnation of Americanism in 1899 effectively put an end to the ecclesiastical controversy but it did little to stop the increasing Catholic absorption in the assumption of American innocence. The condemnation of modernism in 1907 and the repression which followed had a more substantial effect. It did not so much cut Catholics from American culture as it locked them into those nineteenth-century assumptions which Modernism (not simply the theological, but the philosophical and cultural dimensions as well) proceeded to smash.[25]

By the time Richard McCormick was entering the intellectual life of his society, American Catholics were involved in the mainstream of American political and economic life, but they were still steeped in an outdated and inward-looking religious milieu, which was a product of the Thomistic/Scholastic revival initiated by Leo XIII.[26] It was in this intellectually insular world, symbolized by the isolation of West Baden College from the rest of the world, that McCormick had his theological formation and the beginning of his academic work.

THE MANUALIST TRADITION IN CATHOLIC MORAL THEOLOGY

In moral theology, the effects of the Thomistic revival were discernible after 1897 in the textbooks (manuals) that served as the instructional texts in Catholic universities and seminaries up until

Vatican II. Not only did these texts claim that their contents were "based on the work of St. Thomas Aquinas and other modern authors," but there were indications that they did try consciously to appropriate the insights from Thomas's work. McCormick's knowledge of the tradition of the manuals is phenomenal. He described the effect of these texts on his thinking in my interview with him:

> I think that one of the things I would be thankful for was that I started moral theology at a time when we had to teach from the manuals. I got to know the manuals very thoroughly. I read six or seven manuals for every single presentation of every single subject. I got to know the tradition as it was presented in those manuals very thoroughly. I am grateful for that because it exposed me to a point of view which I think had an awful lot of good balance to it. The major defects of the manuals include the fact that they are heavily concerned with sinfulness and the degree of sinfulness. They are confession oriented. This slanted the whole moral view. There wasn't the grand view of the moral life that you hope to find in moral theology. Granted all these limitations, I think there is a great deal of wisdom in the way the manuals went about their casuistry and their qualification of moral obligation. They were very careful.[27]

Because the manuals were of tremendous importance in McCormick's theological formation, it is necessary to highlight the principal characteristics and presuppositions of this tradition in moral theology.

The manuals were a product of Tridentine reforms (1545–1563) and were meant to prepare clerics for their duties as confessors.[28] Influenced by the basic parameters of Scholastic theology, they exhibit remarkable uniformity in many ways. They all treat the same topics—often in the same sequence—and they tend to share a similar position on issues. As one of the best representatives of this school stated, "A writer on Moral Theology today must be indebted beyond measure to the labour of past writers, for the matter is one that has been treated with the greatest acumen and scholarship during well-nigh three centuries, and there is no room for originality."[29] They also tend to follow probabilism and pay a great deal of attention to various views on a matter.

The manuals organized their materials around the exitus/ reditus theme which had been the plan of the *Summa Theologiae* of St. Thomas.[30]

> [The] architectonic idea was the idea of God, considered in his inner being and in his exterior creative and redemptive work. St. Thomas' idea of God was the idea of God who was related to the universe as its originative source and its ultimate end. St. Thomas' God was the triune God, who was at once creator and the satiating supernatural goal, to be possessed by man's intellect and will in the beatific vision which was the culmination of man's life of grace.[31]

This principle, however, made its way into the manuals in a truncated form. Questions related to creation (the exitus theme) and the role of Christ, the mediator, were relegated to dogmatic theology leaving the practical aspects of man's return to the Creator for detailed study. Since moral theology was considered the study of the morality of human conduct in relation to humanity's ultimate end,[32] its aim was to explain the laws of human conduct in reference to humanity's supernatural destiny and to investigate the morality of human acts in relation to this end. Humanity's *raison d'etre* is to know, love, and serve God.[33] Every good moral act has "God's extrinsic glory" and "man's happiness through the vision and fruition of God" as its goal.[34]

The theology of the manuals presumed that some human acts were always morally evil by definition, that is, without regard to circumstances and to the intention of the agent. These were called intrinsically evil acts. Since human nature never changes, prescriptions of natural law make universal and exceptionless demands on the moral agent to act in accordance with its exigencies. As Pope Pius XII wrote, these exceptionless demands pertain to the mysterious dignity of the person's activity. One is capable of fulfilling this demand by single acts, and thus, engage oneself vis-à-vis the absolute. On the other hand, one can refuse to surrender to the absolute and thus dispose oneself in the opposite direction.[35]

Human activity was guided by natural law, interpreted and given by a human authority (positive law). The manuals tried to model their natural law theory on that of St. Thomas for whom every law, including natural law,[36] is a manifestation of the eternal law, which is God's plan for the government of things which are foreknown to God.[37] All laws, insofar as they partake of reason, are derived from the eternal law. The first of these is natural law. As the rational creature's participation in the eternal law, natural law is founded on human nature and pertains primarily to those things which are common to human nature; namely, the preservation of the thing that is possessed, the preservation of the species, and the inclination to the good which human beings possess in accordance with reason.[38] Every agent acts for an end, which is "the good." The first principle of practical reason is based, therefore, on that good which all things seek after. This principle is also the first precept of natural law and the very basis of every other precept of natural law; namely, that good is to be done and pursued and evil is to be avoided. 'Good' must be understood as "that toward which each thing tends by its own orientation"[39] or natural inclination. For Thomas, as I have already indicated, the goods toward which human beings incline are self preservation, self-perpetuation, and the orientation to act in accord with reason.

There is in Aquinas's work both an understanding of nature in regard to essential attributes and nature as a quest for the *humanum*. Both concepts of human nature can complement each other. In any case, they are in tension and must be held in tension. Being and becoming must therefore be held in dynamic tension. Otherwise, any use of the term 'natural' in natural law risks being ideological. The manuals were hardly able to maintain this dynamic tension. While they identified the natural law with 'right reason', that is, with human experience considered in light of the act and circumstances of the agent in other areas of human activity, in matters of human sexuality they reduced the role of reason to discovering the will of God solely on the basis of human biological facticity.[40] Consequently, the conclusions the manuals reached on concrete issues pertaining to sexuality and use of the faculty of speech were invariably the same and always in favor of the view that one should do nothing to interfere with the natural orientation of these faculties.

Human nature, *recta ratio*, the conformity of life to the end willed by God, or all of these dimensions together constitute the norm of morality. Only those actions which are in conformity with human nature are considered right conduct. They are right because by being in conformity with human nature in itself and "in its relations," these actions manifest the agent's willingness to observe the eternal law and will of God. Thus, as I pointed out above, only such actions, which obey God's law, can lead the human person to the end for which God created humanity. Why and in what way this is so and whether there is an intrinsic or extrinsic connection between such actions and the eternal reward is hardly established by the manuals.

The manuals do, however, establish the basis for the consideration of the moral quality of an act. Actions can be considered right or wrong in relation to object, end, and circumstance; that is, an action is morally good if the object, end, and circumstances are good. The manuals refer to these three elements as the *fontes moralitates* (sources of morality). Objects are things to which the will tends. They can be moral or immoral depending on whether they conform or are contrary to the exigencies of rational human nature. The motion of the will takes its quality from the object. A will which tends toward a good end is good, just as one which tends toward a bad end is bad. Consequently, "a good intention cannot make a bad action good." Thomas Slater argues in this regard that "it is not lawful to tell a lie to save one's life. Evil must not be done that good may come of it."[41] The manuals understand circumstances in the Thomistic sense as "whatever conditions are outside of an act and yet in some way touch the human act."[42] In other words, they refer to the accidental (as opposed to the substantial) aspects of an action which can form and complete that particular action. For the manuals, circumstances can affect the intensity, quality, or duration of an act, and thus lessen or heighten its moral significance.

A considerable amount of space was also devoted to the treatment of positive law. Although it seems out of place, the importance of this tract derives from the fact that it helps the manualists to introduce the notion of obligation and sanction into moral theology and thus to take account of the human person as a social being.[43] Despite the fact that all the authors usually began the section on law with the Thomistic definition of law as an ordinance of practical reason for the common good promulgated by one who has care of the community, they did not always display uniform understanding of the source of legal obligation. Most manualists were more Suarezian than Thomistic, in that they tended to subscribe to a voluntaristic rather than a rationalistic conception of law. For these, law was the product of the will (Suarez) more than of reason (Aquinas). This not only meant that "a law is something that comes from outside the individual, determined by someone in authority," but also implied that its binding force did not come from any claim to inherent reasonableness, but simply from the will of the legislator.[44] God as Supreme Will is the supreme lawgiver. In the Church, God has willed that there should be a supreme authority to look after the spiritual and temporal welfare of the faithful. This power resides in the pope as Vicar of Christ. He is the lawgiver for the whole Church.

Laws imply obligation on the part of the governed. The content of this obligation depends, like the law itself, on the will of the legislator: "The legislator may intend to impose a moral obligation under the pain of sin, for God commands us to obey our lawful superiors when they impose a strict precept upon us." To go contrary to the will of the legislator is to offend God and is thus a sin.[45] Authoritarian voluntarism was therefore an essential characteristic of the manuals. It was apparent in their treatment of the role of the pope in the Church, the bishop in his diocese, the superiors of religious orders in their communities, and so forth. Although its basic purpose was to combat what the manuals considered lay or autonomous morality, its effect was to give the impression that an action was right or wrong according to the will of the superior—and ultimately of God. The manuals managed, however, to safeguard the freedom and responsibility of the individual in matters of right and wrong through their doctrine on conscience. Conscience was the authoritative guide of human conduct and "the dictate of practical reason deciding that a particular action is right or wrong."[46] As guide and judge, its role was the clarification of the moral implications of the virtues as well as the discernment of the lawfulness of particular human actions.

Although the ultimate aim of moral action is to please God, it may not always be clear in concrete circumstances which actions can achieve this purpose. This is why the manuals speak of certain, dubious, or probable conscience. When conscience can affirm or assent to what is known without fear of mistake, that conscience is said to be certain. If, however, conscience knows no reason why it should either affirm or deny a proposition, or if it cannot affirm one proposition over another, then that conscience is said to be doubtful. Doubts can arise due to several factors. It is in these situations of doubt that the reflex principles play a part in the theology of the manuals. The reflex principles were important insofar as they helped the agent claim responsibility for his or her actions against a system that was otherwise excessively authoritarian. Following St. Thomas, the manuals maintained that conscience, even an erroneous one, was supreme and the ultimate guide for the moral agent in the subjective discernment of the rightness or wrongness of a particular act.

For the manuals, sin was primarily a free transgression of the law of God. Prümmer, for example, defines sin in Augustinian terms; that is, as word, deed, or concupiscence which is against the eternal law of God.[47] Sins are human and moral acts done or engaged in with knowledge and in freedom. Thus, for acts to be sinful, it is necessary that the agent knows them as such and consents to doing them.

Another important element in the theology of the manuals was their doctrine on the virtues. The section on virtues was usually the only part devoted to the treatment of the character of the moral agent. It was also meant to serve as link between human agent and the meritorious and supernatural dimension of human acts. Virtues are defined by the manuals as permanent human habits and dispositions which incline the agent to follow reason or faith in order to achieve true happiness. The manuals refer to the theological virtues of faith, hope, and charity as infused virtues. These virtues "incline us to act in view of our supernatural duty, and give us the capacity to do so, in imitation of the perfect exemplar of Christian life; namely, Christ our Lord, and so to achieve our supernatural happiness."[48] This class of virtues is grace, because it is the result of God's gratuitous gift, given for a supernatural end. It is this quality that distinguishes these virtues from the 'acquired virtues' such as prudence, temperance, patience, and so on, which can only be acquired through hard work. God is the material and formal object of the theological virtues. It is for the purpose of ordering our lives to their ultimate end that God gives us the gifts of faith, hope, and love.

The manuals teach that human actions have merit. They refer to merit in general as "a certain value in an action which gives the agent the right to be rewarded by the one in whose behalf the action is performed."[49] Since morality is determined in relation to the will's disposition toward the law of God, merit in morality refers to one's right to be rewarded by God. The manuals make a distinction between condign and congruous merit. This distinction helps them establish the basis for considering an action meritorious. An action is condignly meritorious if there is a certain equality between the value of the action and its reward "such that the reward is due to the agent in justice."[50] When, on the other hand, there is no equality between the value of an action and its reward, the merit is congruous. Such is the case with supernatural rewards.[51]

Human actions must meet six conditions to be meritorious. Three of these pertain to the act itself, two pertain to the agent, and one pertains to God. The act must be morally good. It must be free. It must be supernatural; that is, "it must be done under the influence of divine actual grace, because this is necessary in order that human acts may be elevated to the supernatural plane."[52] The agent must be free and still a wayfarer.[53] The agent must be in the state of sanctifying grace. Last, but most important, the notion of merit in regard to human action presupposes the divine promise to accept human acts as meritorious.[54] The manuals manage in the end to hold on to God's freedom, to the gratuitous nature of grace, and to the human capacity, in spite of the fall, to respond to God's initiative.

Since Augustine's time theology has had to tackle the question of the ability of the human person in his or her natural state (that is, unaided by God) to know what to do, and of the human person's capability to do the right thing without supernatural aid.[55] The problem concerns the actual effects of the fall on human nature. What was the prelapsarian state like? Was nature which was neither elevated in Adam, nor fallen through sin, nor redeemed in Christ capable of a 'natural' desire for the Beatific Vision? Was this state of sharing 'owed' to it by God "who had created in him this natural desire"?[56] As John Mahoney points out, Church teaching as well as theological reflection have sought to maintain the gratuitous nature of God's grace. Grace is considered as something God 'owes' no one and to which no one has a right "based on the incompleteness or exigency arising from the nature which God created." Secondly, there has been a constant struggle to maintain that "man himself, even after sin, is somehow capable of actively co-operating and responding to God's overtures of grace."[57] These struggles are all reflected in the manuals' articulation of natural law and in their position on merit.

The problem of merit is therefore that of establishing how human activity can become a token for salvation. Because they have not incorporated the consideration of Jesus Christ as mediator, the manuals have difficulty establishing the merit of human activity and salvation. This is why the question of the role of faith in Jesus Christ in morality is so important and constitutes a logical point of entry into McCormick's work. However, before we come to this question in chapter two, we must first show the impact of the Scholastic manuals of moral theology on McCormick's doctoral dissertation and how McCormick begins his work within this tradition and typically expands its parameters.

MCCORMICK'S DOCTORAL DISSERTATION

STRUCTURE AND ARGUMENT

The question McCormick treated in his thesis is an issue of probabilities.[58] When a state of facts can be established only to a certain degree of probability, what is one allowed to do?

> When the mother is faced with a likelihood of almost certain death (this wording is deliberately general to cover the rather wide concept of certitude found in medical judgments) and her only hope lies in the removal from the uterus of a non-viable fetus probably but not certainly dead, is such a removal permissible?[59]

McCormick answered this question in several steps. First, he surveyed the history of the question and contemporary opinions in moral theology. He found that it did not receive much attention in the manuals and that the opinions of the authors were divided. According to tradition, the right to life is certain when the existence of a subject is certain. When it is uncertain, the rights of the subject also become uncertain. This principle, which antedates Alphonsus

Ligouri, also implies that it is intrinsically evil to expose an innocent subject to the danger of death. When the existence of the
subject is uncertain, one should give the benefit of doubt in favor of
life. In the past, moralists were divided on the moral liceity of
causing death to a certainly living fetus in order to avoid the certain
death of the mother. Some argued in favor on grounds that

> the child was considered as an unjust aggressor, or the death of the
> mother was said to be merely permitted; or again, the mother's right
> was alleged as the stronger of the two conflicting rights, or the child
> was said voluntarily to yield his right. [60]

Following the opinion of Thomas Sanchez, Alphonsus Ligouri
himself concluded that abortion would be wrong even when the life
of the fetus is in doubt. [61]

In the second step, McCormick examined the issue of the
probably dead fetus from the point of view of medicine to determine
whether the problem was a practical one. Although he recognized
that the case occurred only rarely, he argued that it must be studied
because it would lead to a clarification of principles. [62] Then he
proceeded to prove that the question could not be decided by using
the established principles of probabilism. A new approach was
needed, and he took this by arguing on the grounds of "proportionate reason."

Probabilism deals with the applicability of a (moral) law to
action, when its binding force for one's conscience becomes invinc-
ibly (unavoidably) doubtful. [63] McCormick argued that the case of
the probably dead fetus is not an issue of uncertain conscience but of
uncertain fact. The fetus may or may not be alive; it may or may not
be dead. Therefore, the moral law which protects the life of an
innocent subject cannot be applied. The case implies not the use of
probabilism but that of proportionate reasoning. To prove this,
McCormick pointed to the inherent ambiguity that results from
arguments based on probabilism. Many moralists forbade the violation of the life of a possibly dead fetus for the reason of factual doubt
pertinent to life. An action against life in this case implies at least a
virtual or hypothetical willingness to kill. [64] Other authors, however, have allowed the removal of the doubtfully dead fetus on the
grounds that the mother, whose existence is certain, has a certain

right to life, which prevails over the uncertain rights of the fetus. McCormick agreed with the axiom, To do something is the same in moral matters as to expose oneself to the danger of doing it.[65] Temerity or rash judgment occurs when an action is performed with an uncertain conscience or when one exposes oneself or others to probably harmful action without sufficient reason. Conversely, it is absent when the conscience is certain or in the case of probable harm which is done or allowed with proportionate reason. The removal of the probably dead fetus to save the life of the mother, McCormick continues, is not an instance of temerity when it is based on proportionate reason.

> I shall content myself with the opinion that given a proportionate reason, the law forbidding temerarious exposure simply ceases to bind. Hence it is not against the exigencies of justice to remove a fetus in which the presence of life is positively and invincibly doubtful to save the mother.[66]

By resorting to proportionate reasoning in this case, McCormick shows that the action here is not a direct killing of an innocent child and that the probable harm or evil which results from it is an excusable effect in these circumstances.

> In order that the act be licit according to any principle (probabilism or any other), the probable harm or evil result must be shown to be *an excusable effect* [emphasis added]. This is the same as saying that it must be shown that it is not a direct killing; for a direct killing is *always* forbidden. Conversely, if the effects can be shown to be excusable in some circumstances, it follows that it is not a direct killing as understood and absolutely forbidden by theologians.[67]

McCormick understands proportionate reason as a concrete value in relation to all other elements in the act. This value provides the basis for justifying the act itself. In other words, McCormick assumes a hierarchy of goods (*ordo bonorum*). Prudence dictates which of these goods should be chosen in times of conflict. This choice is not made arbitrarily, because some obligations are certain in all circumstances, even if there is a doubt of fact, because the good to be protected and secured "prevails over any good which can

be adduced as *incommodum*."[68] Prudence merely dictates what is
proportionate reason according to this prevalence of goods.[69]

Equally important in the determination of proportionality is
the relationship of the agent's will to the act and the nature of the act
itself. The manuals forbade every direct killing. The authors usually understood direct killing as that "which is chosen or willed
either *propter se* (as an end in itself) or *in se* (not for itself, but as a
necessary means)."[70] McCormick argues that this view ties the
notion of directness too closely to causality, that is, to the relationship of effect to cause. "Hence, whenever we have a *per se* relationship between a *single* effect and the cause, the effect is said to be a
direct killing."[71]

> Such a tendency (sc. to differentiate between direct and indirect by
> careful definition of the nature of the *opus*) has been necessary to
> avoid confusion between the *finis operis* and *finis operantis*. Yet it has
> led, it seems, to a false inference, or at least a false emphasis.[72]

Direct and indirect are designations of the intention of the agent.
However, the nature of the act, that is, the causal relationship of
single evil effect to cause, "indicates when the evil effect *must be
chosen* as a means" and is therefore "a good criterion of what must
be willed."[73]

Thus, McCormick does not base his judgment concerning
direct and indirect killing on intention alone, because there can be
more than one intention—the *finis operis* (the end of the act) and the
finis operantis (the end of the acting agent): "The latter may be
intended; the former, if it is a necessary means, *must be* intended.
This some authors have overlooked; and the oversight has led to a
pernicious misapplication of the terms direct and indirect."[74] A
direct action is thus an action which is causally related to a single
effect, or willed as a means for an effect. For, McCormick concludes, "when a single evil effect (sc. death) has a *per se* relation to the
cause, it cannot be concluded that the effect was willed or chosen *in
se* or *propter se*." Moreover, unless we could reach such a conclusion
about an action, we cannot conclude that the action is (in the case of
killing, for example) a direct one.[75]

The choice of the principle of proportionate reasoning makes
probabilism unnecessary in the determination of the morality of

removing a fetus probably dead to save the life of the mother. In other words, this case cannot be resolved on the probability of either the death or the life of the fetus. Instead, McCormick based the liceity of removing the doubtfully living fetus on the opinion of L. Rodrigo, which states that "the rights of an uncertain subject (uncertain by the uncertainty of the subject's existence) are automatically uncertain rights." Even so, the decision here is subject to the law which forbids the agent to make attempts (*attentare*) on the rights of a person without proportionate reason. McCormick believed that the proportionate reason which justifies the removal of a probably dead fetus is "the certain danger to the mother's life."[76] This reason even makes it an obligation in justice (in this situation of doubt and of danger to the mother) to attend to the certain rights of the mother against the merely probable rights of the probably dead fetus.[77]

In conclusion, McCormick located proportionate reason in a hierarchy of values (*ordo bonorum*). He claimed that the distinction between direct and indirect killing cannot be determined by the cause and effects relationship alone. He only insinuated but did not claim clearly that this intentionality (that is, direct and indirect) also hinges on proportionate reason.

McCormick's use of proportionate reason represents not only a radical departure from the position of the manuals, but it also anticipates Peter Knauer's efforts to reinterpret the principle of double effect. McCormick, however, claims that in the case of the probably dead fetus, the double effect principle has no role.

> The application of the principle of the twofold effect has no place in the problem. . . . There is no question of two effects, one bad, one good, but of an action which may be either (objectively and disjunctively) good or bad.[78]

Considering that McCormick has already decided to risk the possibility of the death of a fetus whose life could or could not be ascertained to save the life of the mother (who could otherwise die), and considering that this decision would be based on the certainty of the right to life of the woman whose life is certain (proportionate reason), it is difficult to see why this was not a case of double effect. McCormick seems, without saying it, to have already decided to consider moral evil as premoral disvalue sanctioned or caused without proportionate reason.

Although he does not employ terms such as ontic or premoral evil or disvalue, he is already engaged in the reinterpretation of the principle of double effect. McCormick himself may not have been aware of this. However, even if he were aware of it he could not have articulated it. For if he even questioned the objectively evil nature of exposing an innocent life to danger of death, on the grounds that there can be proportionate reasons for doing so, he would have been in conflict with the tradition. Only the more tolerant climate of the post-Vatican II era made it possible for Peter Knauer to express in clearer terms the ideas implied by McCormick.[79] It is also obvious in this thesis that McCormick was not yet prepared to question the notion of intrinsic evil. He would have been led to this only if he had made proportionate reason the central focus of the principle of double effect. By not dealing with the connection between proportionate reason and the principle of double effect, he missed the opportunity to initiate the "revolution" Knauer was to trigger a few years later. However, since McCormick had started to think about issues pertinent to proportionate reasoning, he was better equipped than most other interlocutors to bring clarity to the later debate on the issue.

METHOD IN MCCORMICK'S THESIS

McCormick's thesis is a work of casuistry. Its aim is to apply particular moral principles to particular cases. In the dissertation, all of the elements of casuistry come together–the dilemma, the principles, moral rules, the use of axioms to solve difficult cases, attention to the opinion of extrinsic authority, and the careful analysis of arguments for and against a particular line of action to determine which argument carries more weight.

McCormick, however, does not totally fit the mold of the traditional casuist even at this early stage. He respects principles and the tools available for the resolution of cases, but he ultimately engages in the revision of these tools and of the discipline as well. Notice his subtle limiting of the notion of virtual or hypothetical voluntary only to cases where the evil effect is caused without proportionate reason. In this way he frees the notion from an undue dependence on the physical structure of the act and makes it depend instead on intention and proportionality. Secondly, he did not assume the importance of any opinion based simply on the source of that opinion. His stated intention from the very beginning was "to challenge the use of some rather hallowed dicta with the hope of arriving at greater clarity of principle."[80] Thus, while he admitted the usefulness of many of the maxims which have been handed down through successive authorities, he nonetheless believed that some of these maxims could take on expanded meaning in the light of more recent developments and knowledge:

> While it is true that the principles of moral theology do not change substantially (and in this sense, medical fact will simply present requisites for the solutions of cases whose principles are already clear), yet an understanding of these principles can grow with a more profound knowledge of the fact.[81]

We have here an indication of a moral theology that is 'open' to new insights and fresh data – or do we? McCormick devotes the entire second chapter of his work to sampling the opinion of medical experts concerning whether the issue of the probably dead fetus is a practical one. However, even before embarking on this enterprise, he has already concluded that the opinion of medical experts "can add directly very little to the discussion"; in an indirect sense, though, they "throw some light on the principle involved."[82] This brings us to the other aspect of McCormick's methodology: its dependence on the deductive method of the manuals.

In the dissertation there is the element of exposition and disputation and then a systematic construction which only comes after previous opinions have been purified of their undesirable accretions. To this extent we can say that McCormick is employing the Scholastic method in his thesis.[83]

McCormick's thesis is very well written, and his arguments are tightly woven. His survey of theologians and their work is very extensive; his grasp of their views is superb. His analyses are at once fair, deep, disciplined, and vigorous. In many ways, this is a daring work, not only because of his preparedness to challenge hallowed theological dicta and opinions,[84] but also because it reveals his tendency to test and stretch the received tradition to its utmost limit. There are two points to note, however. The first is that in this "theological" work of five hundred and ten pages, the word 'God' is used only four or five times. Moreover, references to 'Jesus' or 'Christ' are totally absent. The warrant for the 'liceity' or 'illiceity' of an action seems to derive from opinions expressed or put forward in the manuals. It would appear there is a magisterium of theologians with precedence even over the authority of scripture.[85]

The other issue is the moral agent. Given the current emphasis on patient autonomy, one is struck by the passivity or even total silence of that figure. Her function is totally taken over by "experts." The mother is supposedly the one at the center of the storm here. However, for all practical purposes, she appears to be already dead, even while the decision is being made by others whether to spare her life or that of her probably dead fetus. In other words, she is not brought in anywhere as a participant in a decision which involves her ultimately. The discussion is between theological and medical experts only, and the decision is ultimately made by moralists alone since the opinion of medical experts "can add directly very little to the discussion." This is after all "a moral decision," and physicians "appear as ridiculous" when "they tamper with the niceties of moral science."[86]

Consideration of the role of the 'patient' is absent, however, not because McCormick denies patient autonomy, but because his declared purpose in the thesis is "the clarification of principles" – a narrow point of view in light of his later works, but quite appropriate for the times before Vatican II. This explains also the role he assigns to the physician as merely a provider of information.

CONCLUSION

I have tried to define McCormick's background and to show how his earliest work reflects the theological context of his formative years. I have indicated also the complex ecclesial context from which he shares – a Church in search of its place in the American socio-political entity and within the wider community of faith. From both its contexts, this Church was left with a desire for independence and dialogue with the wider human culture and at the same time a mentality which deeply distrusted the world.

McCormick's American context would prove very significant in his later years as a theologian, especially in his reflections on *Humanae Vitae* and in his casuistry, especially in the area of bioethics. In the former case, the American democratic ideal may play a more important role than he acknowledges in the search for a community solution (rather than an authoritarian 'imposition') on the issue of contraception. In bioethics, he would engage in dialogue between Church and society, between science and religion, with an incredible sense of urgency.

I have also shown that although McCormick remained faithful to the method of the manuals, he went beyond the scope of the moral handbooks, first, by choosing an issue the manuals considered marginal, and second, by extending moral principles beyond their original meaning. By stretching the method and content of the received tradition this far, McCormick (like many other moral theologians at the time) was making it evident that a revision was necessary within the discipline. The problem was how to go about this process of renewal.

The principal aim of this work is the study of McCormick's contribution to the renewal of moral theology. This task is not made easier by the fact that McCormick is not a system-builder. He approaches problems as they arise in life. He himself acknowledged this in my interview with him in this description of how the late Dr. André Hellegers, the founder of the Kennedy Institute of Bioethics at Georgetown University, used to introduce him and others to visitors at the institute.

> Dr. Hellegers would show people around the Institute and tell them who was there. He'd say, "Well, this is Leon Kass over here. He is our Jewish scholar. He does bioethics from the Jewish point of view. This is LeRoy Walters's office; he does this and that. This is Warren Reich, who is editing the encyclopedia of bioethics, and this is McCormick's office. He puts out fires." People would say, "What do you mean?" Hellegers would say, "McCormick and I put out fires. We respond to problems. We have no eternally valid ten year schemes or methodological revolutions. All we do is respond to fire alarms."[87]

One of my intentions in this work is to construct a system out of McCormick's work. One should embark on such an undertaking by starting where the manuals left off–the importance of faith in Christ for Christian ethics. Such an approach would help in defining the proper nature of the discipline. There are, however, other considerations also which make such a starting point necessary. These include contemporary secularizing trends that emphasize human autonomy in "the manner of understanding, willing, and experiencing morality"; and the seeming intractable problems of war, disease, hunger, poverty, social injustices of unimaginable proportions, technology, and so on, which make people wonder about old answers from the Church and raise the problem concerning the specific contribution of the gospel to the solution of these problems. There are specifically theological reasons as well. These include "the general problematic of the relationship between nature and grace, the natural and the supernatural, the impact of the situation ethics debate and the conciliar emphasis on the 'signs of the times' as a *locus theologicus.*"[88]

McCormick himself has stated the importance of starting the study of Christian ethics with a discussion on the specific nature of the discipline.

> There are few questions in moral theology as fundamental as the issue of a specifically Christian ethic. In practice it raises the question of the relationship between Christian ethics and non-Christian ethics or philosophical ethics. In theory the response to this question says much about the methodological approach used in moral theology and the whole structure of the discipline.[89]

2

THE NATURE OF CHRISTIAN ETHICS

In 1968 McCormick published an article on the characteristics of Catholic moral thought and suggested five themes to organize a discussion on the nature of Christian ethics. These are: the primacy of Charity in Christian morality, the essential interiority of law in the New Covenant, the notion of natural law, the relationship of natural law to gospel morality, and a balanced approach to the determination of moral norms.[1] In my view, all of McCormick's discussion on the nature of Christian ethics properly fits this agenda. Therefore, I will employ them in my investigation. The following arrangement also tries, as much as possible, to take into account the chronological order in which McCormick himself raised these issues. This approach illustrates the process of the development of McCormick's thought on the various themes and maintains the logical links among them.

The Primacy of Charity

Fundamental to McCormick's view is the decisiveness of God's covenant with humanity manifested in the saving incarnation of Jesus Christ.[2] The initial Christian response to God's "stunning and aggressive love in Jesus" is faith.[3] Faith in turn must translate into charity. For McCormick, charity as the heart of Christian moral life, therefore, flows from our experience of God's own love in Christ.[4]

Christian love must lead to ethical commitment in the world. This implies not only loving God but loving our neighbor as well. Love of God is an empty slogan and love of neighbor is incomprehensible without an acknowledgment of the basic demands other

25

people make on us. Failing to acknowledge these demands while at the same time professing our love for our neighbor is to repudiate the human dignity and worth implied in Christ's incarnation. The other consequence of the divine grasp of the human reality is that it has a transformative effect on human actions. This means that every virtue and every virtuous act has become an expression or mediation of "the new-life tendency," love, which we have been called to through the life and death of Christ. In short, our acts of virtue "are simply the interior drive of charity becoming the external gift of charity in the world."[5]

THE PLACE AND ROLE OF LAW

The second essential theme in the discussion of Christian ethics concerns the status and role of law in the New Covenant. McCormick notes that law, for "the new man in Christ," is not a proposition meant to move the person to action from the outside. Instead, it is an "unfolding of the internal motion of the Holy Spirit." Thus, although the law of Christ obliges us, it does so as internal law. The essential interiority of law in the New Covenant implies that mere observance is not justifying and that God's call is made known to a person in a concrete situation. Since knowledge of this call to the individual cannot be adequately formulated, apart from this concrete situation, "the law as externally proposed, and therefore as universal, cannot assert concretely all that the individual . . . here and now must do."[6] Finally, it means that the motion of the Spirit and grace, rather than law, is the principle which governs the present moral order.

NATURAL LAW

Catholic position on natural law implies an understanding that "moral values and obligations are grounded in a moral order known by human reason reflecting on experience."[7] McCormick is convinced that moral order is grounded in the being of the human person as such. In 1965 he wrote that natural law is the law "inscribed in our being by the creative act of God," the dictates of reason "as historical man confronts his inclinations, drives, tendencies, and potentialities."⁸ Besides being inscribed in our hearts, natural law is natural because it is founded in nature and can, for this reason, be known without "supernatural assistance." In that same year he further developed his position in response to John L. McKenzie. In the latter's view, Paul considered a morality of nature and reason a failed morality. Natural law had no salvific effects because, like all other laws, it had been abrogated by the New Testament. Furthermore, he was strongly critical of the view that a moral system of obligations based on a rational consideration of nature could offer solutions to questions on the morality of sex, politics, wealth, slavery, and so forth. The answer to the ethical problems in these areas, McKenzie said, could be found in Christian love alone.⁹

McCormick noted that the claim for the biblical foundation of natural law does not make natural law efficacious for salvation. "There is only one way of salvation: redemption by the blood of Christ." Like Bruno Schüller, he argued, however, that the human person is, logically prior to being addressed by God in revelation, an ethical being. Otherwise, human beings could not make sense of ethical values contained in revelation. For example, we could not understand the biblical meaning of love, humility, or trust if human experience had not provided the ground and the language with which these notions could be understood.¹⁰

Christian love and the concrete demands of natural law are not diametrically opposed. Moreover, given the assistance of reason, human beings can discover the claims which the neighbor's humanity makes on them.

> [This] is all that the authentic natural law tradition asserts. In making such an assertion, it is not endorsing a "natural morality"; it is but insisting that the person's lovability may not be defined short of his full humanity. Being the work of God, man as man is a word of God.¹¹

In 1968 McCormick continued to argue that, not unlike the gospel, natural law is a gift and a challenge from God, an imperative in our being which invites us to become what we are. Thus, there is a relationship between the notion of natural law and that of a personal call from God to the individual at each moment in life. This call is proffered and accepted or rejected in an ensemble of real elements which make up the situation. Within the situation, the human agent is an irreducible element whose relationship with God is based on God's call issued through creation and on God's saving intervention in history.[12] Thus, revelation and natural law are not opposed to each other; both constitute different aspects of a single moral order.

NATURAL LAW AND GOSPEL MORALITY

The relationship of natural law to the gospel or of reason to faith is important in the discussion on Christian ethics. McCormick's view on the nature of this relationship has undergone some changes over the years. In 1968 he wrote that "there is no such thing as a natural law existentially separable from the law of Christ, and there never was. There is only Christian morality, not a natural and a Christian morality."[13] This means that natural institutions like marriage, family, and the state, for example, exist for the service of the kingdom of Christ. It implies also that since the natural law is part of the law of Christ, it is a means to salvation, "not of itself as natural, but by reason of the grace with which it takes place." Furthermore, the material good acts of non-believers "are often or at least potentially performed out of a believing, a Christian love." This love exists at an unreflective level of human consciousness where one disposes oneself in fundamental option before the God of life.

> This basic option is made in confrontation with the grace of Christ.
> Hence the correct moral behavior of non-Christians at least can be an
> expression or mediation of the new life and love which Christ works
> in them even though they do not recognize it as such.[14]

Although McCormick does not say much about it, he presupposes revelation by creation and incarnation. Even when he seems to collapse the natural order into the Christian one he presupposes this distinction. This is the key to understanding how McCormick develops further in later years. Another key to understanding his development is Karl Rahner's theology of the anonymous Christian and his theory of fundamental option, which McCormick himself lists as among the ten most significant theological developments in the past fifty years or so.[15]

Rahner believed that if, as scriptures say, God desires the salvation of everyone, and if this salvation cannot be found outside the Church, as the Church taught, then everyone can somehow belong to the Church historically.[16] Although this has not been so, non-Christian religions have been used by God as instruments of salvation. Prior to their encounter with Christianity, these religions contain elements of a natural knowledge of God as well as "supernatural elements arising out of the grace which is given to men as a gratuitous gift on account of Christ." This grace is not a mere substitute for salvation, it is salvation.[17] Consequently, Rahner concludes that if the salvation proffered to even the non-Christian is Christ's

> then it must be possible to be not only an anonymous *theist* but also an anonymous Christian, and this (since the Church of Christ is not purely interior reality) not in any merely intangible way, but also with a certain making visible and tangible of the anonymous relationship.[18]

Also at issue here is the question of the relation between nature and grace and of the conditions that are necessary for sinful and finite human persons to be able to encounter, receive, or be in communication with the absolutely transcendent God.[19] Furthermore, there is also the question of the value or worth of the behavior of the non-believer. Rahner's position was that non-believers are in fact "regularly the co-operative recipients of God's grace"[20] given through Christ, if they accept their unlimited self-transcendence. When one accepts one's unlimited self-transcendence, one implicitly accepts God. Human transcendence has God as its ground and goal and is mediated historically through a mediating "categorial objectivity," which could be either an explicit religious act or a moral decision in which a person is responsible for and accepts or rejects himself or herself.[21] Every mediation of God's grace occurs through Christ, and every acceptance or rejection of God's grace is also an anonymous acceptance or rejection of Christ.

In moral theology, the corollary to Rahner's theory was that even the understanding of right and wrong as well as all systems of morality are in fact Christian, even if anonymously so. Thus, when McCormick argued that there was nothing but Christian morality, or that the material acts of even the non-believer are done through the grace of Christ, he was, in fact, reflecting the influence of Karl Rahner on his thinking. This influence would have come to him notably through the work of Josef Fuchs, his teacher and friend.[22]

The question of the relationship of natural law to revealed morality and especially of the possibility of Christian ethics became a subject of lively debate in the late 1960s and in the early 1970s. The debate was conducted in the context of the burgeoning renewal movement in moral theology. While some theologians held for a morality that would be completely different from natural law or secular morality, others insisted on a natural law morality as part of Christian morality, but whose central element would come from revelation. This latter group maintained that the Bible ought to be the touchstone of the renewal because it was given to us by God and Christians found what they wanted to do in it.[23]

This view was not left without challenge. Soon, there arose a school of thought which no longer emphasized God as revealer of morality but the human being as discoverer of what constitutes right and wrong conduct. This school of autonomous ethic started to ask whether there was, in fact, a revealed morality different from what Catholic theology had always held to be within the grasp of everyone, pagan and Christian alike. If not, can one still talk about Christian morality? What would be the content of such morality?

Vincent MacNamara suggests three reasons for these questions. The most obvious was the desire to make Christian morality seem less esoteric and childish in the eyes of many outside the Church who viewed the existence of such morality as a childish obedience to the commandments of God. A morality which came "out of the middle of revelation" gave the impression of incarnating a ghetto mentality in a Europe which, in the 1960s and 1970s, favored dialogue and solidarity. Another reason was the increasing awareness of and respect for what Vatican II had labeled "the autonomy of earthly affairs." The Council's statement was a call to Christians to respect the laws and values inherent in society and in created things as a whole. This call echoed among theologians in

general and created "an ethos which was favorable to the development of an autonomous ethic and foreign to the idea of a specific
Christian ethic." The third reason was, of course, the understanding of grace as a universal gift within the reach of everyone. From
this comes a new understanding in the relationship between Christianity and other religions.

These issues all came together in the theology of Karl Rahner.
Their effect in moral theology was first felt in the works of Josef
Fuchs who, in the early 1970s, started to maintain, contrary to his
previous position, that "many questions of Christian morality
are not merely Christian, but universally human problems; consequently, Christians and non-Christians can discuss them together."[24] Fuchs further argued that moral norms are not distinctively Christian just because they are proclaimed officially in
the Church. Instead, to the extent to which norms proclaim truth,
"they are universally human and therefore also Christian–hence,
not distinctively Christian." Furthermore, "when a statement does
not truly address genuine humanness, the norms it sets forth are not
authentically human, hence also not Christian, let alone Christian
ethical norms."[25] The reason is that revelation in Christ presupposes
God's initial self-disclosure in creation.

THE DISTINCTIVENESS OF CHRISTIAN ETHICS

There are several sides to the debate on the distinctiveness of
Christian ethics. One of these concerns the determination of meaning of particular scriptural passages as they are found in scriptures
themselves. An extension of this problem concerns the meaning and
relevance of particular scriptural passages to the modern human
condition. Furthermore, there is the question of the normativity of
the Bible as source of Christian ethics. Finally, there is the question
concerning the influence of scripture on the moral agent and on
moral agency. McCormick's discussion of the distinctiveness of
Christian ethics has focused chiefly on this last issue.

McCormick entered this debate in 1970 in response to Charles
E. Curran, who had denied the specificity of Christian ethics on the
grounds that Christians do not in fact possess any knowledge or
power that others do not or cannot have.[26] McCormick argued that
if, as Curran said, the light of the gospel can aid the discovery of

truly human solutions to our problems, those who have the gospel have a source of knowledge that is unavailable to others not exposed to it. Although he could not state how this knowledge differed from any other, he maintained that whatever this light leads to "will always be utterly human, not beyond or at variance with the human and the reasonable." However, since, as Vatican II taught, "faith directs the mind to solutions that are fully human," the road to the grasping of what is authentically human, for the believer, leads through Christian dispositions and attitudes.[27]

From arguing that there was only Christian morality, McCormick was now moving to a nuanced conclusion which denied any specific Christian morality at the level of innerworldly behavior. In this view the gospel still had a role as a searchlight for the authentically human, whatever that is. From now on, McCormick would continue to hold, like James Gustafson, that faith transforms our attitudes, dispositions, intentions, goals, and norms. Thus our moral judgments can be incarnations of basic prereflective positions.

> Take the case of slavery for example. We do not hold that slavery is humanly demeaning and immoral chiefly because we have argued to this rationally. Rather, first our sensitivities are sharpened to the meaning and value of human persons. We then *experience* the out-of-jointness, inequality, and injustice of slavery. We then *judge* it to be wrong. At this point we develop "arguments" to criticize, modify and above all communicate this judgement.[28]

Such truths are in fact discoverable by intuitive reason and are thus open to anyone.

Since 1979 McCormick has adopted a distinction, first made by Nobert Rigali,[29] between four levels of ethical discourse.[30] This distinction and the traditional concept of reason informed by faith have become the two hinges that hold McCormick's views on the distinctiveness of Christian ethics together. The four levels on which Christian ethical discourse is carried out are those of essential ethics, existential ethics, essential Christian ethics, and existential Christian ethics.

Essential ethics refers to norms applicable to all persons. "One's behavior is but an instance of a general, essential moral norm." Some examples here would be "the rightness and wrongness of killing actions, of contracts, of promises and all those actions whose demands are rooted in the dignity of the person."[31] The level of existential ethics concerns the choice which the individual *qua* individual has to make within unique circumstances. Thus one might, for example, decide that a particular profession or work does not allow the time to grow spiritually and therefore to resign from such work or cease to practice such profession. In essential Christian ethics we are concerned with the choices that all Christians precisely as Christians are called to make – and non-Christians are not. This includes, for example, the necessity of providing a good Christian education for one's children.

> Thus, to the extent that Christianity is a Church . . . and has preordained structures and symbols, to this extent there can be and must be a distinctively Christian ethic, an essential ethics of Christianity which adds to the ordinary essential ethics of persons as members of the universal human community the ethics of persons as members of the Church-community.[32]

Existential Christian ethics refers to the ethical decisions a Christian as an individual has to make based on personal aptitude and in response to the gospel.[33]

The question of the distinctiveness of Christian ethics arises at the level of essential ethics and is concerned with whether explicit Christian faith can add new content at the material or concrete level to one's ethical (essential ethics) perceptions of obligation. McCormick asserts that "faith stamps one at a profound and not totally recoverable depth," affecting the person's perspectives, analyses, and judgment.[34] In other words, Christian faith has an influence on the determination of the good, on the shaping of the moral agent, and on the formulation of moral judgment. This is what McCormick means when he speaks of "reason informed by faith."[35]

Reason informed, not replaced, by faith as a moral epistemological principle is central to McCormick's moral theory because it illumines his casuistry as well as his anthropology. With reference to casuistry, this means that although Christian emphases do not yield concretely different norms or rules for decision-making, they affect them. In anthropology, it signals the "new man" of whom Paul speaks, one with sometimes a profoundly different outlook and attitude to the world.

Therefore, Christian faith can affect the human dispositions, intentions, and goals in several ways. First, it can be transformative. That is, it can transform our view of persons and their meaning as well as our style of performing the moral tasks common to all persons.[36] In this sense, faith is much more a value-raiser than an answer-giver, because it affects the values of the person at the spontaneous, pre-thematic level.[37] Secondly, faith can be disclosive. It opens up "surprising and delightful new insights about the human condition as such," revealing the deeper dimensions of the universally human as well as the meaning of the world.[38]

Faith is also directive. It tells us who we ought to be, what values we ought to pursue, what disvalues we should avoid, and the type of world we ought to seek. In short, it provides the framework that ought to shape the individual decisions which the Christian makes. If these decisions are separated from the context of the Christian story, they lose their perspective, and they become a

> merely rationalistic and sterile ethic subject to the distortions of self-interested perspectives and cultural drifts, a kind of contracted etiquette with no relation to the ultimate meaning of persons.[39]

However, insight from faith brings "confirmatory" rather than "originating" warrants to moral reflection. The warrants of faith are confirmatory because they provide the Christian with a privileged articulation or objectification in Christ of what everyone does or can experience. Furthermore, they stand in judgment over "all human meaning and actions."[40] They are not originating, because they do not and cannot add to human ethical self-understanding as such any material content which is, in principle, "strange or foreign to man as he exists and experiences himself in the world."[41] Therefore, whatever is distinctive about Christian morality as such is so only in style and in the manner of accomplishing the moral tasks common to everyone. Moral norms whether generated by a person or community of faith are inherently intelligible and cannot be impervious to human insight.[42]

McCormick maintains further that this conclusion does not deny that Christianity has something to offer in moral judgments.

Therefore, he contends that "reason informed by faith" gives the Christian an edge in difficult ethical cases. In fact, faith can powerfully shape the character of the moral agent and constitute the touchstone for moral discernment.

With all this, McCormick's position on the relationship of faith and reason, or gospel and natural law, needs further clarification; this occurs in his discussion on the relationship of Christian ethics and bioethics. The following discussion on faith and bioethics is not only an example of what he says on the role of the faith in matters of life and death but also shows a peculiar characteristic in his method, in which he uses one position to develop a point of view which he then applies to other aspects of his theology.

CHRISTIAN FAITH AND BIOETHICS

In a 1989 address,[43] McCormick isolated some key elements of the Christian story that he believes are important to the discussion of the ethical issues of life and death. These include: (a) the notion of God as author and preserver of life in whose image all human beings are made; (b) the idea of life as a gift given by and received in trust from God–a fact which constitutes life's worth and value; (c) the idea that the human being is a pilgrim with no final refuge or home here on earth; and (d) the understanding of Jesus as the ultimate epiphany of God and as someone whose life, death, and resurrection have a transformative impact on our lives. These elements influence our judgments and decisions in various ways in bioethics.

Belief in the resurrection of Christ and in our own resurrection yields a general value judgment about the meaning and value of life as we know it. This should lead to an understanding of life as basic but not absolute good. This means that although life is a necessary condition for every human activity and for society, it can be sacrificed for such higher goods as the glory of God, the salvation of souls, the service of one's brothers and sisters, and so forth. Jesus' example in this regard is a very powerful one, which has motivated men and women to great accomplishments for hundreds of years. This theme stands as a corrective against the tendency to preserve life at all costs or to do away with life when it becomes dysfunctional, onerous, or boring. This implies, as McCormick says elsewhere, that "there are higher values in the living of it [and] there are also higher values in the dying of it."[44] However, McCormick is insistent that although the Christian story makes us sensitive to the meaning of life, it does not provide us with direct answers to questions about the means to use or not to use in any particular situation to preserve life or what to do about "now incompetent, and always incompetent patients in critical illness," for example.[45]

Also, reason informed by the nativity story can teach us to think specifically of unborn children. McCormick maintains that, although this does not settle the moral rightness or wrongness of any particular abortion, it rules out a simple pro-choice position for a Christian. Furthermore, reason informed by faith attests to the essential equality (regardless of functional importance) and radical sociality of all persons, as a further indication of our interconnectedness and interdependence, and as a reminder that one's well-being cannot be pursued independently of the good of others. Although the fact of human equality and sociality does not provide ready-made answers to dilemmas about organ transplantations and non-therapeutic experimentations, for instance, it does provide a context in which to judge the morality of these procedures.[46]

Further insights from the Christian faith that can influence concrete norms in bioethics include the understanding that the procreative and unitive aspects of human sexuality should not be separated. Although McCormick denies that this inseparability applies to individual acts of love-making within marriage rather than to the entire marriage itself, he states that the Christian story has significance for the way one understands contraception, sterilization, and the morality of reproductive technologies like artificial insemination by husband (AIH) or donor (AID), *in vitro* fertilization (IVF), surrogate motherhood, and so on.[47] The Christian story also establishes the normativity of heterosexual marriage. Without implying that every such marriage will be happy or successful, it insists that monogamous marriages offer the best opportunity "to humanize our sexuality and bridge the separation and isolation of our individual selves." Therefore we all ought (normative) to try to make monogamous marriages the context for the expression of our full sexuality.[48] While this norm cannot always provide us with concrete answers, it can at least help us in the evaluation of transsexual surgery, teenage sexuality, homosexuality, and so forth.

As a countercultural influence, faith can help fight the modern cultural tendency to regard nature as "alien, independent of human beings and possessing no inherent value." Such a worldview encourages human beings to believe it is their right to manipulate nature and put it to their use in whatever way they can. It also creates a climate in which the value of human persons is predicated on functionality. Thus, in Western societies, the aged are cast aside when they are no longer considered functionally useful, and retarded persons are considered a burden and socially worthless. Christian faith can protect against such a collapse of the worth and dignity of the human person into social usefulness and desirability "by steadying our gaze on the basic values that are the parents of more concrete norms or rules."[49]

McCormick also believes that charity, "as the shape of the faith," can influence the way the Christian physician understands the notions of beneficence, autonomy, and justice in medicine generally and in the patient-physician relationship. The Christian physician sees himself or herself called to perfection, to imitate Jesus's healing. In this perspective, appeals to exigency, fiscal survival, self-protection, or the canons of a competitive environment are morally feeble, even totally unacceptable. Similarly, where justice is concerned, 'faith-full' Christians will go beyond the strict calculus of duties and claims and exercise a "preferential option" for the very ones whose moral claims on society are difficult to establish: the poor, the outcasts, the sociopaths, the alcoholic, the noncompliant in the care of their own health.[50]

How does the Christian perspective affect dialogue and the general relationship with persons who have other or no faith stories at all? Can an ethical position arrived at on the assumptions of the Christian faith also apply to them? What use can such an ethical position be in public policy issues aimed at people of other or no faith persuasions?

McCormick believes that the themes he has isolated from the Christian story are intelligible to non-Christians. The Christian story is not the only cognitive source for the radical sociality of the person or for the immorality of abortion, "even though historically those insights may be strongly attached to the story." In this epistemological sense, others can and do indeed share these insights. But even when they do not share them by unanimous consent,

Christians expect the Christian story "to have some persuasiveness in general experience."[51]

> The Catholic tradition reasons about its story. In the process it hopes to and claims to disclose surprising and delightful insights about the human condition as such. These insights are not, therefore, eccentric infractions limited in application to a particular historical community. For instance, the sacredness of nascent life is not an insight that applies only to Catholic babies – as if it were wrong to abort Catholic babies, but perfectly all right to do so with Muslim, Protestant, or Jewish babies. Quite the contrary. Reasoning about the Christian story makes a bolder claim.[52]

Stanley Hauerwas has argued that McCormick's reduction of Christian ethics to human ethics is based on the assumption that "Christian ethics will never be radically anti-world – that is, aligned against the prevailing values of their culture."[53] The emphasis on the human character of Christian ethics smacks of a deep fear of a radical discontinuity between Christians and their culture. This, he says, is an ideological use of the natural law theory to sustain the presupposition that contemporary societies – "particularly societies of Western democracies – are intrinsic to God's purposes."

Hauerwas does not see any support for McCormick's contention that if Christian faith adds material content to morality there would be problems with discussions and deliberations in the public forum.

> Why does he assume that the public forum is shaped by "human" values? Why does he assume that Christians should be able to contribute to the "public forum" on its own terms? What, for example, would have been the result if Christians had approached their entry into Roman society with McCormick's presupposition? Isn't it possible that Christians, because of the ethos peculiar to their community, might find themselves in deep discontinuity with the ethos of a particular society?[54]

Therefore the question of the specificity of Christian ethics is, for Stanley Hauerwas, a question of the relationship of the Christian Church to the world. The claim of a distinctive status for Christian ethics is not an attempt to underwrite Christian assumptions of dominance and superiority. It is a recognition of the radicalness of the gospel. The claim is not even a denial that there are points of contact between Christian ethics and other forms of morality. It is a statement of the insufficiency of these points of contact to provide a universal ethic grounded on human nature *per se*.

David Hollenbach also believes he has detected an ambiguity in McCormick's approach to the question of the distinctiveness of Christian ethics. The problem stems from McCormick's position that Christian faith discloses the truly human and that insights from the faith are confirmatory rather than originating sources of moral knowledge. Hollenbach points out that there "is a difference between the statement that the Christian story 'discloses' the meaning of the normatively human and the statement that this story 'confirms' insights into this meaning."[55] Also, Hollenbach continues, McCormick's understanding of Christian ethics as the objectification in Jesus Christ of each individual's experience of subjectivity assumes that Christian symbols and faith "express the contours of this inner experience, rather than adding something distinctively new to the inner awareness of what it is to be human."[56] Such a view, he maintains, does not do justice to the reality of the incarnation, because it stresses only the confirmatory aspect of that mystery. For, while the incarnation shows that the Christian faith is not strange or foreign to the human condition, it also is an indication "that human particularity, historicity, and diversity must be taken with equal seriousness."[57] Thus, views like those of McCormick do not sufficiently acknowledge the historicity of human experience but base themselves on an assumption of the timelessness of human subjectivity.

I believe that McCormick's position on the disclosive and confirmatory nature of faith insights must be carefully listened to in order to be understood. Faith insights disclose what is authentically human and direct the mind to it by sensitizing our moral affectivities. When we make judgments on the essential level they also act as checks to establish that those judgments are human, not merely according to what the culture or current fad considers human but according to what it is to be human in Christian terms. As McCormick says repeatedly, such judgments must be tested against the notion of our radical equality with one another, the sacredness of human life, human interconnectedness, human eternal destiny, and so on.

Therefore, although Christians cannot claim that they have an arcane source of moral insight into the problems of the human condition, they can recognize a good moral judgment when they see it, based on the confirmatory warrants of the faith. Furthermore, although it is correct to argue against converting human subjectivity into a timeless paradigm for interpreting the meaning and assessing the truth of religious traditions and the way of life they imply, as George Lindbeck does against Rahner and Lonergan,[58] I doubt that such criticism applies to McCormick. He tries to steer a middle course between the subjectivity that can arise from espousal of the experiential-expressive view of religion and the denial of universality, or the possibility of any common grounds for moral discourse, which can also result from the cultural-linguistic model. Thus, he maintains, as the Catholic tradition has always done, the ability of the human person, regardless of religious or cultural affiliation, to make morally right judgments. At the same time he argues that what is right can only be decided on a much wider canvas. What this wider canvas involves is a central issue in McCormick's position on moral norms as well as in his understanding of Christian ethics.

Determination of Moral Norms

Moral norms are concerned with how to determine the meaning and significance of human action. As attempts to capture and validly formulate the good, they must be marked by a certain amount of tentativeness, because, no matter how hard we try, we can never capture this good totally or formulate its significance with complete accuracy. However, beyond the refractoriness of the good, there is also the epistemological reality that the objectification of our knowing is inadequate to the experience itself.[59] Finally, there is also the fact that human beings are historical beings and that moral norms as generalizations upon the significance of actions are affected by our definition of self. In other words, they are conditioned by "a host of personal and social factors whose limitations we are incapable of perceiving with the clarity we would like."[60]

McCormick also insists that moral significance is to be determined by relationship to personal value. By this he means that since human beings form the basis for the assessment of the moral significance of human action, norms are formed to protect and foster human welfare and dignity.

> For instance, reflection has led us to the conviction that the meaning and purpose of expressive powers is not simply the communication of true information, but a communication between persons that respects and promotes their good precisely as persons in community. Whether a concrete act contains a malice of a lie (and is therefore an unloving act incompatible with the Christian idea) must be determined by reference to this over-all purpose. There are times when spoken untruths are demanded by and protective of these personal values. That is, there are times when material truth destroys the very values that veracity is meant to protect.[61]

More recently, McCormick has found support for his person-centered thinking in the teaching of Vatican II that human acts must not be judged merely from a biological aspect but "insofar as they refer to the human person integrally and adequately considered."[62] McCormick has understood this to mean that our formulation of moral norms must take cognizance of the human person as a conscious, embodied subject who is part of the world, essentially directed toward others, and lives in community and within institutions and structures worthy of the human person. The human person is a historical being who is utterly original but fundamentally equal to all other human beings.[63]

Also, the determination of the meaning or significance of human acts can benefit from attention to other human sciences. McCormick notes the help of the depth sciences (for example, psychology) in the better understanding of human sexuality. They have shown that we can no longer talk of human sexuality in terms of the human organs alone, that sexual acts are an engagement of the whole human person and that sexual intercourse is the expression of a total personal donation and sharing.

> Far from undermining moral norms, this evidence has provided a more realistic and adequate basis in which to anchor them. Thus, the

rejection of adultery and fornication must be based on an analysis of sexuality which does justice to its true depth. Similarly, if one is to condemn contraception, his rejection can hope to be credible only if it grows out of awareness of the awesome depths of human sexuality.[64]

Another important consideration in the determination of norms must be the consequences of the act as well as the empirical evidence which can be adduced (in light of the consequences of such acts in the past) to determine whether the act in question is supportive or destructive of value. McCormick also points to the subjective aspect of significance. This implies, as I stated above, that our story (for example, as Christians) colors our perception of reality. Our moral disposition is reflected in the unreflexive choices and concrete affirmations we make as persons. Finally, there is a communal aspect to our grasp of moral significance. As persons in communion with other persons, we cannot exist except in community. This is also true of the Christian who cannot exist as such except in a community of faith. The Christian instinctively draws upon the ethos of the community for the meaning of human actions. Finally, it is McCormick's conviction that even when these factors have been weighed, our efforts at the formulation of behavioral norms must be considered tentative and only more or less adequate and "inherently revisable."[65]

FORMAL AND MATERIAL NORMS

With other contemporary theologians McCormick maintains that moral norms function on two levels of human consciousness because they approach moral goods from two different perspectives—the general and the concrete, or the formal and material, respectively. Formal norms articulate value in a general or universalizable manner by leaving out the consideration of concrete circumstances wherein a given value is found. They describe the demands in abstract or universal terms. Consequently, they are universally valid, relevant to all circumstances, and always binding on our conscience. However, due to their abstractness and universality, they do not say much about how the content of the action would realize or destroy a particular value.[66] For example, while everyone would accept such norms as "one must be humble," "one must be kind," "thou shalt not murder," "do not commit adultery," "do not be unjust," there is no similar consensus on actions which would realize or destroy these values in given concrete situations.

The purpose of formal norms is therefore parenetic, intended to remind people of what they are supposed to know and to exhort them to do to avoid sin. Parenetic discourse is different from explanatory discourse. While the latter deals with the pros and cons of a position as well as with the argument and normative validity of a precept, the former takes such validity for granted and employs the precept to pass judgment on a particular behavior.[67] Since they presume genuine agreement about what is right and wrong, parenetic discourse or formal norms can only invite, exhort, judge, strengthen, or implore. Ordinarily, they do not inform or instruct.[68]

While formal norms reflect the accumulated experience of the community by stating in a general and exhortative tone that it is good for the community and its members that moral values be respected, material norms, by contrast, express the same moral truth but as it is discovered in our own conscience given a particular set of circumstances or situations. The difference between formal and material norms is at the basis of a crucial distinction which McCormick, with many other moralists, has started to make in recent years between moral goodness / badness and moral rightness / wrongness.[69] Since the realization of a moral value presupposes the free surrender of the person to the value, only the action which corresponds to the character of the person and the action which contradicts it will disclose the characteristic of moral good or evil.[70] Thus, the chief function of material norms is to specify in concrete situations what amounts to right or wrong conduct.

> Formal norms (parenetic discourse) remind of the right and exhort to it. Material norms (explanatory discourse) attempt to state specifically what the formal norms state in compact value judgments. They attempt, e.g., to specify what is to account for 'murder.' They are instructional.[71]

Like Josef Fuchs, Richard McCormick points out that when we talk about moral goodness and evil, we refer "to the vertical dimension of our being,"[72] that is, to our openness to or rejection of

the self-giving love of God. By contrast, moral rightness or wrongness belongs to the horizontal level of human existence.

> This refers to the proper disposition of the realities of this world, the
> realization in concrete behavior of what is promotive for human
> persons. We refer to this as the rightness (or wrongness) of human
> conduct.[73]

Moral goodness discloses "an inclination, an intention, a
goodwill, a readiness to do what is right."[74] Moral goodness is
salvation. Therefore what we can say about the moral goodness of a
person is a "truth of salvation." In speaking of the rightness or
wrongness of human conduct, on the other hand, we articulate the
relation of this-worldly realities. The "innerworldly activity," that
is, the moral rightness or wrongness of human conduct, is moral
only in an analogous sense, since doing the right thing "is not
directly and *in itself* concerned with personal moral goodness."[75]
However, moral goodness and moral rightness are related to each
other as a tree to fruit. For although doing right or wrong does not
ordinarily and in itself determine salvation or perdition, a morally
good person would try to behave in this world in the right way.

The term 'ordinarily' has to be stressed because even the
morally good person experiences moral ambiguity in the process of
expressing openness to good through pre-moral right or wrong
actions. However, the person who is totally open to transcendence
and is thus less selfish and more readily available to the *other* can do
the right thing with greater ease than someone who is not as open to
transcendence and is therefore more inclined to be self-seeking.

CONCLUSION

We have seen that McCormick believes that the center of
Christian ethics is a responsive love which undertakes to love the
neighbor in gratitude to God for God's engendering deed in Jesus
Christ. Further, he believes in the ability of the human person to
decide between right and wrong behavior without explicit reference
to revelation. However, there is a dialectical tension between revelation and reason in morality. For, although the revealed Word of God

in scripture represents a full articulation of the mind of God, "man's [moral] obligation is founded on man's being."[76] Biblical revelation contributes three basic elements to moral discourse: the notion of God's gift to humankind, the centrality of love in morality, and the understanding of moral action as an empowered (graced) response.[77] McCormick also believes that Christian ethics does not establish moral significance merely on the basis of external acts. Christian ethics 'listens' to various sources and voices in making moral determination. However, whatever it determines must be in the interest of the human person "adequately considered."

The first three themes discussed in this chapter–the primacy of charity, the interiority of law, and natural law–seem to represent a Trinitarian aspect or focus in McCormick's theology. Primacy of charity roots Christian ethics in God's love in Christ. The interiority of law relates Christian ethics to the work of the Holy Spirit and shows that Christian ethics is also founded on the belief in the Spirit who is at work in the world. Natural law is an essential aspect of Christian ethics because Christians believe that God is not only revealed in the Son, not only that the Spirit gave us grace, but also that God is Creator of all humanity. These three points make McCormick's ethics Trinitarian in the way every Christian ethics should be. The rest of the themes pertain to the issue of emphasis. They raise the issue of relationships between charity and law, between revelation and reason, and so forth. Which is prior? Where does one place emphasis? Differences in answers to these questions and to other related issues explain the different conceptions of Christian ethics.

We are left with three unanswered questions. The first concerns the goal of moral striving. In the manuals there was a conscious effort to relate morality to the Beatific Vision by reference to issues of reward and punishment. This provided their theology with a focus. In McCormick's understanding of moral theology there is no room for such consciousness. And, although there are allusions to Christian life as being *in via*, there does not seem to be much evidence of the "eschatological awareness" one author speaks of.[78]

Also, although McCormick is aware of the importance of scripture for ethics, he is not inclined to use particular texts to buttress his points or even to ask questions about the meaning of particular texts for contemporary society. It is not that this does not matter. For him, scripture is a "moral reminder,"[79] and a privileged articulation of what everyone can know through human reason. Apart from the danger that this attitude may fail to see that sacred scriptures command us to love our neighbor in a particular way, it makes McCormick's work no more scriptural than the theology of the manuals.

Finally, McCormick's use of the distinction between essential human ethics and other levels of ethical discourse raises the problem of the proper role of the Church as moral teacher, especially when viewed against the traditional teaching, which insists that the Church's power to teach morality is without restriction even in those matters that, according to McCormick, belong to the level of essential ethics. This problem is even more acute considering that in the manuals, tradition (the Church) is judged to be one of the three sources of morality. The question is whether McCormick accepts this. McCormick's insistence that much of the contemporary discussion about moral norms focuses not on moral goodness or badness but on moral rightness or wrongness, which is the level of behavioral or material norms, and raises the question of ecclesial competence in morality even further. If the entire area of material concrete behavior is not one where the Church has special competence, where *does* the Church's competence lie? This is one of the key questions to be addressed in the next chapter.

3

THE CHURCH AS MORAL TEACHER

McCormick assumes a close connection between ecclesiology and moral theology: "How you conceive the Church and how you conceive its teaching function will always be very closely bound to how you proclaim the Church's moral conviction."[1] This chapter intends to show that McCormick's notion of Church has changed from a juridical one with a pyramidal structure of teaching to a communal one in which all the elements that make up the Church contribute to the Church's teaching function. Another aim of the chapter is to trace the course of these changes. Finally, at the end of the chapter, I intend to note some deficiencies in McCormick's understanding of the Church as moral teacher. Some of these inadequacies are indeed open questions begging for more consideration than this study can handle. However, even as they are, they contribute to the understanding of what McCormick says about the proclamation of the Church's moral convictions.

The role of the Church as moral teacher has become a hotly debated issue since Vatican II. There are basically two aspects to the debate. One concerns the subject of ecclesial teaching authority; the other concerns its nature and scope. McCormick's positions on these issues have been considerably shaped by three events: the birth control debate, which has continued to rage in the Church especially since the publication of *Humanae Vitae*; the teaching of the Second Vatican Council; and the censure of Charles E. Curran. Thus, the first section of this chapter will provide a historical overview of the development of his position vis-à-vis the birth control debate. In the second and third sections, I will present his position on the nature of the Church's teaching office and on the scope of the ecclesial magisterium. The fourth section will be concerned with the issue of dissent.

McCormick wrote a good number of articles on birth control before the publication of *Humanae Vitae*.[3] These articles were generally in support of the Church's ban on contraceptives and direct sterilization. For example, in an article he wrote in 1964 he argued that, since sexual intercourse is communication between persons,

> acts that do not preserve a completeness of donation (e.g. condomistic intercourse and *coitus interruptus* or withdrawal) fail to express the relationship of total oblation. By more or less detracting from the total self-gift, such acts do not create unity in one flesh, and to that extent are separative.[4]

Also, his response to Louis Janssens on the controversy over the contraceptive pill is indicative not only of his traditional bent at this period but also his juridical attitude to authority and teaching in the Church. In 1963 Louis Janssens wrote that the pill was an acceptable form of contraception because like periodic abstinence it was not a form of direct sterilization but a positive intervention which conserved rather than destroyed the ova and left the natural structure of the sexual act intact.[5] In his response the following year, McCormick wondered what Janssens understood by direct sterilization and argued that the pill was considered objectionable by the pope because it conformed to "those procedures which by sterilizing the reproductive system, strip the conjugal act of its productive potential." He cited approvingly the teachings of Pius XII against any form of direct sterilization and maintained that they "provide authoritative (though not necessarily exhaustive or final) guidelines (not shackles) within which theologians continue their study."[6]

McCormick not only believed that the Church's teaching on sterilization and contraception was right because it was authoritatively taught, but he sometimes chided those theologians who dissented from the Church's teaching on the matter for the reason that it was not infallibly proposed. For example, in his review of Louis Dupré's *Contraception and Catholics*, he objected to the author's suggestion that since the doctrine on contraception was not infallibly proposed one could hold a dissenting position if the arguments which supported the Church's position were not persuasive. McCormick wondered why lack of persuasive arguments should force the Church to remain silent on moral problems.

> What if the arguments have not been and are not likely to be decisive? Is the Church muted on that account in the area of morals? Can she not take a truly authoritative position when there exist not decisive arguments but only Rahner's "reasonable theological justification."[7]

Notice McCormick's move from the consideration of the issue of ecclesial competence over contraception to a discussion of ecclesial competence in moral theology as a whole. It is either that the Church can teach decisively on contraception or that it cannot teach morality at all. However, by 1966 he was beginning to soften his views. Although he still defended the Church's stand on contraception as authentic and as "the present understanding of God's law itself by a divinely commissioned teacher," he was at the same time stating that such teachings were always "open" simply because "the Church exists in time and its formulations will always contain the limitations inseparable from immersion in a historical moment."[8]

The major reason for the "softening" in McCormick's view was Pope Paul VI's attitude to and utterances about the work of the Birth Control Commission. In 1964 Paul VI enlarged the Birth Control Commission which his predecessor set up. On June 23 of the same year the pope talked about the delicate and painful nature of the birth control issue and stated that the norms which Pius XII had taught

> must be considered valid, at least until we feel obliged in conscience to change them. In matters of such gravity, it seems well that Catholics should wish to follow one law, that which the Church authoritatively puts forward. And it therefore seems opportune to recommend that no one, for the present, take it upon himself to make pronouncements in terms different from the prevailing norm.[9]

Did the pope consider changing the norms on birth control? Was he ever in doubt about the intrinsic and absolute validity of that teaching? Supposing he was, could a pope consider that he had the authority to tamper with such norms? When McCormick reported the pope's speech in his first installment of the "Notes" he said:

> I have been of the opinion that Pope Paul's intervention meant both to encourage theological thought and yet to repeat *authoritatively* the norms of Pius XII, especially with regard to the pill. I have never been able to read this intervention as merely disciplinary. Hence, I have felt that the official position of the Church as a guide of conscience has been the norms of Pius XII. Practically this would mean that those who claim the privilege of enlightenment from the magisterium could reflect this magisterium in their advice and actions.[10]

McCormick pointed out that the pope had reserved to himself alone the right to speak on the issue and had in fact promised to speak soon and authoritatively on the matter. McCormick then argued that if the pope failed to make an authoritative pronouncement soon, this would be sure evidence that a state of practical doubt existed in the Church on this matter, in which case it would be hard to deny application of the principles of probabilism.

> This would mean that the confessor or priest would indicate to an enquirer that the matter is still under discussion and that he must be ready to receive with open and grateful heart the ultimate authoritative teaching of the magisterium.[11]

McCormick did not discard his caution or his juridical attitude to ecclesial pronouncements. This attitude was still evident one year later (1966) when he returned to the pope's statement. However, an important change was evident in his views on papal teaching authority. While he maintained that the pontiff's statement implied that there was yet no persuasive or sufficient argument to bring the traditional teaching, as laid down by Pius XII, into doubt, he stated that the teaching itself was an act of the noninfallible but authentic teaching magisterium of the Church. It was not just a disciplinary ruling. It was binding. Therefore it was for the pope as ultimate judge to determine whether the arguments and analyses which supported the traditional norms were persuasive and conclusive or not.[12] This does not mean that the pope would reserve to himself alone the ability to recognize the clarity of an argument. However, deference to papal authority was a good ground for assessing any new analyses and arguments against the traditional position on contraception to find out whether they were cogent enough to supersede the norms laid down by Pius XII and Pius XI "or at least to have rendered them doubtful." If the new analyses were sufficient to establish the moral liceity of contraception, then traditional arguments had all along been inadequate as support for the Church's position on the issue. Such a shortcoming would suggest that theologians had not done their work sufficiently well. In McCormick's opinion, this would be understandable "in the light of the strong curial controls which, in the view of many, prevented adequate free discussion of this matter for a fairly prolonged period."[13]

Supposing that theological discussions were not as free as they ought to have been, and the arguments behind the traditional teaching on contraception were not sufficiently cogent or persuasive, what would this do to the status of the teaching of the Church on this matter? Was this fact enough to establish at least the probable liceity of contraception as some theologians were then saying? McCormick at this point would not say anything on this issue. Nor would he, as yet, say whether contraceptive acts could be justified by "a sound and consistent analysis of conjugal intimacy."[14]

However, by 1967 McCormick had come to the conclusion that the Church's teaching on contraception was at least in a state of practical doubt and therefore subject to an interpretation based on the theory of probabilism. He was also, at this point, starting to lean toward the position of the majority report of the Birth Control Commission. Not unlike that report, he started questioning the soundness of an analysis "rooted in the notion of *actus naturae*."[15] His inclination toward this report was important because it indicated that McCormick had started to rethink the role of the Church as moral teacher not just in regard to contraception but in other areas as well.

Challenged on his views that the teaching on contraception was practically doubtful and therefore subject to probabilism,[16] McCormick responded by pointing out that this conclusion was based on the pope's actions and utterances on the matter so far. He believed that the pope's actions and utterances had given the impression that the Church was still searching for the will of God on the case. In an allocution to the Italian Feminine Center in 1966, for example, he said,

> The magisterium of the Church cannot propose moral norms until it is certain of interpreting the will of God. And to reach this certainty the Church is not dispensed from research and from examining the many questions proposed for her considerations from every part of the world. This is at times a long and not an easy task.[17]

This speech indicates that the magisterium was not certain that the ecclesial norm represented the will of God, and thus the Church needed further research on the question. Therefore, what prevailed, for the time being, was a situation of uncertainty or practical doubt. Consequently, he concluded,

> If certainty is required to teach moral norms, and if research is required to achieve this certainty, and if the research sources produce anything but certainty, then the conclusion must be that required certainty about these norms did not exist—hence that these norms could not be proposed (taught).[18]

The encyclical finally published by Pope Paul VI raised more questions than it actually settled.[19] Two of these have occupied McCormick ever since: concern with the nature of the teaching authority in the Church, and the scope of that authority.

NATURE OF THE MAGISTERIUM

McCormick first elaborated his views on the question of the teaching office in a paper he presented in 1969. The nature of the magisterium, he claimed, cannot be conceived independently of the prevailing notion of teaching in the church in any given era. This notion is in turn dependent on the self-definition of the Church, the way or manner of the exercise of authority in the Church, the educational status of the clergy and laity, and the educational theories and styles which are predominant in the era in question.[20]

NOTION OF TEACHING

McCormick notes that the view of authority in the pre-Vatican II Church was predominantly pyramidal. An important characteristic of such attitude was the belief that truth descended from the pope and bishops to rank-and-file believers. Another was the frequent identification of Church with a small group of people in positions of authority. One result of such ecclesiology was a questionable notion of teaching and of what it meant to be a teacher.[21]

According to McCormick, a number of other factors also helped to produce this type of teaching. One such factor was the generally poor condition of communications resulting in limited access to information, thought, and opinion from other parts of the world. Another was the fact that educational institutions were often cloistered from the major currents of secular life and intending to foster and maintain "Catholic attitudes" apart from the enlightenment that contemporary science could bring to them. This prevented them from obtaining full awareness of the complexity of issues. Furthermore, Church authority was highly centralized in Rome and at the diocesan levels, and papal documents were produced "from a single theological emphasis." Theologians were often so overawed by the fact of papal infallibility that they could not muster enough courage to question even the teachings of the noninfallible magisterium. The clergy were the best educated in the Church. Non-Catholic religious groups were considered adversaries to whom Catholics could hardly turn for theological enlightenment; they were simply not a reliable source of knowledge. Finally, the pre-Vatican II Church, like the rest of the world then, regarded education as "the handing down of the wisdom, experience, and resources of the professor to a rather passive and non-participative audience of students."[22]

McCormick notes that the cumulative effects of these were: (a) an undue separation of the teaching (*docens*) from the learning (*discens*) function in the Church, with the result that much was said about the right to teach and too little about the teacher's duty to learn; (b) an undue identification of this teaching function with the ecclesial hierarchy; (c) an undue stress on the judgmental aspect of the teaching function, which led to the narrowing of the meaning of the term *magisterium*, making it "synonymous with the hierarchical issuance of authoritative judgments." Other effects included: (d) an extremely disproportionate stress on the authority of the teacher rather than on evidence and the process of evidence-gathering, which in turn gave rise to a theology of response to authoritative teaching that was heavily obediential in emphasis; and (e) a view of theologians "as agents of the hierarchy whose major, and perhaps even sole task, was to mediate and apply authoritative teaching." Their creative efforts–their more proper educational and theological task–were viewed with distrust. The result of this was the "polarization between theologians and hierarchy, a growing lack of exchange and communication."[23]

Much later McCormick labelled this notion of authority a form of ultramontanism, which powerfully fosters "an ecclesiastical gnosism," which in turn exempts the hierarchy from standard criteria of scholarly accountability and reduces the theological task to merely explicating authoritative documents. This mentality, he says, peaked in the highly authoritarian and obediential motifs of *Humani Generis* and other statements of Pius XII.[24]

THE INFLUENCE OF VATICAN II

McCormick is convinced that Vatican II forever changed this notion of Church and of teaching in the Church from the juridical to one which is more open and less legalistic with respect to the authority of the magisterium. The Council, he believes, portrayed the Church as *communio* and described its structures in concentric terms by recognizing the special competence of the laity in various aspects of life as an indispensable enrichment of the Church. Vatican II explicitly recognized this competence when it directed the laity to shoulder its responsibilities "under the guidance of Christian wisdom and with eager attention to the teaching authority of the Church."[25] Therefore, it is the people of God who are the collective repository of Christian revelation and wisdom.

Through greater participation and involvement in the social and intellectual currents around them, Catholics have become more aware of the complexities of contemporary theological and social problems. They have also become more aware of the need to employ many competencies for their adequate analysis, and of the very tentative character of some earlier doctrinal formulations.[26] Due to cultural progress, the clergy is no longer the best educated group in the Church. Members of the laity enjoy special expertise in various fields, are capable of relating their expertise to doctrinal issues, and can often express themselves articulately in religious and theological matters. McCormick insists that this reformed understanding of Church "suggests, among other things, the need of broad communication if the wisdom resident in the Church is to be gathered, formulated, and reflected to the world."

Other contributing factors include the influence of television and other forms of mass media; the new ecumenical spirit, which is willing "to seek answers from and in association with other non-Catholic ecclesial groups"; and the modern styles of educational theories, which aim "to stimulate the student to self-involvement, to creativity (and) to experiment."[27]

McCormick believes that to be satisfactory the new view of teaching must consider teaching and learning as equal components in a dialectical process that leads to an ever deepening appreciation of reality. Judgment must be considered only one limited aspect of this process. Since teaching must persuade and not merely command, teaching in the Church must devote more attention than was hitherto the case to evidence and to the process of evidence-gathering and analysis. This is important in order to assess properly the ultimate meaning and authoritative value and character of collegial-episcopal pronouncements.[28] The new notion of teaching must emphasize docile assimilation and appropriation rather than unquestioning assent as the appropriate response to authentic non-infallible teaching. It must also include the creative reflection of theologians and the prophetic charism of all Christians in order to secure a meaningful and persuasive expression of the Christian faith in contemporary times.

Therefore, the aim of the teaching function in the Church is to search for new understanding of the faith, to discover the action of the Spirit in the Church, to determine the identifiable dimensions of Christian life in contemporary society, and to use whatever media are available to proclaim the Church's authoritative expression of its faith. This is a gigantic task; no single group in the Church can carry it out alone.[29]

Who speaks for the Church? McCormick believes that the Church's hierarchy does. Theologians as theologians are not authentic teachers, because they do not have a divine commission or mandate to function as authoritative judges of the Christian faith or to determine its application to conduct in our time. Only the pope and the bishops acting collegially are authentic teachers, that is "teachers endowed with the authority of Christ." They alone possess the promise of the guidance of the Spirit in their essential task."[30] The task of the theologian is to reflect systematically upon revelation in order to deepen its understanding in the Church; to prepare the beginning of a clear, precise, consistent, topical and persuasive formulation. Bishops *qua* bishops do not possess this scientific competence, this charism. Therefore, to measure up to their pastoral responsibilities and role as authentic teachers, they must draw on the best theological knowledge available.

> That is, the teaching function of the Church cannot occur without the contributions of all components. If we say it can, we have denied that they are true components of the teaching process. The theologian, therefore, has a teaching role not only in the sense that he mediates and applies decisions of the hierarchy, but in the more authentic sense that he analyzes the Christian message in contemporary times by exploring, questioning, innovating, hypothesizing. His reflection, analysis and formulation is a necessary pre-requisite for the proper (contemporary and persuasive) expression of the faith by hierarchical leaders. In this sense, he educates the hierarchical magisterium.[31]

Thus, although McCormick considers the Church's hierarchical magisterium a privilege given by Christ to his Church, and an "irreplaceable value" without which the Church would not be the Church, he also believes that the magisterium needs rehabilitation so that it can adequately face contemporary realities in the world. This refashioning must result in a magisterium in which all elements in the Church have a greater responsibility.[32] The point is that a healthy magisterium would be one that draws on all sources of wisdom which are resident in the entire Church.

> This is exactly what is not going on now. The International Theological Commission is a packed commission. Consultors on documents

like the one on reproductive technologies are not exactly known. When we have come to such levels of secrecy where consultors on such major documents are not known, then we are in trouble. At that point, the presumption the Church ought to enjoy in its official teaching has been undermined to such an extent that it no longer is a presumption of truth.[33]

THE SCOPE OF THE MAGISTERIUM

In the treatment of this question, McCormick has moved through three different stages. First, he argued for the inherent reasonableness of the magisterial claim to authority in matters pertaining to all aspects of the natural law, including its applications to concrete cases.[34] He believed such a voice of certainty was needed in view of the disagreements over concrete applications of natural law. The disagreements by reasonable and well-meaning people over the moral evaluation of premarital sex, homosexuality, adultery, and so on, were proofs of the incomplete nature of our perception of the implications of the primary principles of moral conduct. The difficulty arises from the fact that "certain truths about man's nature penetrate his consciousness gradually by historical processes and for the same reason are maintained only with difficulty."[35] The Church, on the other hand, is "divinely commissioned to consciences." Therefore,

> Because of this divine commission and the promise of aid in its execution, authentic Church interpretations of natural law morality enjoy the presumption of certainty and it is this presumption which founds the duty in prudence to accept in a human way (as contrasted with a merely mechanical conformism) these teachings.[36]

Second, McCormick also held that the Church could teach natural law infallibly on the grounds that natural law was integral to the gospel. Thus,

> the Church's prerogative to propose infallibly the gospel morality would be no more than nugatory without the power to teach natural

law infallibly. One could hardly propose what concerns *Christian men* without proposing what concerns *men*.[37]

McCormick gave up his position on the Church's infallible competence over the detailed prescriptions of natural law partly through the influence of Daniel Maguire. In an article he published in 1968, Daniel Maguire disagreed with McCormick on his view that the Church can teach natural law infallibly.[38] The Christian experience can and does enrich the natural law. And the magisterium, if it is faithful to the Christian experience, "has much to offer those who struggle for the realization of human values." However, this contribution can hardly be regarded as infallible.[39] Maguire considered McCormick's claim of ecclesial competence over natural law insufficiently nuanced and lacking in modesty, because it fails to distinguish between the general aspects of the natural law and their particular applications.

> The certitude of the general principle does not pass over into the discussion of cases such as the liceity of certain abortions or pills that prevent implantation. Here moral intuition, empirical data, philosophical probings, and the various forms of expertise are relevant, and the certainty of unapplied principle does not obtain.[40]

McCormick reacted positively to this criticism:

> Maguire is right, I believe, in saying that the infallible competence of the Church does not imply the power to proceed infallibly through the multiple judgments and informational processes required to apply these natural and gospel values to concrete instances. This restriction does not solve the question about the competence to define the natural law. It merely suggests that, regardless of what position one prefers on this point, he should distinguish between the natural law in its basic imperatives, and derivations or implications of this law. It also suggests that a more realistic and fruitful avenue of inquiry is the authentic noninfallible moral magisterium.[41]

Since the publication of *Humanae Vitae*, McCormick has approached the question of the Church's competence in morality under two aspects, an ecclesiological one, and a methodological one.

ECCLESIOLOGICAL CONSIDERATIONS

On the ecclesiological level, McCormick has continued to insist that the notion of competence must be understood analogously. The idea has a different meaning when used in regard to the "substance of the Christ-event" or revealed truth and when applied to "detailed prescriptions of the natural law."[42] These two senses represent two distinct spheres of moral evaluation, which McCormick, like Fuchs, characterizes as moral goodness and rightness.

Moral goodness refers "to the person as such, to the person's being open to and decided for the self-giving love of God. It is the vertical dimension of our being, it is salvation." This vertical realm is covered by and co-extensive with "the treasures of divine revelation" – the *depositum fidei*. Moral rightness, on the other hand, refers to the innerworldly behavior of human persons. This is the horizontal level, the realm where material moral norms are determined based on human experience, evaluation, and judgment.[43] Because this level refers to proper disposition of the realities of this world and to their realization in concrete behavior, it does not *per se* belong to the realm of the *depositum fidei* but to the realm of natural law and its application to concrete situations. The Church is not equally competent in this area as it is in regard to matters pertaining to personal goodness, because what happens in connection with moral rightness is not directly connected with "truths of salvation." The Church's claims to knowledge about what constitutes moral rightness or moral wrongness in any given situation of innerworldly behavior must, therefore, be made with caution and tentativeness, because her teachings on issues in this area are not buttressed by the certainty and stability that truths of salvation can enjoy.[44]

METHODOLOGICAL CONSIDERATIONS

McCormick believes that two types of confusion arise when the Church claims equal competence over the horizontal and vertical aspects of human existence. The first confusion comes from failure to distinguish between a principle and its application. Consider, for instance, the presumption in Catholic tradition against taking human life. This, says McCormick, represents the principle. However, what this principle enjoins or forbids in the concrete is difficult to define due to "the broad sense in which the very understanding of the principle shifts or is modified" or to new insights arising from the "assessment of contingent facts in relation to the principle's term of reference." Applications can change in the very understanding of the principles themselves or in the assessment of the contingent data which are relevant to the case.

A second problem arises when the particular application of a principle is confused for the principle itself and is consequently elevated to the level of a principle. The results are that

> the changeable is taken to be unchangeable, the contingent to be abiding, the formulation to be the substance. Revisions and modifications suggested by changing data, times and cultures are resisted as threats, and sclerosis of the thinking body settles in. The past becomes exclusively normative and moral leadership quietly shifts into other hands, a victim of incredibility.[45]

These confusions are possible, first, because of the human tendency to accord normative status to established practices on the bases of longevity or, second, due to the authoritative presentation of what initially was in fact an application but has become elevated by authoritative fiat or mistake to the status of a principle. The third and most important reason is that principles and their applications are in fact close and very malleable and may easily be confused. McCormick claims that in the Church's teaching, this confusion occurs more frequently in areas related to sex–birth control, reproductive technologies, abortion, homosexuality, masturbation, divorce and remarriage.

Since official formulations dealing with these issues are heavily dependent on human reason for their support, and given that the issues are remote from the core of the faith and are often very complex and specific, the Church ought to show "something more modest than absolute certitude" as it goes on with its mission of offering moral guidance. Therefore, we should not expect total agreement on the level of concrete applications of natural law. Pluralism on the level of concrete issues is an inescapable dimension of being human, that is, limited but committed, alert, and honest.

McCormick points to a number of significant developments that he believes to have contributed to our heightened awareness of pluralism as an inevitable fact of life since Vatican II. First is the development in magisterial awareness about its own competence evident in the Conciliar admission that the Church "does not have ready answers to every question" but is eager "to associate the light of revelation with the experience of mankind in trying to clarify the course upon which mankind has just entered."[46]

Second, a shift has occurred in moral methodology since Vatican II from an essentialist to a person-centered presupposition. In the explanatory notes approved by the council for interpreting the document on the Church in the modern world, it is noted that the subject matter in the second part of the document was made up of both permanent and contingent principles. The constitution, the Council said, was to be interpreted "according to the general norms of theological interpretation, while taking into account, especially in part II, the changing circumstances which the subject matter, by its very nature involves."[47] Also, while speaking of the harmonization of married love with the responsible transmission of life, the Council stated that good intention and motive are not the only considerations to take account of in judging the morality of human acts. Instead, "objective criteria must be used, based on criteria drawn from the nature of the human person and human action, criteria which respect the total meaning of mutual self-giving and human procreation in the context of human love."[48] McCormick insists that the official commentary on this passage indicates that the principle applies to all human actions, not just to sexuality and marriage, and that the choice of expression means that "human activity must be judged insofar as it refers to the human person integrally and adequately considered."[49] He maintains that this shift in methodology calls for a different type of evidence in our assessment of human actions. This evidence will be obtained also from the sciences and from general human experience and will be "a more gradual, inductive, time-consuming, messy, uncertain and ultimately pluralistic process." The process of evaluating human actions in this case, therefore, presupposes a different awareness of reality than the deductive method we inherited from the manuals would ever want to acknowledge.[50]

Other reasons for the heightened awareness of pluralism are the emergence of lay voices in the determination of right and wrong and the ecumenical spirit, both of which the council fostered and encouraged.[51] Finally, McCormick contends that the change in the understanding of authority in the Church makes allowance for possible error and distortion in the ordinary teaching of bishops and the pope. This was not the case previously.

The convergence of the above and other factors must therefore lead to lowered expectations about clarity and certainty in the application of moral principles to human life.[52] They must make us wary of monolithic and all-encompassing positions on moral matters. We no longer need a grand and sweeping ecclesial claim to moral authority. Instead, says McCormick, "there are good reasons in our time to restate a moderate ecclesiology on authentic Papal moral teaching–moderate in that it states the presumption of faith in such teaching."[53] Such ecclesiology will be manifest in a careful attention to the traditional distinction between grades of teaching. This is important if we must avoid what, in the words of Yves Congar, he describes as "creeping infallibilism," that is, the tendency to see every statement of the authentic magisterium as infallibly taught. McCormick accuses Germain Grisez and John C. Ford of perpetrating this in their interpretation of Church teaching on contraception.[54]

For Ford and Grisez, the teaching on contraception is infallibly proposed because it meets some important criteria set by Vatican II for such qualification. They believe in this regard that even if the norm on contraception is not contained in revelation "it is at least connected with it as a truth required to guard the deposit as inviolable and to expound it with fidelity." In support of this assertion they point out that no one "has seriously tried to show that anything in revelation is *incompatible* with the Church's teaching on the morality of contraception." Furthermore, although it is not a revealed doctrine, it has been handed down over the centuries "in one way or another" and more or less explicitly as revealed, that is, as something to be definitively held by the faithful.[55] To be definitively held, a doctrine does not need to be expressed in the language of solemn definition. The bishops scattered throughout the world do not in their day to day exercise of the ordinary magisterium use "the language of solemn definition, except when they quote some solemn definition previously made by the Church."[56]

It has been noted that the position of Ford and Grisez amounts to saying that once the magisterium has spoken in a definitive way about something, "it must necessarily be the case that what they speak about is a proper object of infallible teaching."[57] Therefore, the question of object would no longer constitute an independent criterion for determining whether or not the magisterium had spoken infallibly. In other words, once the magisterium decides that the matter on which it has spoken is matter for infallibility, it becomes so whether the subject has to do with the morality of war or of the marketplace, for example. It is one thing to teach that something involves a serious moral obligation and "quite another to claim that this teaching is now definitive, and demands an irrevocable assent." Were Ford and Grisez right, the implication would be that "the Church could not declare any mode of conduct wrong unless it were prepared to make an irreversible judgment on the matter. This would practically rule out any ordinary, noninfallible exercise of the Church's teaching authority on moral issues.[58]

McCormick believes that whereas everything authoritatively proposed which pertains to the deposit of faith belongs to the sphere of infallibility, this is not true of everything which has been authoritatively proposed in the moral sphere. His claim that material moral norms do not pertain to the Church's infallible teaching competence thus takes a much more radical view of the different grades of teaching in the Church than Grisez's views would seem to imply.

Such differences imply varying degrees of binding force as well. "Some very few are things 'to be definitively held,' others are more provisional and reformable."[59] Positions such as that expressed by Ford and Grisez tend to blur the distinction between the grades. They represent a form of "creeping infallibilism" or "magisterial maximalism," which tends to assimilate the ordinary magisterium into the extraordinary one. Whereas the proper response to infallible teaching in the Church is an act of faith, in the other case it is a presumptive certitude of the correctness of such teaching.[60] Even so, not every moral teaching of the Church calls for the same level of "presumptive certitude," as McCormick argues:

> I think that there are levels of authority with which the Church can impose things. For example, I think that the Church's teaching on abortion is a teaching of inherent soundness. I think it has tremendous amount of authority behind it, in terms of papal, episcopal and traditional presentation, etc. I do not think it is infallibly proposed

because the teaching involves the use of such philosophical concepts as direct and indirect. You do not want to say that the Church defines philosophical concepts as a part of revelation. However, I think that the teaching is a very high authoritative teaching. This is not the case with capital punishment. This is at a different level altogether. This is an application of a more general principle where people of goodwill could disagree in the Church. The bishops in this country have opposed it, the pope has also, but I do not think with the same authority. I think the matter of contraception is unique. The pope is trying to escalate that to the point where it is connected with dogmas of the faith. Carlo Caffara is behind this move. "You deny the Church's teaching on contraception and you are denying God's goodness." Well, come on, that's not correct.[61]

In some matters the teaching of the Church calls for even a lower level of submission on account of the newness or of the complex nature of the issues involved in these areas.

I think the teaching of the Church on reproductive technologies is very low grade in terms of authority. We have new problems on hand (for example, in the area of genetic technology), and if you are going to say really helpful things about them, you better get the expertise that is available around the world together to talk about this. That's not what they are doing in the Vatican. They are starting with the idea that certain past pronouncements are to be extended into the present and the future, and they control these developments. Therefore, the document on reproductive technology was more about contraception than it was about reproductive technology. To the authors of that document, what was at stake was the integrity of the unitive and procreative aspects of the sexual act. "If you have babies by *in vitro* fertilization, you give up on contraception right away." That's not the way to do these things. People see that. Unfortunately, it is our obligation, as moral theologians, to say these things, to point them out. We get the reputation of being Vatican bashers and everything else for saying what we have to say.[62]

Every teaching of the Church demands presumptive certitude, more or less. Therefore, "prudence demands the acceptance of the conclusion in defect of prevailing contrary evidence." However, since this certitude is only presumptive, circumstances can arise which will create a duty for the agent to treat such teaching differently in the light of changing fact and increasing understanding of ethical theory, and so on.[63]

Dissent

NATURE OF DISSENT

Eagerness to accept and adhere to official teaching will manifest itself in various ways: (a) respect for the person and office of the teacher, including a form of external behavior that fosters respect and support for the magisterium; (b) openness to what the teacher as teacher has to say; (c) readiness to evaluate critically one's position on the issue in question in light of this teaching with the intention of finding whether it can be "supported on grounds other than those presented"; and (d) a great reluctance to conclude to the erroneousness of the moral teaching of the magisterium even when one is clearly convinced of the inadequacy of the evidence and analyses which led to it. Thus, one would rather conclude that this teaching was positively doubtful rather than erroneous. A Catholic who follows these steps, McCormick argues, has responded to authoritative teaching in a proper way.

> Such procedural respect and reverence will generally lead to assent, but assent is not the immediate proportionate response. And if dissent occurs, one would suspect that it would occur, as a general rule, only after the passage of certain amount of time, since time is needed for the arduous reflection suggested here.[64]

Dissent is therefore not a personal right but a possible outcome of a long, arduous, respectful, and docile reflection on noninfallible teaching. Such a reflection constitutes a powerful help in the Church's search for truth and is the very condition for progress in understanding in the Church. Consequently, it must be viewed as part of the learning process in the Church. To consider dissent as a challenge to papal authority or as disloyalty would be to rule personal reflection out of court and to compromise our growth in understanding.[65]

At the end of *Humanae Vitae* Pope Paul VI exhorted priests to be good examples of loyal internal and external *obsequium* and insisted that the authoritative character of the Church's teaching should not be identified with the reasons adduced for the teaching. While accepting this, McCormick argues that the certainty of authoritative teaching cannot prescind from the analyses and arguments provided. Two extremes ought to be avoided—one which says that the teaching of the Church's magisterium is as good as the argument offered, and the other which considers it totally independent of the argument. The first attitude employs a one-sidedly rationalistic epistemology of moral cognition which makes the pope another theologian and shows little regard for genuinely authoritative character of the papal charism. The second one makes the pope an arbitrary issuer of decrees and edicts with no need for theological reflection.[66] If a teaching is valid independent of the reasons and arguments, then the possibility of dissent is eliminated in principle; if dissent is impossible, it is not clear in what sense one can say a teaching is noninfallible.

The middle ground consists in granting the presumption of correctness to the authentic noninfallible statements. This involves going through the various stages already indicated above. However, if at the end one is still not convinced of the correctness of the doctrinal conclusions, the presumption of correctness still prevails, at least until "a large number of loyal, docile, and expert Catholics share this same difficulty." At this point it would seem that this presumption of correctness has been weakened and that therefore the doctrine could be considered doubtful. "At this point one would wonder whether such a doctrine could give rise to a certain obligation in conscience."[67]

Dissent is therefore a statement about the possibility of error in the day-to-day exercise of the teaching function of the Church. This consequently raises questions about the meaning of the continual presence of the Holy Spirit promised to the Church by Christ and to which she often refers as proof for the validity of her teaching.[68] According to McCormick, again, two extremes must be avoided.

> The first would explain the assistance of the Holy Spirit in a way which dispenses with human processes. The second would simply reduce this assistance to human processes. The first is the notion of a

special assistance by the Spirit which represents a new source of hierarchical knowledge, arcane and impervious to any criticism developed out of a Christian experience, evidence and reasoning. Such a notion of assistance results in a form of fideism which makes it difficult, if not impossible, to see how any authoritative utterance is not thereby practically infallible. Furthermore, this notion is a summary edict of dissolution for the scholarly and theological fraternity. The second extreme is such an emphasis on analyses and reasons that the action of the Holy Spirit is simply identified with the shrewdest thinkers in the community and ultimately imprisoned in the best reasons they can unravel.

McCormick believes the best course of action is "one which would associate the activity of the Holy Spirit with human processes without identifying it with them."[69]

Error can occur in the magisterial function of the Church either as a result of inadequate evidence-gathering or inadequate evidence-assessing. Evidence-gathering becomes adequate when consultation is broad enough to allow the full wisdom stimulated by the Spirit's activity in the Church to emerge.

Evidence-assessing breaks down when consideration of the evidence is insufficient to allow the Holy Spirit to aid in the emergence of its meaning. In the contemporary world these inadequacies would seem to be traceable to a failure in the fullness of the collegial process at all levels.[70]

Therefore, the pope and the bishops must constantly strive to go beyond the isolation of their own reflections or those of particular restricted groups and engage the total resources of the community in the search for moral truth. Such a process cannot of course guarantee that genuine error cannot occur, considering that human beings are still human, with all that that entails. However, since the wisdom of the entire Church had apparently gone into its formulation, error would be detected as certain error only after a considerable time. Moreover, such error would be attributed to human frailty and failure in evidence gathering and the analyses, not to the Holy Spirit. For this reason, McCormick argues, theologians must continue to subject the principles and arguments used in magisterial documents to close and careful critique. This is the only way to distinguish between truth and error in moral judgments.[71]

Since dissent is "the terminus of a sincere attempt to assimilate authentic teaching,"[72] it must not be equated with mere advocacy, resistance, or violence. Nor must it be made to suggest "a kind of muscular tactic in the face of the entrenched establishment." It is a struggle for truth, not a struggle between superiors and subjects, a fact which tends to give it independent value and presents it as courageous, enlightened, honest, and forward-looking "almost regardless of the inherent merits of the dissenting point of view."[73] Dissent has no independent value in itself. Its lasting significance is in its relationship to truth. Dissent is worthwhile only if it contributes to the interplay among those elements which are essential for a vigorous magisterium. For this interplay to occur a certain atmosphere is necessary within the Christian community.

> This atmosphere is constituted by the preservation of certain values within the teaching-learning process: respect for the authority of the teacher, a pastoral devotion to truth and its sources, the freedom of scholarly research and publication, the existence of broad consultative procedures as the basis for the exercise of authoritative teaching, good relations between persons exercising various functions within the teaching process. If public dissent is to contribute to the learning process, its overall effect must be to support and strengthen these values which constitute the atmosphere just mentioned.[74]

McCormick is aware also that rather than strengthening the various charisms within the teaching function, dissent can polarize different groups in the Church, undermine confidence in the hierarchy of the Church, and consequently impair its effectiveness. Dissent can also prevent the faithful from having the opportunity to think through particular issues in the Church. Furthermore, it can even lead to a situation where people "associate theology with popular media rather than with serious, scholarly reflection." Consequently, one should dissent openly only if "other forms of less sensational dissent are ineffective and only in circumstances where an opposed error would cause great harm."[75]

THE THEOLOGIAN AND DISSENT

The silencing of Charles Curran by the Vatican in 1986 gave fresh impetus to discussion on dissent in the Church. McCormick has maintained that the issue had nothing to do with whether one agreed with Curran on every issue or not, because theology would not be worth that name without discussion and disagreement, and "the magisterium itself would be paralyzed by the sycophancy of theologians."[76] Infallibility was not the issue either, since the Church's authentic teaching on concrete moral issues "does not, indeed cannot fall into the category of definable doctrine." At issue is the question of the right of the Church to safeguard teaching by taking away a teacher's mandate to teach as a Catholic theologian. When and under what circumstances should this measure be taken? For the theologian the problem is what to do "if one judges a teaching authoritatively proposed to be one-sided, incomplete, partially inaccurate or erroneous."[77] Keep silence and avoid "the risk of causing scandal"? Or speak up and be "punished"?

McCormick also sees in the action against Curran a strong statement that one may not dissent from any authoritatively proposed teaching; an understanding of "authentic theological instruction" to imply presenting Church teaching "and never disagreeing with it, even with respect and reverence"; and a sense "that sound theological education means an uncritical acceptance of official Catholic teaching."[78] Furthermore, he is concerned about the pain that the Curran affair and other such incidents inflict on the Church. He believes that the 'coercive' atmosphere which they create weakens the episcopal magisterium, marginalizes theologians, demoralizes priests, reduces the laity by telling lay people that their experience and reflection count for nothing, and compromises the future of ministry through the imposition of rigid orthodoxy on seminaries and thereby jeopardizes their ability to minister to post–Vatican II Catholics. Also, it encourages the loss of the Catholic leaven by insisting that the term 'official teaching' "is simply synonymous with right, certain, sound, and unchangeable" – a situation which McCormick believes could lead to the public perception that the role of Catholic scholars is an "intellectual form of public relations."[79]

One important concern of the Vatican in the Curran case and in similar cases is the fear that certain theological speculations as well as the attitude of some theologians to Church authority on some moral questions might confuse the faithful, the majority of whom are not schooled in the niceties of theological thought. McCormick understands the injunction against scandalizing the faithful to mean that anyone who holds a dissenting view is by that very fact creating the occasion in the minds of others for neglect of, or disrespect for, the teaching authority of the Church. McCormick argues that "whether or not encouraging dissent in others is morally wrong depends on what the dissent is aimed at. If it is aimed at a teaching that is incomplete or inaccurate, it is quite appropriate, even obligatory."[80] In other words, McCormick believes that dissent is inevitable given the confusing nature of reality, the need for free speech which allows for differences in perspectives, the changing times, and the fresh problems which arise because of it.[81] Other factors are the varied cultural composition of a world Church, the Church's openness to the sciences and its recognition of the autonomy of earthly affairs, the acknowledgment of legitimate pluralism in the Church, and so on.[82] McCormick believes the faithful who are liable to confusion in the face of dissent must be educated to the idea that "our unity as a community does not ride or fall with absolute uniformity on the application of moral norms to very detailed questions." They must also be taught "to take theologians seriously, but not all seriously." They are not ultimate teachers in the Church.[83]

CONCLUSION

This chapter discussed McCormick's views on the role of the Church as bearer of moral tradition and shaper of moral character and established that McCormick has modified his position on many of the issues over the years. First, his notion of Church changed from a juridical understanding to one that was more in keeping with the sense of communion which Vatican II envisioned the Church to be. In keeping with this change, and in view of the fact that the notion of teaching in the Church is influenced considerably by other non-ecclesial factors, McCormick also believes there ought to be a change in the notion of teaching in the Church. The teaching and learning functions of the Church must not be separated, the hierarchical magisterium is the authentic but not the only element in the teaching function of the Church, and the judgmental and juridical aspects constitute one aspect of the notion of teaching. His notion of teaching in the Church also implies that more attention should be paid to the process of evidence-gathering and analysis than was hitherto the case and that theologians must be accorded proper recognition as teachers in their own right.

Notwithstanding the problems it would create vis-à-vis the teaching of the First Vatican Council, McCormick also moved from the position that the Church could teach natural law infallibly to one where he now states that the Church should be tentative and cautious in its pronouncements on the particular application of natural law.

McCormick certainly values the Church's moral magisterium. It is clear, however, that he thinks the teaching office of the Church needs reform in its self-understanding and in the way it is actually exercised. He wants to see a change from the juridical notion of authority in the Church to one that is concentric and allows for greater involvement of the various charisms in the Church, including those of the laity.[84] He wants a teaching office which jealously safeguards its authority by speaking rarely and only after wide consultation on those issues which do not belong to the deposit of faith. The reason is that, given the complexity of human reality and of human experience, no single institution can claim unbridled competence or speak to every human experience with unquestionable competence. In short, McCormick believes there are good reasons in our time "to restate a moderate ecclesiology on authentic but noninfallible" magisterial teaching.[85]

By insisting that the new concept of teaching implies that magisterial teaching must persuade, not command;[86] that docile appropriation, rather than unquestioning assent, must characterize the response of the faithful to episcopal teaching,[87] and that the magisterium should draw from the work of theologians;[88] McCormick does not seem to me to be asking for the subordination of the magisterium of the bishops to that of theologians, as Germain Grisez assumes.[89] Nor is he "forgetful that faith is a presupposition of theology."[90] McCormick is only suggesting safeguards against arbitrary use even of the divine mandate to teach. He is thus acutely aware of many instances of such abuse of power in our history.

Grisez is, too, although he seems to consider that fact inconsequential.[91]

Finally, I see no evidence of the "political attitude" concerning magisterial authority to which Grisez refers.[92] On the contrary, it is evident in McCormick's work that he is concerned for accountability and responsibility from theologians. Aside from his point that theologians are not authoritative teachers, he also sees the need for greater self-criticism within the theological community.

> We theologians need to be more critical of one another—in a courteous and disciplined way, of course—so that the hierarchy does not bear the whole responsibility of correcting one-sidedness or irresponsibility, and therefore get forced into a dominantly negative role.[93]

In conclusion, I want to highlight some deficiencies and difficulties I see in McCormick's position on the Church as moral teacher. First, McCormick makes no effort to develop an ecclesiology. Rather, he clings to bits and pieces from Yves Congar, Avery Dulles, Francis Sullivan, and Richard McBrien. Therefore, his view of the Church as moral teacher is not all-encompassing. It ignores the fact of the Church as a shaper of moral character and pays too much attention to the role of theologians and the hierarchical magisterium as teaching voices in the Church. One wonders whether encyclicals and authoritative statements from the magisterium do, in fact, teach louder than the lives of the saints or the witness of martyrs, past and present. And what is the role of worship and celebrations in the Church?

McCormick also pays too much attention to dissent. The problem with this is that it distracts from other equally important issues and gives rise, as McCormick himself states, to a class of theologians whose only claim to fame is that they are dissenters and who, unlike McCormick, present their views as a form of neo-orthodoxy, even when untested by time or by their peers.

Perhaps the most complex of the issues treated in this chapter is the idea of moral goodness and moral rightness. To a considerable degree this distinction has brought some clarity to the discussion on moral norms and the extent of ecclesial competence on norms. The question is how far the distinction can be carried without introducing, at least for the Christian, an unacceptable dualism into human experience. One result of the incarnation is the merging of the orders of creation and redemption. Thus, every action of the Christian has eternal implications. This is the reason why even such 'mundane' actions as feeding the hungry or clothing the naked assume eternal spiritual significance. For this reason, one wonders whether the moral rightness or wrongness of an act can be analyzed in abstraction from the goodness or badness of the agent. Is contraception, for example, totally an issue of moral rightness and thus completely unconnected to the salvation of the agent? Or can it also be indicative of the agent's disposition toward the Absolute? If so, to what extent can we rule the Church out of it?

Indeed, McCormick was able to maintain a balance earlier when he argued simply that since the Church's competence in matters pertaining to the practical application of natural law is not absolute, that it must approach issues in this area with tentativeness. However, incorporating the notion of rightness and wrongness through the influence of European philosophers and theologians seems to have offset this balance. Therefore, there are three pitfalls to avoid. One is the pre–Vatican II ecclesiology, which believed that the teaching was valid as the authority was legitimate, and that formal authority was sufficient validation for moral teaching even at the concrete level. The second is rendering the Church irrelevant in moral matters. The third is the dualistic approach to human experience that can result from excessive adherence to the distinction between moral rightness and moral goodness.

However, one must appreciate McCormick's attempt to maintain a balance between the role of the (faith) community and that of the individual in moral determination. Because for McCormick moral theology is a study of the behavioral implications "of Christian beliefs about man – his origins, his destiny and his world"[94] – we shall devote the next chapter to an examination of McCormick's anthropology.

4

ANTHROPOLOGY

Since we have so far discussed the nature and sources of Christian theological ethics, I now intend to bring together McCormick's dispersed thought on the human person as both the subject of moral evaluations and as moral agent. A chapter on 'man' as 'he' exists and acts in the world is necessary for several reasons. The search for the good of the human person, adequately considered, is a recurring theme in McCormick's moral theory. It is, in my view, the architectonic idea of his moral theory; even proportionate reasoning is subordinate to it. McCormick has also paid considerable attention to the moral agent, as we discovered in our discussion on the role of faith in moral experience.[1] In that discussion we spoke of McCormick's view on the role of faith in transforming the agent's view of persons, in motivating him or her to follow Christ, and in imbuing the agent with a style of performing the moral tasks common to all people. Finally, this chapter is intended as a link between the discussions on the nature of moral theology that the previous chapters represent, and the issue of moral agency which will occupy us in the next two chapters. It is necessary to provide such a link not only because the human person, adequately considered, is a pivotal theme of McCormick's moral theory but also because ethics is about human persons. Consequently, every ethicist must, at some point, explain the underlying anthropology of his or her work so that readers can be adequately informed concerning the assumptions which guide the author's work.

WHAT DEFINES THE HUMAN PERSON?

McCormick often refers to Louis Janssens's view of the person. It is difficult to tell whether these references constitute dependence,

74

because often the ideas he attributes to Janssens have been present for many years in his own work.[2] The unresolved issue of dependence aside, a search for McCormick's anthropology should take note of Janssens's anthropological constants at least for the fact that McCormick connects many of his ideas with Janssens's writings since 1980.

Anthropological constants refer to the "constitutive conditions which must always be presupposed in any human action" and taken into account in the "creative establishment of specific norms for a better assessment of human worth and thus for human salvation."[3] A search through McCormick's works yields the constants discussed below.

CREATED IN GOD'S IMAGE

Not unlike Janssens's, McCormick's anthropology is primarily predicated on the creaturehood of the person.[4] Not only do human beings have their origin in God the Creator, but they are redeemed by and destined for God.[5] Creation in the image of God confers dignity and makes everyone equally valuable. As the foundation of human dignity, it "dictates *who* is to be considered worthy: every individual, regardless of condition,"[6] and highlights human equality, regardless of functional importance. The question, of course, is whether creation in the image of God also confers personhood. McCormick's view on this issue becomes clear when one examines his position on the status of the fetus in the abortion debate. The discussion which follows is not concerned with abortion but rather is meant to highlight the author's answer to the question whether the human status is an achievement or an endowment.

There are three discernible approaches to this question in the literature.[7] One approach links both the ontic and moral status of the embryo to its possession of some internal characteristics like human parentage and genotype, or to the embryo's developmental capability. Proponents of this view generally defend a developmental theory of human personhood. Another approach, a relational one, bases the worth and value of the embryo on the goodwill of the host, the mother. When the mother accepts pregnancy,

> it is then that its [the fetus's] potentiality for relationality and sociality is activated, because it is brought into a personal relationship with

a human person, with the only human person who can actuate this potentiality while the fetus is still in the mother's body and in a previable state.[8]

The third approach relies on performance or functional characteristics. Joseph Fletcher, a prominent proponent of this position, states,

Neocortical function is the key to humanness, the essential trait, the human *sine qua non*. . . . Without the synthesizing function of the cerebral cortex (without thought or mind), whether before it is present or with its end, the person is nonexistent.[9]

Although McCormick espouses the developmental approach and considers fetal personhood dependent on the acquisition of individuality, he grants full humanity to the embryo even prior to individuation because the embryo is in the process of becoming a person.[10]

On the basis of the evidence I have seen (though I have not seen it all, by any means), I am inclined to see individualization as the crucial developmental stage – and individualization seems to occur prior to the development of the cerebral cortex. Be that as it may, what calls for our protection is *personne en devenir*, a contemporary rendering of Tertullian's "he is a man who will become a man."[11]

Genetic individuation and developmental individuation of the embryo are important markers in McCormick's views on personhood. While the former is present from "the earliest beginnings," the latter "is completed only when implantation has been completed, a period of time whose outside time limits are around fourteen days."[12] Until the developmental individuation is completed, the embryo, though human, is not yet a person. Therefore, respect for nascent life does not make the same demands at this stage as it does later. It is on this ground that McCormick would allow "preliminary research aimed at eventual safe transfer," as well as "the loss of embryos in attempted clinical application of in vitro fertilization," although "not without fear and trembling."[13]

In summary, the principal thrust of McCormick's position on the source of personhood is that the ontological status of a being does not depend on a subjective decision exterior to its being. Furthermore, the value of the human individual does not depend on its physiology, as Fletcher believes, or merely on the fact that this physiology will eventually lead to functional differences which are morally relevant, as the classical position holds. Neither physiology or potentiality alone nor both of them together constitutes source for human personhood or gives the reason for respecting the human being. Each human being has an intrinsic dignity which is not subject to whims or calculations.

> The greatest affirmation of this alien dignity is, of course, God's Word-become-flesh. As Christ is of God, and Christ is *the* man, so all persons are God's, his darlings, deriving their dignity from the value He is putting on them. This perspective stands as a profound critique of our tendency to assess persons functionally, to weaken our hold on the basic value that is life.[14]

This consideration which is basic to the Judeo-Christian tradition, McCormick argues, must lead to special care for the weak, defenseless, powerless, and unwanted members of the human race. For example, McCormick believes it robs a person of his or her worth to be left to die for institutional or managerial reasons, such as the inability of the family to pick up the cost of an otherwise ordinary treatment. It is equally inhuman to refuse medical treatment to a child owing to retardation. On the other hand, respect for human dignity demands the withdrawal of treatment when such treatment causes excessive pain and the prognosis is poor.[15]

Although McCormick believes that human personhood is not dependent on the decision of any other human being, he is also convinced that personal status requires minimal achievement not only genetically but also in the form of developmental individuality. Therefore, he gives the following summary of Janssens's definition of the human person as his understanding also of the human person in all his or her essential aspects.

> The human person is (1) a subject (normally called to consciousness, to act according to conscience, in freedom and in a responsible way);

(2) a subject embodied; (3) an embodied subject that is part of the world. (4) Persons are essentially directed to one another (only in relation to Thou do we become I). (5) Persons live in social groups, with structures and institutions worthy of persons. (6) The human person is called to know and worship God. (7) The human person is a historical being, with successive life stages and continuing new possibilities. (8) All persons are utterly original but fundamentally equal.[16]

FINITUDE

Creatureliness implies finitude as well. That is to say, it imposes limitations on our being and on our doing. Thus, although we are capable of choices, our choices are limited by time, space, and matter. In these circumstances therefore, good and evil are closely intertwined, and the good we achieve often comes at the price of deprivation and imperfection. Thus

> we must kill to preserve life and freedom; we protect one through the pain of another; our education must at times be punitive; our health is preserved at times by pain and disfiguring mutilation; we protect our secrets by misstatements and our marriages and population by contraception and sterilization.[17]

Every choice is therefore a sacrifice that could bring about mixed and ambiguous results. Furthermore, finitude implies a practical limitation on human capacity to love. Although McCormick believes that the ideal to love one another as Christ loves us must be pursued constantly, he also understands there are limits to what each finite creature can do. To refuse to accept this limitation is to fail to recognize that to impose perfect love on imperfect creatures is a disproportionate demand capable of turning creatures from God and in fact turns them into God.[18]

A HISTORICAL SUBJECT

McCormick also speaks of the human person as a historical being. He refers to our being rooted in time and space and to our characteristic as changing beings whose self-definition and experience of self emerge "from a consciousness in contact with a rapidly changing world."[19] More than any other consideration, the awareness of human historicity is the basis of McCormick's belief in the dynamic nature of natural law and of his recommendation to the magisterium for great caution in descending to detailed specifications of the demands of Christian love.[20]

SOCIALITY

The human person is also a social being, one who lives in the world and in relationship with others. Sociality is closely tied with human creaturehood. The person's dignity is rooted in the relationship with God. This relationship is pursued and nurtured only through relationships with other persons. Like everyone else, the Christian cannot exist except in community. As McCormick says, the person's potentialities are conditioned by "the authenticity of the other members of the community, and vice versa – that is, the community exists for the individual." It is not an independent entity to which the individual is subordinated or into which the personal good is absorbed. "It does not serve an abstract ideal; rather that ideal is incarnate in each of its members."[21] Therefore, the individual and the community are not two separable and competing entities.

> The individual and the community are related like only partially overlapping circles. At points there is identification of concerns and goods, at other points there is distinction. Thus, while the individual is an integral part of the community and must take it into account in defining his or her own prerogatives and rights, still the individual does not exist for the community in a way that *totally* subordinates him or her to it.[22]

This balance between the individual and community can only be maintained with delicate care. Here, we are merely concerned with the question of obligations which are part of the requirements of membership in society. There are many such obligations. It is clear, then, that McCormick understands that the other side of sociality must keep in mind the implications of the Bantu proverb, "I am because we are." Such a philosophy takes for granted that while the individual derives his or her identity from the group, he or she is also involved in safeguarding the common good. Thus, individual membership in human communities goes hand in hand with some obligations. "Individuals ought to–indeed, can–be rightfully forced to make certain sacrifices for the common good (for example, conscription, proportionate taxation)."[23] Such demand is understandable when we are dealing with a person who is free and capable of making informed and free decisions. The difficulty arises when the person is incapable of such decision because of legal (e.g., age) and mental incompetence. Since such subjects cannot be regarded as moral agents if we are to follow the classical definition, the question is whether they have any responsibilities to the community. The reverse side of this question is whether the community has a right to make certain demands on such individuals.

For McCormick, sociality implies as well that every individual

> *ought* also to take into account, realize, and make efforts in behalf of the lives of others, for we are social beings, and the goods that define our growth and invite it are goods that reside also in others. Therefore, when it factually is good, we may say that one *ought* to do so (as opposed to not doing so).[24]

This is also true of children and other incompetent individuals. The argument is simple: one *ought* to choose to contribute to support the goods which define our common flourishing because we owe this to the rest of humanity. Indeed, one's own flourishing depends on this. McCormick also uses this argument to justify limited experimentation[25] on children and other noncompetent research subjects as well as cases of organ donation. Since children and other noncompetent individuals are human subjects they ought, *up to a point*, "share in the general effort and burden of health maintenance and disease control" that is "part of our growth and flourishing as humans."[26] Although such subjects cannot give consent, it is reasonable sometimes to presume that the child would wish this procedure because *he ought to*. One wonders whether McCormick is laying too much of the burden of the maintenance of human relationship on the child's shoulders. Here is how he reacts to this suggestion:

A construction of what the child *would* wish (presumed consent) is
not an exercise in adult capriciousness and arbitrariness. . . . It is
based, rather, on two assertions: (1) that there are certain values (in
this case, life itself) definitive of our good and flourishing, hence
values that we ought to choose and support if we want to become and
stay human, and that therefore these are good also for the child; and
(2) that these "ought" judgments, at least in their more general
formulations, are a common patronage available to all men, and
hence form the basis on which policies can be built.[27]

McCormick's position therefore hinges on one important notion, namely "the common good." We all have to contribute to it, to
the best of our ability. His position on this issue is highly nuanced.
There are things we all, children included, have to do in virtue of
social justice. Involvement in non-therapeutic experimentation
(even in the case of children and other noncompetent subjects) is an
issue of social justice if it does not involve undue burden. In fact, in
the case of children, as I pointed out, McCormick allows only
negligible inconvenience.[28] Therefore, involvement of children in
non-therapeutic experiments with negligible risk is not an issue of
charity, as Paul Ramsey would hold.[29]

For Ramsey, Christian covenant-fidelity calls for actions "that
embody righteousness in the relations of man to man."[30] Such
faithfulness yields "informed consent" as the morally relevant consideration in medical practice. Ramsey believed that the rule re-
quiring informed consent in medical experimentation is needed "to
ensure that [for the sake of future beneficial consequences to hu-
manity] no man shall be degraded and treated as a thing or an
animal in order that good may come of it."[31] Children are to be
protected in a special way against any consequentialist incursions.

Where there is *no* possible relation to the child's own recovery, a child
is not to be made a mere subject of medical experimentation for the
sake of supposable good to come. . . . To begin to experiment on
children in ways that are not related to *them* as subjects is already a
sanitized form of barbarism; it already removes them from view and
pays no attention to the faithfulness-claim which a child, simply by
being a sick or dying child, places upon us and upon medical care.[32]

Ramsey's theological concern is obviously with the protection of the 'neighbor' whose interests he wants to protect from "long-range social ideals"[33] achieved through a series of "curious exceptions." As Lisa Cahill points out, the concept of the common good from which McCormick argues

> is distinctive in its comprehension of all persons equally and by its ordering to a transcendent communion, that of persons in God. McCormick defines justifiable experimentation on the premise that communal interaction is an essential component of the realization of values, and proposes it with the conviction that those values persons "tend towards" or seek are common ones.[34]

Although McCormick believes that we ought to perform certain acts on grounds of social justice, he also states that there are works not all of us are expected to make. To this category belong "choices involving notable risk, discomfort, inconvenience." Such works are done based on "individual generosity and charity."[35] Children ought not be exposed to such tasks. This caveat shows McCormick's awareness of the possibility of abuse by sacrificing the rights of the individual to the welfare of the whole community. That is why, in the case of children, he cautions that to justify consent in experimental procedures which do not directly benefit the child, the experiment must involve no discernible risk or undue discomfort to the child.[36] In case of fetal experimentation, he adds the condition that the experiment must be necessary[37] and cause no discernible risk for the mother or added discomfort or pain for the fetus.

What McCormick has done is to take human sociality seriously as part of human nature and to argue that we can also determine moral agency based on it, if there is proportionate reason.

THE HUMAN PERSON AS MORAL AGENT

Catholic moral tradition holds that freedom and knowledge are the two necessary conditions for moral agency. Thus, not all acts done by human beings are moral acts.[38] McCormick, too, shares this conviction.

Central to McCormick's discussion on freedom is the theory of basic (fundamental) freedom, which, as he points out, "entered systematic theological reflection largely through the anthropology of Karl Rahner."[39] Fundamental or basic freedom is generally described by theologians as

> the freedom that enables us not only to decide freely on particular acts and aims but also, by means of these, to determine ourselves totally as person and not merely in any particular area of behaviour.[40]

Basic freedom presupposes that the moral order "is properly and primarily constituted by the order of personal response," which involves the exercise of a basic choice between the self and God and between love and selfishness.[41] Therefore, it refers to the relationship between the agent as a free person and his or her actions. Like freedom of choice, it is expressed through choice of particular goods. However, whereas freedom of choice concerns the psychological motivations or principles behind our choice of *particular objects,* fundamental freedom involves a basic orientation or a fundamental option on the part of the self-conscious subject to realize himself or herself either in openness to God and thus to other self-conscious subjects or through withdrawal from them.

An important challenge involved in the theory of the fundamental option is to maintain a balanced formulation of the relationship of basic freedom to the freedom of choice exercised in individual acts. McCormick tries to steer a middle course between the view that one cannot totally commit oneself in a single brief act and the belief that a single act can describe one's standing before God, regardless of any other consideration. He maintains that both views represent a distorted notion of human acts because they fail to consider them integrally.

> Take adultery, for example. This can be described in two ways, abstractly or integrally. Abstractly, adultery can be said to occur in a very brief period of time. It is as brief as its mere physical occurrence. But more integrally viewed, adultery includes a larger

experience: the meetings, thoughts, desires, plans, effects as foreseen, the vacillations, and so on. In other words, realistically viewed,
adultery is a whole relationship brought to this culmination. Most
often it is the culmination of a process including many components.
Is it not this totality which a person must be said to choose, not
simply and abstractly extramarital intercourse? If the entire experience is understood as the full meaning of the action, then is there
not good reason for thinking that adultery could indeed and presumably does elicit a serious moral response? This same analysis is
true in other areas if the single act is understood in more human and
integral terms. I believe that this is how "grave matter" must be
explained to remain true to contemporary psychological data on
freedom.[42]

In short, not only does serious moral choice not always correspond with the performance of an individual act and vice versa, but
the full meaning of the action can be ascertained only by taking the
entire experience into consideration. One inference from this, in
McCormick's view, is the need realistically to assess actions before
we relate them to the use of our basic freedom. Furthermore, in
spite of such assessment, human definition of particular actions can
only be abstract and general because "it does not and cannot tell us
what the individual is meaning, doing, suffering, experiencing as he
performs the realistically defined actions."[43]

In summary, basic or fundamental freedom has the following
characteristics: (a) It is free. It is within the power, and it is the
responsibility of the moral agent to realize "the fundamental posture or orientation toward the ultimate good of human life" through
object choices and a fundamental option or self disposition.[44] (b) It is
supernatural because the radical disposition of the self characteristic of fundamental option is inconceivable without divine empower-
ment under the grace of the Spirit. (c) It is obscure. Fundamental
freedom is located at the deepest level of human consciousness and
thus excludes adequate conceptual and propositional formulation.[45]
(d) Although it defies total conceptualization, basic freedom is still
conscious without objective formulation. Even so, the agent can
only infer about his or her state before God by conjecture.[46] (e) We
cannot say with certainty when a moral agent opts for openness
toward God and the world or makes a negative commitment against

them. (f) Fundamental freedom is a definite and total commitment, which "excludes the possibility of a series of quickly repeated transitions between life and death."[47]

In response to the objection that the theory of fundamental option cannot account for the distinction between light and grave matter but rather trivializes sin and all but obliterates the sense of sin in people,[48] McCormick points out that all acts do not carry the same weight and that not all wrongful acts are equally disruptive of the good, whatever that is construed to be. However, the theory of fundamental freedom is not a proposal for distinguishing between light and grave matter.

> That distinction is found in the objective nature of the "action against our own good," whether it is seriously disruptive of personal or communal good or not. Fundamental option enters to explain the existence and gravity of personal *sin*, which cannot simply be equated with the gravity of the matter.[49]

Concerning the accessibility of fundamental freedom to consciousness, McCormick argues that the theory of fundamental freedom does not say that basic freedom is unavailable to thematic awareness. It only asserts that "it is not *completely* available to conceptual awareness."[50] He believes that the opponents of the theory generally misunderstand its underlying anthropological basis.

KNOWLEDGE

McCormick considers two types of knowledge: prediscursive and discursive.

Prediscursive knowledge

This type of knowledge, in McCormick's words, is prereflective,[51] or pre-thematic, or connatural.[52] It is prior to cultural differentiations, although its judgments can be "affected by cultural distortions." McCormick also equates prediscursive knowledge, in Rahner's words, with the "moral instinct of faith." As James J. Walter points out, the various terms McCormick uses to describe this notion seem to create two slightly different senses of the idea.[53]

As connatural, prediscursive knowledge (intelligence) "without reflection grasps the possibilities" to which it points.[54] As the moral instinct of faith, it is "chiefly responsible for one's ultimate judgment on concrete moral questions."[55] Ultimately, we are not speaking of two distinct realities. Prediscursive knowledge described as connatural knowledge or as the "moral instinct of faith" "cannot be adequately subject to analytic reflection." In spite of possible distortions due to personal or cultural biases they remain "a more reliable test of the humanizing and dehumanizing, of the morally right and wrong, of proportion, than our discursive arguments."[56]

Discursive knowledge

This type of knowledge is concerned with analysis and the adoption of a hierarchy of values. Discursive knowledge, in McCormick's terms, is an extension of our sociality. An important implication of our sociality is that we cannot know in isolation. Being Christian, for example, entails belonging in a world of shared knowledge concerned with the moral implications of God's self-disclosure in Jesus Christ.

> Just as the Christian's mode of being is a sharing, so the moral knowledge necessary to its continuation and development is the result of a communal experience, a communal discernment that prolongs knowledge into the twilight human areas where there are no sharp contours, no bright colors.[57]

The Christian comes to knowledge of moral rightness or wrongness in the light of the gospel and human experience. The light of the gospel is mediated through the believing community in a number of ways, namely, "tradition, the magisterium of the Church, personal reflection and prayer, reflection and discussion with other Christians and even non-Christians (e.g., Catholics with non-Catholic Christians), theological scholarship,"[58] and through attention to the sciences. Although discursive knowledge is largely communal in its source, judgment of right or wrong is largely a personal judgment. Therefore, even though the moral teachings of the Church are especially important in the agent's formation of conscience, it is conscience itself which can determine the proper course of action.

McCormick defines conscience in its broadest sense as "judgment about the moral licitness or illicitness of an individual's concrete action." In this sense conscience functions as subjective norm of morality. As objective norm of morality, it "provides general information about the moral character of human actions." As a dictate about personal concrete action, conscience has roots

> in the depths of the person where a person is innately inclined to the good, to the love of God and neighbor. This inclination takes more concrete form in general moral knowledge and becomes utterly concrete and personal when a person judges about the loving or unloving, selfish or unselfish – briefly, about the moral quality – of his own action.[59]

McCormick also upholds the traditional belief in the supremacy of conscience. However, the moral agent must take pains to educate and properly form his or her conscience in the wisdom resident in the entire Christian community. In this regard the question arises concerning the weight of theological opinion in the formation of individual conscience when this opinion is at variance with the official formulation by the magisterium of the Church. There is usually no problem when the agent is sure which position to take. However, the answer is not so simple in situations of conflict. Again, McCormick resorts to the traditional teaching of the manuals on this issue and insists that the doubt must be resolved, since it is immoral to act with uncertain conscience.[60]

Following the manuals, McCormick lists three steps toward the resolution of the doubt. First, we have to solve the doubt directly by consulting expert opinion and arguments on the issue and weighing all the available evidence. If this fails, we would have recourse to proximate reflex principles.[61] If these cannot help, then the agent may have recourse to the principle of probabilism. McCormick acknowledges that sometimes even probabilism cannot work, not only because it is not always clear what opinions constitute genuinely probable opinion but also, as we have seen, because sometimes probabilism cannot apply, owing to the nature of the case. It is in such situations of ambiguity and conflict that McCormick suggests the use of proportionate reasoning.

Conscience is neither a dictator nor a slave. It is a discerning guide. As such, it must use all available means of enlightenment to dispel ignorance. However, it cannot be dictated to even when it is in doubt or clearly erroneous. Instead, it must be allowed to assume its rightful place in moral decision-making. Says McCormick, "The articulated wisdom of the community—the teaching of the magisterium—*enlightens* conscience; it does not *replace* it."[62] It is for this reason that McCormick regards dissent as a fundamental right of the human person. Dissent can become inevitable owing to tension between the role of the community as moral teacher and the responsibility of the moral agent to remain faithful to his or her own best judgment. This applies not only to theologians but to every informed and committed Christian as well. The right to dissent stems from the agent's being as a free, responsible, and knowledgeable Christian.

Conclusion

I have presented the principal elements of McCormick's anthropology. There are two sides to his understanding; namely, the person as subject of moral deliberation and as agent. I have stressed both sides because of their importance in McCormick's work. This distinction shows continuity and discontinuity between his thought and that of the manuals. The manuals extensively treated the person as moral agent but paid little attention to the person as subject. This is understandable considering that they were more concerned with seeking "eternal truths" and searching for "immutable essences" than with the human person as subject of moral deliberation.

Unlike the manuals, McCormick now makes the human person integrally and adequately considered the focus of his moral deliberation. In this, he is in line with many other contemporary theologians around the world who, since the Council, have made the same change. These theologians who subscribe to a person-centered morality find support for their position in the general orientation of the Council but especially in the following passage from the document on the Church in the modern world (*Gaudium et Spes*):

> When there is therefore, a question of reconciling marital love with the responsible transmission of life, the moral character of the behavior does not depend simply on good intention and evaluation of motives, but ought to be determined by objective criteria, derived from the nature of the person and its acts, which take account of the whole meaning of mutual giving and human procreation in the context of true love.[63]

Official commentary on this passage explains that the acts must not be judged merely according to their biological aspects but insofar as they pertain to "the human person integrally and adequately considered."[64] McCormick began to subscribe to some form of personalist morals even before the Council, as shown by his conviction that charity, not law or human acts alone, should form the center of moral determination.[65]

I showed in chapter 1 that although he had solved the problem of the removal of the probably dead fetus on grounds of proportionate reason, he was not prepared then to forgo the idea that some human acts are intrinsically evil, that is, regardless of other human considerations. However, by 1968 he had clearly become an advocate of the determination of moral significance based on other considerations than mere external acts. He now maintained that based on the order of values, making a false statement, for example, could sometimes be the morally right thing to do if it was demanded by and protective of personal values. We are all obliged to seek for and always protect values which promote the good of human persons, precisely as persons in community. "Therefore, moral significance does not refer to mere physical acts. Rather it is an assessment of an action's relation to the order of persons, to the hierarchy of personal value."[66] The personalist orientation was also evident in his concern, in the same year, that contemporary attitudes to sexuality were taking sex away from the sphere of the truly personal marriage and thus depriving it of its significance.[67] Since 1968 the personalist criterion has become the central idea of McCormick's moral theory.

The turn to the search for the good of integral humanity as the chief concern of moral theology also raises a considerable number of questions. How does one, for example, relate to a being who possesses an 'alien dignity'? What actions are destructive or promotive of the good of the person? How can such determinations be made? As McCormick himself puts it, "If *persona integere et adequate considerata* is the criterion for rectitude, it means that a different (from traditional) type of evidence is required for our assessment of human action."[68] While the evidence for the rightness or wrongness of human conduct should be as all-encompassing as possible,[69] the assessment of such evidence in a conflict situation would be carried out teleologically, using proportionate reasoning. While McCormick's espousal of proportionate reasoning is motivated by the need to discover what best promotes the good of the person integrally and adequately considered in the circumstance, the debate over proportionate reasoning, as we shall see in the next chapter, hinges on the role of human intentionality, interconnectedness, embodiment, finitude, sinfulness, cultural conditioning, and so on, which define the person's role in the determination of right and wrong.

5

PROPORTIONATE REASON

In chapter 1, we saw McCormick's earliest use of proportionate reasoning to solve a difficult case. We also saw that he understood proportionate reason as a concrete value in relation to other elements in the situation. This value, such as the certain life of the woman vis-à-vis the uncertain life of the fetus, provides the basis for justifying the action. I argued in that chapter that McCormick's understanding of proportionate reason implied a revision of the principle of double effect. The principal elements of this revision are: (a) the assumption of a hierarchy of values on the basis of which one has to make a prudent choice of what to do in times of conflict; and (b) the argument that the traditional understanding of what constitutes directness in human action is too closely tied to causality. McCormick came to the conclusion as early as his dissertation that the terms 'direct' and 'indirect' refer to intention. Even so, he refused to base his judgments on intention alone, because there can be more than one intention – the *finis operis*, or the end of the act, and the *finis operantis*, or the end of the agent. McCormick maintained that unless we could determine that the effect of an act is chosen or willed either as an end or as necessary means we cannot conclude that the act is direct and therefore immoral.[1]

Although McCormick had taken steps toward the revision of the principle of double effect, the credit for drawing attention to the difficulties in the use of that principle rightfully goes to Peter Knauer.[2] As I stated earlier, McCormick's refusal to accept proportionate reason as the primary element of the principle of double

91

effect cost him this honor. For him, at this time, they were two distinct principles.

The debate over proportionate reasoning can only be appreciated within the context of the person-centered turn of Roman Catholic theology since the Council. This is especially true in the case of Richard McCormick. His involvement in this debate is a significant element of his search for ethical insights to promote or protect the good of the human person "adequately and integrally considered." The reader of this chapter has to keep in mind that I do not intend to cover all aspects of the debate on proportionate reasoning. There is no need to duplicate the efforts of many authors. What I intend is to indicate McCormick's contribution in the debate as well as to show how his involvement in the debate hinges on his presuppositions on the human person as the center of moral decisions. Although the link between his views on proportionate reasoning and his person-centered approach to ethics becomes more obvious when one turns to his casuistry, it is also well illustrated in the difference between his two responses to Knauer's argument on commensurate reasoning.

PETER KNAUER

The principle of double effect was employed in traditional theology as a tool for determining the morality of actions in conflict situations where good could be achieved or a particular evil could be avoided only by causing another evil. Such action was considered morally licit only if it met all of the following conditions:

1. The act directly performed is in itself good or at least indifferent.
2. The good accomplished is at least as immediate as the evil.
3. The intention of the agent is good.
4. There is proportionate reason for causing the evil.[3]

The first condition of the principle of double effect in its traditional form assumed that some actions were evil in themselves; nothing could make them good or justifiable. The second requirement was meant to ensure that the agent does not desire the evil effect directly. Thus, in the classical example of removing the uterus of a pregnant woman to save her life, tradition argued that the death of the fetus was unintended and indirect. Consequently, it was morally justifiable since it followed the removal of the cancerous uterus, which threatened the life of the woman. As some contemporary authors point out, this interpretation ignored the obvious fact that the death occurred concurrently with the removal of the fetus. In other words, the one act which cured the woman also killed the fetus. This fact in turn put a great strain on the third requirement of the principle. Was the death of the fetus not primarily causing evil to achieve good? The fourth condition of the principle also created difficulties on account of its vagueness. Germain Grisez captures the problem in the following words:

> What is to count as a "proportionately grave reason" mentioned in the fourth condition? Does the physical proximity or probability of the bad effect have something to do with this? Is the justification in the cancerous uterus case simply that one life is as good as another? Should one take into account the probability that the child could live many more years than the mother? Or can one consider here factors such as the woman's responsibilities for other children?[4]

Peter Knauer believed that the principle of double effect was "the fundamental principle of all morality."[5] However, he too believed it had been misunderstood and misused. His chief contribution was in reducing all the four conditions of the principle to the last one. For him, moral evil consists simply in causing or permitting evil without commensurate (or proportionate reason). Commensurate reason is the dividing line between physical evil and moral evil.

> In fact, a physical evil, such as a sickness, or an error or any injury, is not yet in contradiction to nature in a moral sense; such an evil is not a moral evil, even if moral evil is definable only in relation to it.[6]

Physical evil becomes moral evil if there is no commensurate reason for causing or permitting it.

> Moral evil, I contend, consists in the last analysis in the permission or causing of a physical evil which is not justified by a commensurate reason. Not every permission or causing of physical evil is a moral evil, but every moral evil depends on the causing or permission of physical evil.[7]

Knauer read the term 'effect' in Thomas Aquinas's treatment of self-defense not as that which follows a cause but as 'aspect'. The defense of one's life against an unjust aggressor is only an aspect of the whole action. We cannot determine the morality of this act of self-defense merely on the external act. As Knauer puts it, "by *finis operis* there should not be understood—as unfortunately often happens—only external effect, the effect that could be photographed."[8] It is rather to be understood as "the act which is willed and intended as such." Consider almsgiving for example. The physical fact of giving money to someone could be a bribe, the repayment of a loan, payment for a good purchased, or a service received. It could also be almsgiving. The meaning of the act can only be determined based on the intention of the person transferring the money. A person who cuts another person with a knife is doing something wrong, but if this person is a surgeon removing unhealthy tissue with the intention to restore the health of the person, his action would be permissible. The difference in both examples is in the intention and in the presence of commensurate reason and not merely in the physical act.

Commensurate reason alone determines the entire moral content of an act. "If the reason of an act is commensurate, it alone determines the *finis operis*, so that the act is morally good."[9] Commensurate or proportionate reason exists when the act is proportioned to the value which is being pursued; that is, when the value sought "is achieved in the highest possible measure for the whole."[10] To put it negatively, "the reason for an act is not a commensurate reason if there is a contradiction in the final analysis between the act and the reason."[11] Therefore, "the entire act must correspond to its end." An immoral act is so because it contradicts its end in relation to the whole of reality. In such a case, "a short run 'more' of the value is paid by a 'lesser' achievement of the same value in the long run."[12]

Like McCormick before him, Knauer also argued that the notion of direct and indirect voluntareity, as employed by scholastic thinkers, was too closely tied to physical causality. Knauer maintained that proportionate reason should determine the directness or indirectness of an act. Thus, an act which causes physical evil is morally wrong and therefore direct if there is no commensurate reason for allowing or permitting the evil. Therefore, "the physical series of events is irrelevant to the moral determination of good or bad."[13] For example, in the case of self-defense against an unjust aggressor, the death of the aggressor may be caused if there is no other way to save oneself. The formal intention of the agent in this case, that is, the reason which determines what aspect of the act is willed, may not be inferred by the external act alone. Also, although one who takes the property of another because it is necessary to save his or her life is doing externally what a thief would do, yet the action assumes a different moral significance because of proportionate reason. However, there is proportionate reason only when the act corresponds to the value sought "not only in the short run but in its existential entirety."[14] Furthermore, the means by which the value is achieved must be justifiable in itself "without reference to a further objective as having a reason in itself which suffices for the positing of the act."[15] In a much later work Knauer explained that

> an act which is already "evil in itself cannot subsequently become justified by the fact that it is additionally used for the realization of a further act which would have been faultless in itself. What is more, the second act would also become "evil in itself" by participating in the badness of the means.[16]

In other words, "a good end does not justify an evil means—even in a teleological ethics."[17]

Contrary to the manualist tradition, Knauer insisted that no moral significance should be attached to any physical evil (such as death, falsehood, sickness, loss of property, etc.) until it could be determined whether or not there was a commensurate reason for causing it. This is the case even if the physical evil is directly intended psychologically, as in the surgical operation where the doctor removes a patient's limb for some necessary medical reason. In a psychological sense the doctor intends to amputate the limb. In the moral sense the act is a healing intervention that can be justified by 'commensurate reason'. The psychological intention in such a case is premoral and beyond intention. What Knauer did in effect was to deny the possibility of intrinsic evil acts, the claim that certain actions could be wrong regardless of circumstances or consequences. McCormick was quick to point this out.

MCCORMICK'S INITIAL RESPONSE TO KNAUER

Considering that McCormick had espoused some views which were similar to Knauer's in his doctoral dissertation, one might wonder about his initial negative reaction.[18] However, the reasons for this are not difficult to perceive. For one thing, McCormick thought that Knauer extended the application of the principle far beyond its traditional limits. This view is in keeping with the position he expressed in his dissertation concerning the limited application of the principle of double effect. He sensed that Knauer made proportionate reason a constitutive factor of the object of the act in such a manner that neither causality nor the external act retained any moral significance. By making proportionate reason so unconditionally the object of the act Knauer also had made it "theoretically possible to assume into an act as indirect and licit any means, providing it is necessary to a value or end envisaged."[19] He also argued that Knauer's position was inconsistent and imprecise.

Inconsistency was a result of what McCormick believed to be Knauer's failure to give a proper definition of commensurate reason.[20] Since commensurate reason could mean "a good effect *as produced immediately by the cause*" or "motives introduced from outside" and superimposed on a physical act with an already determined meaning of its own, Knauer should have been careful to distinguish what the notion means. Lack of such distinctions could result in the introduction of arbitrary motives into an act which in human terms has a basic meaning of its own. For example, to destroy a child to save its mother could be termed "mother-saving." However, this is a "verbal-shuffling," which hardly obscures the fact that the destruction of the child is willed directly because it is "the single immediate effect of the agent's action."[21]

Most important, McCormick was convinced at this time that making proportionate reasoning the basis for the determination of every moral significance "would destroy the concept of that which is intrinsically evil *ex objecto*."[22] As was the case in his dissertation, he was not yet ready to forgo the notion of intrinsically evil acts, or the deontological methodology inherited from the Catholic theological tradition.

Events between 1965 and 1972, however, compelled McCormick to give increasing weight to teleological thinking. Among these one has to single out the birth control debate that surrounded the publication of *Humanae Vitae*, the issues brought into consciousness by the Vietnam War, his increasing exposure to problems created by scientific and technological developments in various fields of medicine, and his dialogue and interaction with other theologians.[23] Undoubtedly, the single most important catalyst was the publication of *Humanae Vitae*.

When McCormick reviewed *Humanae Vitae* he concluded that the encyclical's argument that every act of sexual intercourse must be open to procreation and its condemnation of contraception as intrinsically evil was flawed because it measured the meaning of an act merely "by examining its physiological structure." The basic criterion for the meaning of human actions "is the person, not some isolated aspect of the person. . . . Physical objects as such have no relation to the moral order. . . . The materiality of the act is not the same as its meaning." While McCormick maintained that sexuality is founded in biological realities and that the sexual act, materially considered, "has some orientation toward fecundation," he also stated that "it is not the sexual organs which are the source of life, but the person."[24]

McCormick's position in this review of the encyclical was the clearest indication yet that he deemed the human person adequately and integrally considered to be the basis for determining moral significance. As he points out in the following passage, he was not the only one who was taking the personalist turn at this time.

> Authors have always admitted that the total object (or significance) of action cannot be identified merely with the physical object. Physical objects as such have no relation to the moral order. Thus "taking another's property" is only a physical act; it is not yet a moral truth. Similarly "uttering an untruth" is only a physical act or object.[25]

These acts become morally wrong if after careful consideration they are found to constitute an attack "on the person through those things which are necessary for personal growth and good."[26]

The change to the personalist orientation was a major paradigm shift for Catholic theology. Like all such shifts it also came with the realization that former categories which had been employed for measuring reality can no longer perform that task adequately. In McCormick's case it not only compelled him to move toward a teleological methodology but it also affected his views on the role of authority, especially in the Church, in determining the meaning of human actions. It also affected his views on moral agency; that is, on how the agent comes to a right decision especially in conflict situations. It is therefore no accident that McCormick's wholehearted embrace of proportionate reasoning as the only viable option in moral determination was subsequent to his rejection of the act-centered approach employed by *Humanae Vitae* and to his conviction that the significance of human actions must be determined in all instances (including the area of sexuality) "by relating the physical act to the order of persons and by seeing it as an intersubjective reality."[27]

The Pére Marquette lecture of 1973 was McCormick's most comprehensive statement on the debate that Knauer's reinterpretation of the principle of double effect had generated.[28] To put it another way, it was McCormick's most comprehensive statement yet on *how* to relate the physical act to the order of persons. Three of the issues McCormick raised in this lecture constitute the pillars around which his contribution to the debate has progressed till now. These are the place and meaning of direct/indirect intentionality in moral determination; the meaning, extent, and manner of determining proportionate reason; and the notion of absolute or intrinsic evil.

The Direct / Indirect Distinction

McCormick reviewed Knauer's work a second time in the Marquette lecture. By then he had been persuaded by events of the recent past to accept "the substance of Knauer's presentation"[29] that moral evil consists in permitting or causing of physical evil without commensurate reason, and that "the meaning of an act is not derived simply from its external effect but is really that aspect of the act which is willed."[30] On the other hand, McCormick still had difficulty with Knauer's use of the terms 'direct' and 'indirect'. He thought these notions were so closely identified with commensurate reason in Knauer's work that they ceased to function at all. They seemed devoid of any psychological intent.[31] The other problem with Knauer's work was its failure to indicate the limitation of intention in the determination of the meaning of concrete human actions.[32] The same failure is also apparent in the moral theories of William Van der Marck[33] and Cornelius Van der Poel;[34] they rooted it in intersubjective or social relationships alone. McCormick was convinced that the limitation of intention must also be gauged by the agent's attitude to the basic goods, as Germain Grisez had said.[35]

Grisez maintains that human choice in some ways always involves one of these goods. As ideals to be realized, they clarify the possibilities of choice but do not determine its moral quality. What determines this is the attitude with which the choice is made. In other words, to make a morally right choice one has to choose a particular good "with an appreciation of its genuine but limited possibility and its objectively human character."[36] This attitude also implies that none of them would be belittled or impeded in the course of realizing another, since all of them are equally important. Given that to act against any of the basic goods is to subordinate the good to whatever leads to that choice, the question is whether every action which inhibits a basic good constitutes a direct inhibition of that good. No, says Grisez. Since some inhibitions are unsought and unavoidable side effects of an effort to pursue another value, only directly intended inhibitions are destructive of the basic good. In determining the difference between direct and indirect intention Grisez dissociates himself from the manualist position that an evil is directly produced and therefore directly intended if it is the sole immediate effect of the physical act. Grisez is convinced that

> from the point of view of human moral activity, the initiation of the *indivisible* (emphasis added) process through one's own causality renders all that is involved in that process equally immediate.[37]

Therefore, all things being equal, when an agent posits a natural cause he or she also simultaneously posits its foreseen effects.[38]

McCormick finds Grisez's notion of an indivisible process correct because it implies that "the evil effect is not a means, morally speaking, to the good effect," and so it is not and need not be "the object of an intending will." However, the question is why it must be said that one has turned against a basic good when the evil occurs as a means and is the object of an intending will, even if there is proportionate reason for permitting or intending it.[39]

Proportionate reason is ultimately more decisive in the determination of the morality of an act than the difference between direct/indirect intention. Since Grisez refused to accept the centrality of proportionate reason in moral determination he is unable to offer much help, McCormick argues, when human beings are forced to choose between basic goods in situations of moral conflict. McCormick is convinced that the untenable nature of Grisez's disdain for proportionate reasoning stands out clearly in the case where we are faced with the following alternatives: an operation which saves the mother but kills the child versus one that saves the child but kills the mother. In both procedures the evil and good effects occur in an indivisible process. The obvious preference for saving the mother's life, however, is difficult to justify by Grisez's reasoning.

> If Grisez would say that in this instance we may save the mother, I ask: Why? Why prefer the mother to the child when I have a choice? On the other hand, if Grisez says that I may do neither since to do either would involve one in a preference of one life over another, then it seems that what has functioned as proportionate reason in instances where he allows abortion to save the mother is this: it is better to save one life than to lose two. Or more generally, a proportionate reason exists because that choice represents the lesser evil.
>
> Frankly, I do not know what Grisez would say to an either/or case of this kind. But I suspect he would hesitate long and hard. But he would not and does not hesitate in the simple instance where abortion (of a fetus who will perish under any circumstances) is necessary to save the mother's life.[40]

The lack of hesitation on Grisez's part in the latter case is for McCormick a clear indication that even for Grisez the crucial and decisive consideration is that it is better on all counts to save one life rather than lose two. The preference for saving the mother in the first case must be rooted in the same proportionate reason: her death would cause greater damage than the death of the fetus. Thus, although McCormick considers Grisez's analysis of the direct/indirect distinction very subtle, consistent, and plausible,[41] he is also convinced that acting against a basic good should not be understood within Grisez's deontological interpretation of the meaning of direct and indirect voluntareity.

The direct/indirect distinction was also the subject of Bruno Schüller's inquiry in 1972.[42] Schüller's argument in this study was that the distinction has little relevance in determining the morality of human actions. He noted that traditionally this distinction has been applied especially to evaluation of suicide, killing, contraception, causing scandal, and cooperation in the sin of another person.[43] However, his conviction is that in spite of what appears like absolute prohibitions, these actions, except scandal and cooperation in the sin of others, have been forbidden on teleological considerations, that is, on the basis of their intended or foreseen results rather than on the modality of the actions themselves or the posture of the will.

Leading others to sin was always considered an absolute disvalue because its intended result is the sin of another, which cannot be justified on any grounds. Although it would seem to follow on this premise that all actions which one knows might cause an absolute disvalue would be forbidden, Schüller is convinced that such prohibition might lead to the absurd situation where the lawgiver could no longer enact any penal laws if it could be foreseen that someone somewhere could possibly use such a law to blackmail people who had broken the law.[44] Schüller notes that the tradition got around this problem by admitting of differences in the posture of the will, that is, by distinguishing between direct and indirect intention.

> The absolute non-value of sin demands only that one not positively desire or intend it in any circumstances or any price; granting this, it is thoroughly consonant with the absolute non-value of sin that one permit it, if one has a proportionately grave reason.[45]

Therefore, the distinction between an intending will and a merely permitting will is relevant only when one is dealing with moral evil. Non-moral evils, such as pain, sickness, error, or death may not be intended because they are only relative disvalues. As a rule, a relative disvalue only should be avoided if "it does not occur competitively with another relative value but one that is to be preferred to it, or with an absolute value."[46] Sickness, for example, ought to be avoided, but not at the cost of sending the whole family into the most dire straits. Insofar as it is necessary for the realization of a preferable value, one is allowed to cause a relative disvalue, and at times one *should* cause it. For a proportionate reason one may permit a moral evil and directly will and cause a non-moral evil. Furthermore, Schüller insists, when we justifiably cause a relative disvalue in our conduct we should not describe it as indirect because the term has no relevance in this case. What is relevant is the presence or lack of proportionate reason.[47]

Although McCormick had earlier stated that Schüller was absolutely correct in his analysis and conclusions,[48] in the Marquette lecture he argued that Schüller had not clearly resolved the question of the moral significance of an intending and a merely permitting will when a nonmoral evil is concerned. Granted it is true, as Schüller says, that the will relates differently to what it wills and what it merely permits whenever that distinction can be legitimately made, McCormick wondered whether it is correct to say, as Schüller did, that the direct/indirect distinction is meaningless and arbitrary because in all instances (whether one permits or intends the nonmoral evil), the moral rightness of the act can only be secured by proportionate reason.

McCormick concluded that what constitutes proportionate reason for indirect action (descriptively speaking) might not constitute a proportionate reason for direct (descriptively speaking) acts.[49] In other words, the direct/indirect distinction can not only tell us what kind of action we are performing, "but can have enormously different immediate and long term implications, and therefore generate a quite different calculus of proportion."[50] McCormick believed that his contention is supported by the issue of the death of noncombatants in warfare. Tradition has permitted attacks on the enemy's war machine even though some noncombatants might be killed in the process. The same tradition has also forbidden targeting these noncombatants as a means to bring the enemy to its knees. Although the death of civilians is involved in both cases, there is a difference in the posture of the will. In the first case the intention is indirect. In the other it is direct. Such difference in the posture of the will is morally significant even in a teleological calculus.

> The difference is not in the numbers of the deaths here and now. They could be numerically the same—for instance, one hundred

civilians killed incidentally, one hundred directly killed. The deaths are equally regrettable and tragic simply as deaths and *in this sense* how they occur does not affect their status as non-moral evil. But how they occur has a good deal to say about the present meaning of the action, the effect on the agent and others, and hence about the protection and security of life in the long run.[51]

By maintaining that there is a difference between a permitting and an intending will McCormick remained consistent with his earlier views on the matter. It may be recalled that in his doctoral dissertation he had stated that a permitting will may refer to the posture of the will when the effect is *per accidens* or "a *per se* but second effect." In such a case the effect is not intended. That is to say, it is neither willed as an end nor as a means.[52] In the dialogue with Schüller he illustrates this difference in the postures of an intending will and a permitting will by arguing that if cancer made the removal of ovaries necessary, the resulting sterility is unintended, but if tubal ligation becomes necessary to avoid complications arising with pregnancy, sterility is chosen. In the second case "the non-moral evil is chosen as means; in the other it is not."[53]

There is also a different awareness at play in each of the two cases. In the latter case the awareness is one of intentionality. In the former it is that of permission. This much he concedes to Schüller. The question is whether the fact that in one case the intending will is more closely associated with the evil and more willing that it exist constitutes enough ground to impute morality. Is the obliqueness of intention enough reason to impute a superior moral quality or to determine rightness or wrongness? No, says McCormick. To make such an assessment, human action must be examined, and morality must be imputed, against a much wider canvas than intention or the external act. The action must be measured by its relation to or impacts on the goods which define our flourishing.

In a subsequent reply to McCormick's critique, Schüller continued to argue the limited relevance of the direct/indirect distinction. The distinction retains significance only for the realization of moral evil (sin). Although, like McCormick, Schüller believed that killing noncombatants "as a means to bring the enemy to his knees and weakening his will to fight" is "morally condemnable," he states that this is so not because the action is direct but because it violates the principle of moderation of a justified defense. One should not do more harm than necessary to defend oneself.[54]

Although Schüller did not intend totally do away with the relevance of direct/indirect distinction, he maintained there is no morally significant difference between intending moral evil as means and permitting it only. An action which induces others to sin can either be intended or permitted; that is, it can either be approved or disapproved. To permit another's wrongdoing is to disapprove of it but not prevent it. Such action (that is, the permitting of or failure to prevent another's wrongdoing) is morally justifiable only if there is proportionate reason. Intending an action means more than not preventing it. It means approval. Therefore,

> to intend the wrongdoing of others and to permit their wrong doing are mutually exclusive in the same way as the basic moral attitudes which express themselves in intending or permitting the wrong behaviour of others.[55]

One may not intend moral evil as means, but one may permit it (since permitting implies that one could not prevent it).

In response to Schüller, McCormick agrees that the key to understanding the direct/indirect distinction is intention/permission. He modified his position and accepted that one could neither prove the difference between direct/indirect killing by appeal to the deleterious consequences of the act nor even assert that these consequences are reprehensible simply because they result from the directness of the act. Furthermore, the practical absoluteness of norms which forbid direct killing of noncombatants in warfare cannot be established teleologically on these consequences. Instead, "such killing is disproportionate to the good being sought because it undermines (through the association of basic goods) the very good of life" and therefore lacks proportionate reason.[56] Thus, from believing in the wide-ranging relevance of the distinction between direct and indirect voluntariness in the determination of moral significance, McCormick came to the conclusion, following Schüller's persuasion, that it has relevance only for the causing of moral evil, which may be permitted only, and for proportionate reason. In the moral evaluation of causing nonmoral evil, such as destroying the lives of noncombatants in a war, proportionate reason is the only relevant criterion.

PROPORTIONATE REASON

I have shown that in his dissertation McCormick understood proportionate reason as the value in a situation, the achievement of which justifies the causing of some harm. In that work, the removal of the probably dead fetus to save the life of the mother was justified on the grounds that the protection of the certain value, the life of the mother, is to be preferred over the uncertain value, the probably dead fetus. Later, in the Marquette lecture, McCormick justified this conclusion by setting out the criteria by which proportionate reason can be established:

> (a) a value at least equal to that sacrificed is at stake; (b) there is no less harmful way of protecting the value here and now; (c) the manner of its protection will not undermine it in the long run.[57]

Proportionate reason is, therefore, not reducible to a simple utilitarian calculus. The answer to what actions would best promote a value in a given set of circumstances is dependent on how one defines 'circumstances'. An adequate account of the circumstances must consider "not just how much qualitative good can be salvaged in this particular situation of conflict of values."[58] It must weigh the social implications and the aftereffects of the action, and it must apply the rule of generalizability and consider the cultural climate of the place – the reactions it is likely to generate and the biases it is likely to run up against. It "will draw as much as possible from the wisdom and experience of the past," particularly as embodied in the rules peoples of the past have found a useful guide in difficult times and from other mature, experienced, detached, and distant reflections whose ideas will serve as counterbalance to the often short-sighted and self-interested tendencies we experience when we are proximate to and closely involved in a case. Also, "it will take full force of one's own religious faith and its intentionalities to interpret the meaning and enlighten the options of the situation."[59]

Consequently, it is never left to the individual whim alone to discover what constitutes proportionate reason. Rather "the individual will depend on community discernment" to a large extent.[60] All these notwithstanding, there may be procedures in which we know very little "and must proceed to normative statements gradually by trial and error."[61] Our limited capacity to know must lead sometimes to tentativeness in moral judgments and to preparedness to revise our views and judgments where new insights or fresh data call for it.[62]

There will therefore be different criteria for determining adequacy in proportionality because proportionate reason is an analogous concept with three possible and distinct senses. One connotation of proportionate reason is evident in a situation where causing or permitting an evil is the only alternative to causing a greater evil. McCormick gives two examples to explain his point. One is the classical abortion dilemma—save one or lose two. The second example is the case of a swimmer allowed to drown because the only person around to help cannot swim. The mother cannot save the child no matter how she tries. Nor can the bystander who cannot swim save the drowning swimmer. There would be no need even to try because to do so would go against the *ordo bonorum*. McCormick therefore concludes that

> love (as involving besides *benevolentia*, also *beneficentia*) is always controlled by the possible. There is no genuine *beneficentia* if no good can accrue to the individual through my sacrifice. An act of love (as *beneficentia*) is not measured by the mere desire or intention (*benevolentia*). Therefore, in instances like this, abortion and not attempting to save the drowning swimmer are proportionately grounded decisions precisely because the harm cannot be avoided, whereas harm to the mother and prospective rescuer can and should be avoided.[63]

Another meaning of proportionate reason is evident in situations where the alternatives are not so obvious. In a case where a person lays down his life for another, the one who lays down his life does so not because the other's life is preferable to his but because in such cases of conflict it is human and Christian to seek to secure this good for a neighbor, even at the cost of one's life. Indeed, other things being equal, such a self-sacrifice is the ultimate act of human love and a very Christlike pointer to the way we should all be going.[64] In a sinful world the most mature choices are those, like that of Christ, which prefer the good of the neighbor to that of the self. Also, it is this sense of preferential love which distinguishes the readiness to die for others from mere suicide, the attempt to escape from life's burdens.

The third sense of proportionate reason comes from the fact that no one should be required to give more than his or her capacity allows. "Love one another as I have loved you," is an ideal to be pursued constantly. But, at each time and in each place and for each person there can be a limit to what can be done in the name of charity. To refuse to accept this is to fail to recognize that to impose perfect love upon imperfect creatures is a disproportionate demand capable of turning human beings from God. On the other hand, to assert the limit of charity is not to emasculate the gospel message but to recognize that the ideal was proclaimed to imperfect human beings who must grow into its fullness.

> The ideal remains. It is there—to be sought, pursued, struggled after. But it is precisely because its achievement demands constant pursuit that it would be inconsistent with the charity of the gospel message to assert that its demands exceed the limitations of the human pursuer.[65]

Still, the question is this: What constitutes the proportionate reason in any given conflict situation? Is proportionate reason "something in addition to a clearly definable action," some good which is outside the action and which is achieved without any consideration to the significance of the evil means? John Connery believed that contemporary revisionist theologians would give an affirmative answer to the above question.[66] He believed that for theologians such as Knauer, Schüller, and presumably McCormick, proportionate reasoning implies that "an act would be morally bad only if the evil it contained outweighed the good it was expected to accomplish."[67] Thus, all that was required of the means is that it be proportioned to the end.

McCormick believes that Connery's position distorts the views of revisionist theologians on proportionate reason. The proportionate reason in a conflict situation, he argues, "is not in addition to an act already defined; it constitutes its very object, but in the full sense of that term."[68] He insists that in the case of the amputation of a cancerous limb to save the life of the patient, for example, saving the patient's life (the proportionate reason) is the object "in the full sense of the term" and not merely the motive for the amputation. Amputation is not the object of the act.

> In other words, proportionate reason enters into the very definition of *what* one is doing. If one conceives proportionate reason as *in addition to an act already definable by its object*, then one does indeed get into some mischievous results. For instance, it makes it possible for Connery to attribute to proportionalists the notion that a *ratio proportionata* can justify a morally wrong act.[69]

Thus, proportionalists are not saying that the morally wrong action can be justified by the end. Besides insisting that proportionate reason is not a motive "superadded to an act with its own definition,"[70] McCormick also stresses that a definition of proportionality must take the object and the circumstances (side effects, possible consequences, intentions, and so forth) into consideration. As Lisa Cahill puts it, proportionalists in general are saying that "the unconditional force of a moral rule depends on specification of circumstances adequate to constitute a disproportion between the end sought and the value sacrificed, not on the abstract meaning of a material act."[71]

Furthermore, proportionate reasoning is not about discovering whether adultery or stealing, for instance, would "produce more evil than good," as Connery suggests.[72] Rather, it is a search for what should count as adultery or stealing in the first place.[73] Of course, central to this search for what constitutes proportionate reason in a conflict situation is the *ordo bonorum* or the hierarchy of values. I do not share Cahill's view that the difficulty in discerning and agreeing on a hierarchy of values constitutes "an undeniable shortcoming" in McCormick's teleology.[74] Instead, it indicates that there is no other route to ethics but through responsible teleology. This is so because the difficulty she points out stems from the human condition–our individual, social, and cultural differences as well as our finiteness. Although determining a hierarchy of values might involve "an intricate conceptualization of relative values and disvalues,"[75] it is not foreign to any normal adult. Nor is it something "theoreticians" instead of "decision-makers" do. Thus even the "moral instinct of faith," which McCormick speaks so often about, is not totally free from conceptual analysis.

The answer McCormick gives to the notion of proportionate reason and the criteria for determining adequate proportion reveals something of his understanding of ethics. It is prudence in action to protect the basic human goods as much as possible within the often tragic and ambiguous situations in which human beings find themselves. Ethics is about persons and how to protect and promote their good, integrally and adequately.

As I stated earlier, the reader is asked to bear in mind the connection between the personalist turn in moral theology and McCormick's conviction that proportionate reasoning constitutes the only route to all moral determination in conflict situations. So far we have established the major aspects of his position on the issue. The bid to determine the relevance and meaning of the direct/indirect distinction and of proportionate reason is an effort to find the demands of love in the circumstances as opposed to the search for what is licit. The search for love's demands presupposes that the subject of moral action is a person. The search for what is licit, on the other hand, presupposes law and fixed essences. These two emphases account both for the reason McCormick was not able to apply proportionate reasoning in all cases earlier than he did and the reason he applied it when he did.

Without implying that McCormick had clearly spelled out every detail about the meaning of proportionate reason in his dissertation, it is clear that he recognized and valued its importance then. However, until he came to the clear conclusion around 1968 that moral significance is "an assessment of an action's relation to the order of persons, to the hierarchy of values,"[76] he could not accept the validity of proportionate reasoning in all aspects of morality. As I indicated above, his rejection of the notion of intrinsic evil in his critique of *Humanae Vitae* was crucial for his acceptance of proportionate reasoning as applicable in all areas of morality. It is instructive that it was after 1968, the year of the publication of *Humanae Vitae*, when he again gave serious consideration to the reinterpretation of the principle of double effect. The rejection of intrinsic evil in that encyclical was, in turn, tied to his espousal of the need to determine moral significance on the human person adequately considered and not just on the basis of physical acts.

INTRINSIC EVIL

The notion of intrinsic evil involves the conviction that some acts are wrong in spite of circumstances. Catholic tradition has maintained that adultery, unjust killing of the innocent, and the use of contraception are intrinsically wrong. The norms against these actions are believed to share the same characteristic: "The types of action they identify are specifiable, as potential objects of choice, without reliance on any evaluative term which presupposes a moral judgement or the action."[77] In traditional theology such actions were regarded as evil either because they were against nature (for example, masturbation, killing of the innocent, divorce and remarriage) or because there was defect of right (for example, suicide).

McCormick's attack on the notion of intrinsic evil is prefaced with a distinction between premoral evil and moral evil. Premoral evil, in Louis Janssen's words, refers to "any lack of a perfection at which we aim, any lack of fulfillment which frustrates our natural urges and makes us suffer."[78] Moral evil occurs when a premoral evil is caused without proportionate reason.[79] Thus, the notion of premoral evil is an admission of imperfection and conflict of values. As McCormick puts it, every good we achieve is rarely untainted by hurt and deprivation. As I stated above, the thrust of proportionate reasoning in moral theology is to determine when premoral evil can be allowed and when an action which contains premoral evil can be allowed. Furthermore, the point of proportionate reasoning is precisely to prove that the notion of intrinsic evil cannot be sustained. McCormick himself says this much.

> Proportionate reason represents above all a structure of moral reasoning and moral norming, teleological in character, whose thrust is that concrete norms understood as exceptionless because they propose certain interventions dealing with nonmoral goods as *intrinsic evils* cannot be sustained.[80]

Although there cannot be exceptionless moral norms, there can be norms which are held to be "virtually exceptionless." These norms are considered virtually exceptionless because although we cannot conceive any exceptions to them, we cannot prove "with a syllogistic click" that under no circumstances can exceptions occur.[81] Since McCormick argues, like some other ethicists, that what had been regarded as exceptionless norms in traditional theology were in fact established on teleological grounds, he believes that calculation of consequences is vital to establishing what norms can be classed as "virtually" or "practically" exceptionless and what actions one is allowed to take in situations of conflict.

The calculations of consequences are often demonstrable prudential judgments "based on the certainties of history and the uncertainties of the future."[82] Moreover, McCormick refuses to equate consequences in proportionate reasoning "with the later-on effects of an action one performs here and now."[83] Rather, consequences apply to "the immediate intersubjective implications of an action."[84] Consequently, the decision to regard a norm as virtually exceptionless would be based on the prudential validity of "a lex lata in presumptione periculi communis."[85] In other words, the validity of such a norm would be judged on its intersubjective implications. McCormick maintains that the principle of noncombatant immunity is on these grounds a virtually exceptionless norm because to allow indiscriminate and willful killing of innocent populations poses a common and universal danger. Put differently, due to the consequences (understood as immediate and intersubjective implications) of such an action, there are no readily imaginable exceptions to it.

CRITICS OF THE THEORY

Criticism of McCormick's position on proportionate reasoning has ranged from the charge that it honors neither the formulation nor the substance of received moral theology to the view that it leads to unbridled subjectivism.[86] Some critics accuse proportionalists in general of basing their calculations solely on consequences and claim that the method itself is comparable to the earliest form of utilitarianism, where pleasure and pain "were considered the only intrinsic good or evil."[87] McCormick himself has been called "a utilitarian of some sort,"[88] and his approach to moral decision-making has been referred to as "a consequentialist methodology" which fails to bear on the question of exception-making considerations of human rights.[89] Questions also have been raised concerning the practicality of proportionate reason,[90] the notion and manner of determining the proportionality of consequences.

Early in the debate, John Connery argued that Knauer, Schüller, Fuchs, and Nicholas Crotty were part of a movement in Catholic theology tending toward "a consequentialist response" to the question of right and wrong.[91] He understood them to say that "what one ought and ought not to do depends entirely on the consequences of the act. If the consequences on the whole are undesirable, the act ought not to be done."[92] Furthermore, Connery argued that Knauer and other revisionist moral theologians are act-utilitarians because they make "the judgment of an act depend solely on its consequence."[93]

The calculation of consequences causes problems in regard to acts such as the direct killing of the innocent for whatever reason or adultery, which have traditionally been regarded as intrinsically wrong. It is generally believed that act-utilitarians cannot deal satisfactorily with such issues or with cases of justice.

In response to Connery, McCormick pointed out that the authors in question are not constructing a morality based solely on consequences.[94] McCormick did not deal satisfactorily with the issue of consequences as intended consequences in this response. However, he returned to it three years later. He noted this time that the idea of consequences implied in Connery's article suggests that the authors in question believed torture or adultery may be morally right if it produces "sufficiently good results or net good." In other words, it suggested in an undifferentiated form that "a good end justifies an evil means."[95] However, McCormick argued that besides being a rejection of the notion of intrinsic evil, the intention of those authors was to show that the moral significance of actions cannot be determined independently of their consequences and of particular circumstances alone. "All things must be considered before a final moral judgment of rightness or wrongness can be made." The things which must be considered comprise more than mere 'welfare values' (or net good). They must include dignity values or expressive actions as well as institutional obligations.[96]

Paul Ramsey was convinced that proportionate reason cannot apply to issues pertaining to human life. Like Grisez, Ramsey maintained that human life is a basic good which is conditional to all other goods.[97] Therefore the destruction of 'embodied life' is tantamount to the destruction in and for that person of "the whole scale of goods and values, the whole world of worth he knows."[98] Consequently, human life is not commensurate with any other value. One should therefore not destroy life with direct intention. Ramsey, however, concedes that it may sometimes become necessary to cause the death of others indirectly "in course of actions which inseparably also save many other lives."[99]

At issue then is the commensurability of values or goods[100] and the moral relevance of the direct/indirect distinction. For Ramsey, situations which involve us in the commensuration of life with other values call for the principle of double effect, not proportionate reason. This principle, with its distinction between direct and indirect action, prevents us from turning against basic goods and enables us to face indeterminate choices.[101] The importance of the direct/indirect distinction lies not so much in the fact that it brings out the difference between a proper attitude toward moral and nonmoral evil as in the fact that "it brings out an important difference among the attitudinal positions of moral agents and the intentionality of their actions in cases in which incommensurable values are conflicted, whatever these may be."[102] Although this restates the debate between McCormick and Schüller, it also strengthens Ramsey's case for the dismissal of proportionate reasoning as a valid principle for the determination of moral significance.

In addition, Ramsey also dismisses the relevance of proportionate reasoning on the grounds that it does not provide sufficient protection against individualistic or even communitarian whims and caprices as do feature-dependent principles which state the behavioral norms and only subsequently go on to "bring in exception clauses that are also feature-dependent in terms of the conflicting values that put a limit on that valid principle or rule of behavior."[103] Behind Ramsey's position is the assumption that life is an absolute and inviolable good as well as a basic one. While granting that life is a basic good McCormick has maintained that it is not an absolute one. In his response to Ramsey he argues that in a situation where the taking of human life is "truly life saving and life-serving in the circumstances," death cannot be regarded as "turning against a basic good" of life[104] because the basic warrant for the taking of life in such circumstances is that "all things considered, such taking is a life-saving action" and the lesser of two possible evils.[105] Thus, although life is a basic good, it is not more basic than moral evil or moral good. For example, although God can command the death of a person, as tradition says, God cannot command or force a person to sin.[106]

In proportionate reasoning "it is the end that measures." The question always is whether the end being sought by the nonmoral act in this case is promoted and not undermined by the means.[107] Thus, in the classical abortion case where the choice is either to save one or lose both mother and child, what is being weighed is "the relationship of a killing intervention (abortion) to the end (saving life)." What is not being weighed is one life (the mother's) versus another (the child's). The means is judged proportionate because "*in these circumstances* it is consistent with the end."[108]

There is room for commensuration even in cases involving apparently incommensurable and indeterminate goods. McCormick argues that even in those real cases of incommensurability and indeterminacy we do not always succumb to decisional paralysis. Instead, we manage somehow to overcome indeterminacy and incommensurability by means of a hierarchy or order of values.

> We go to war to protect our freedom. That means we are willing to sacrifice life to protect this good. If "give me liberty or give me death" does not involve *some kind* of commensurating then I do not know what commensurating means. Our tradition allows violent, even, if necessary, lethal, resistance to rape attempts. If this does not mean measuring *somehow* or other sexual integrity against human life, I fail to see what it means. Our tradition allows (perhaps incorrectly) capital punishment as a protection deterrent. That involves weighing one individual's life against the common safety which he threatens.[109]

McCormick agrees that while these goods are incommensurable, they are "associated" to each other in such a way that harm to or protection of one or the other will probably or necessarily harm or enhance others.[110] Establishing proportionate reason through the theory of associated goods helps McCormick to give persuasive answers to critics who charge that proportionate reasoning cannot apply to cases of justice without employing a utilitarian calculus. In the case of a sheriff with an innocent black prisoner, this would imply that he must hand over the innocent black man or risk the 'greater evil' of widespread rioting, murder, and arson. Applying the principle of associated good, McCormick insists that the sheriff ought not to give in to the mob demand because to do so would imply that the protection of the human good, in this case life, property, and so on, by framing an innocent person will undermine that good in the long run "by serious injury to an associated good (human liberty)."[111]

McCormick is not just speaking of the personal liberty of the black suspect in this case. He is also concerned about the freedom of the rioting mob as well. Killing an innocent person just to appease a mob supposes that the cessation of others from wrongdoing is necessarily dependent on another's wrongdoing. Also justifying obliteration bombing, as Harry Truman did in Nagasaki and Hiroshima, in the understanding that it might end the war and thus save more lives in the long run, is to do serious injury to an associated good, liberty, because "making innocent (non-combatant) persons the object of our targeting is a form of extortion in international affairs that contains an implicit denial of human freedom."[112] The bombing has no necessary connection to the good being sought.

Thus, beside the principle of associated goods, McCormick also introduces a principle of *necessity* to explain more clearly the meaning of proportionate reason.[113] The principle of necessary connection as an aspect of the notion of proportionate reasoning expresses a conviction that "it is wrong to do evil when the evil has no necessary connection to the good being sought." This connection does not exist when evil is done "to convince a free and rational agent to refrain from evil."[114]

> Let us put this in another way and explicitly Christian terms. It is the Christian's faith that another's ceasing from his wrongdoing is *never* dependent on my doing nonmoral evil. For the Christian believes that we are truly what we are, redeemed in Christ. We are still threatened by the *reliquae peccati* but we are free and powerful in Christ's grace.[115]

Thus, although McCormick could perceive a connection between abortion and saving the one who can be saved, he sees no such necessary connection in the instance where an innocent man has to be framed to appease a mob. In other words, the rioting mob can cease its evil without the death or the unjust suffering of one person. As regards obliteration bombing, the aggressor nation can and ought to desist from wrongful aggression without our harming innocents to make that nation do so.

CONCLUSION

I have in this chapter shown the extent of McCormick's involvement in the debate on proportionate reasoning. I have pointed out that, in some sense, he had already drawn attention in his doctoral dissertation to the importance of the traditional notion of proportionate reason in solving cases to which the theory had been thought to be inapplicable. This was an important move, which prepared him to accept subsequently its application to a few more cases, like contraception, where he had hitherto believed it did not apply. I have also shown his growth in understanding of the key components of proportionate reason through detailed attention to his conversations with other ethicists. It must be concluded that although these conversations helped him clarify or modify certain aspects of the theory, they did not make him abandon it completely. Instead, they made him even more convinced of the importance of proportionate reasoning in the determination of moral norms.

McCormick does not believe he has found the answer to all moral dilemmas through the use of proportionate reasoning. First, he believes that the importance of the debate on proportionate reason is exaggerated when it is referred to as a revolution because it gives the impression that this is a whole new way of determining moral significance.

People are making a huge splash out of that [the debate on proportionate reason] as if it were a whole revolution when in nine out of ten areas of moral theology we have interpreted moral norms in that way: You must keep your promises unless there is a proportionate reason for not doing so. You shouldn't kill people unless there is a proportionate reason. It is our tradition. We have a theory of just war, we have a theory of capital punishment, of self defense, and so on. The structure is always the same in all these cases.[116]

What proportionalists have tried to do, McCormick says, is to apply this mode of moral reasoning, which has been used in the Church for centuries, to areas from which it was excluded up to now.[117]

Also, proportionate reasoning in moral theology takes second place to the "instinct of faith." In other words, there is a limit to analysis. Or, put differently, McCormick believes that moral analysis in Christian ethics becomes sterile if it does not pay careful attention to the gospel and to the faith of the Church. What organizes and gives meaning and unity to moral life in Christian terms is the sense that we have been loved by God. Proportionate reasoning is a tool for working out the implications of this love in concrete circumstances. Even then it is not an adequate tool for all cases. For this reason McCormick believes that the theologian cannot afford to ignore the prophetic voices in the Church.

> People like Dan Berrigan who speaks with a prophetic poetic voice in the area of war and peace without feeling the need to justify what he says, disturb us. Berrigan takes it for granted that the Church is a Church of peace. He doesn't argue that point. He just goes out and acts upon that assumption, out of his faith instinct. People like him make us nervous because we are used to the idea that implications of our faith are things that you work out by human reason. I never felt comfortable dealing with Dan Berrigan during the Vietnam war because I never got satisfactory answers to questions. I think he was proved right in his judgments. He saw, long before most of us that war was morally wrong. I can now admit that.[118]

Thus, for McCormick, the limitation of the type of analysis involved in proportionate reasoning (and of the notion of faith informed by reason) is the limitation of theology as conceived within the academy, as an academic enterprise.[119]

Finally, proportionate reasoning is principally a device for determining what promotes the good of the human person, integrally and adequately considered. In the next chapter we will explore, with a few examples from the area of bioethics, how Mc-Cormick has been able to put it at the service of the architectonic idea of his theology. In other words, our interest in the next chapter will be to determine the way Richard McCormick has made moral decisions, particularly in the field of bioethics.

6

CASUISTRY

We have so far examined the theoretical underpinnings of McCormick's work. In this chapter we intend to examine the way he makes moral decisions. For this study we will concentrate on his casuistry in order to show how he brings his theoretical presuppositions to bear on practical moral questions and to examine the level of consistency between theory and practice in his work.[1] I am using the term 'casuistry' in a broad sense to include not only a study of particular cases but also the approach to dealing responsibly with "the contingencies and ambiguities of contemporary human experience."[2]

Although casuistry does not exhaust McCormick's moral methodology, it represents the most consistent tool in his moral decision-making; proportionate reasoning is an essential component of this tool.[3] As we shall see, other principles (for example, the distinction between ordinary and extraordinary means of treatment) also form part of McCormick's casuistry. Ultimately, even casuistry itself as a tool for moral decision-making is employed by McCormick in the search for the good of the human person integrally and adequately considered.

For our study of McCormick's casuistry, we shall examine two issues related to sanctity of life, abortion and life-end questions, and two issues connected with sexuality and family, sterilization/contraception and reproductive technologies. The limitation of space notwithstanding, these issues are sufficient for our present purposes because they represent a significant part of McCormick's interest in bioethics.[4] Our interest in bioethics is, in turn, justified on the ground that most of McCormick's work on practical moral problems is done in this area.[5]

119

ABORTION

Methodological Considerations

McCormick's position on abortion has been affected by the methodological shifts which were the subject of our discussion in the previous chapter. Initially, his position was developed on the basis of the traditional prohibition of direct taking of innocent life. The sole criterion was the difference between the directness or indirectness of the killing act. Therefore, in his earlier writings on abortion he was concerned with determining when the evacuation of the uterus could be considered a direct killing of the innocent.

> The word "direct" in this context refers to the type of action or intervention that has as its single immediate effect destruction of innocent life. Here destruction of life is the deliberate aim, whether in service of a laudable end or not. Not all actions that result in fetal death, however, involve direct destruction. For example, the removal of a cancerous but pregnant uterus (where the fetus is not viable) will produce fetal death. But this can be an unintended and regretted by-product of a legitimate therapeutic procedure, what is called technically an "indirect abortion."[6]

As McCormick understood it then, the argument about abortion was an argument about objective injustice. The Catholic tradition maintains that the only warrant for taking the life of another is unjust aggression. It is this element of objective injustice alone which can make the taking of someone's life justifiable. In theory, one is "empowered to resist forcefully an 'aggressive' act even if the aggressor is pursuing a genuine right."[7] Such a resistance to aggression would make the resultant injury or death only an indirect result of a justified action. The question in regard to abortion is when or whether an unborn life can become an unjust aggressor to merit resistance from the host—the mother.

McCormick saw two main benefits from the direct/indirect distinction. As we saw in the previous chapter, he believed, until convinced to the contrary by Schüller, that the distinction gave an indication of the will's posture toward the evil which results from the action and was thus important in determining the morality of the act. To abandon it would be to deprive us of the only means of recognizing the difference between "legitimate military targeting, with collateral civilian death, and counter-society bombing."[8] Especially with regard to abortion, the direct / indirect distinction still seemed to him to be "a reasonable and charitable effort to respect the equal sanctity of both or several lives that may be in conflict,"[9] because it forces us to take account of the relation of means to ends in the discussion on abortion.

In an argument with William Van der Marck, McCormick insisted that there is a limit to what the end of an action can justify. Van der Marck had argued that the termination of pregnancy could become only a 'means' and therefore justified if it promoted intersubjectivity.[10] In such a case, termination of pregnancy would be no more than "the removal of the effects of rape, or saving the life of the mother."[11] In reaction to Van der Marck's position, McCormick asserted that such a subsumption of ends to means would open the way to the justification of any action whatsoever on very flimsy grounds. For example, he wondered why, on Van der Marck's terms, "the emptying of the uterus of a non-viable fetus cannot at times be called 'relief of psychic pain' or saving and increasing income."[12] In short, whatever way we characterize the action, the question remains whether the effects are morally appropriate.[13]

Since the Marquette lecture McCormick has turned to judging the appropriateness of moral actions generally on the basis of proportionate reasoning. Considering that, like the Catholic tradition itself, McCormick had previous to the Marquette lecture applied teleological reasoning to some aspects of the abortion debate,[14] the principal methodological change in his approach to abortion is not the introduction of proportionate reasoning but the exposing of the redundancy of the direct/indirect distinction in the determination of the morality of certain actions. We have already discussed the process that led to McCormick's rejection of this distinction.

The rejection of the direct/indirect distinction as pertinent to defining the morality of abortion implied that one may in regard to abortion, intend nonmoral evil as a means to achieving good.[15] Furthermore, it removes certain cases of abortion from the category of justice/injustice. By considering the morality of abortion in regard to the directness or indirectness and within the innocence/non-innocence category, the tradition had "by implication" limited permitted killing "to the *ratio* of injustice." The absence of such injustice meant that the killing was unjust because it took innocent life. McCormick now insists that this reasoning "overlooks the fact that there can be instances where there is "innocence" (no harm), yet killing would involve no *injuria*."[16] Thus, the bombing of noncombatants might kill innocent civilians and yet involve no moral wrong because there is proportionate reason for dropping the bomb in this area. In regard to abortion, however, this does not mean the endorsement or rejection of any particular abortion. All it means for McCormick is that the traditional prohibition of the direct killing of the innocent, "tied to the notion of justice as it is, may not be as all-encompassing and far-reaching as making it a 'bed-rock' would suggest."[17] The all-encompassing principle in all cases involving the causing of death (self-defense, abortion, active euthanasia, attack on noncombatants in warfare) would be proportionate reasoning.

Moral Considerations

McCormick's current moral position on abortion is based on a few key assumptions, the principal one being that human beings possess their "right to life" from God and not from society or any other human person or institution. In 1965 he expressed the implication of this conviction in the following manner:

> There is thus no man, no human authority, no science, no indication (whether medical, eugenic, social, economic or moral) that can justify deliberate and direct destruction of innocent human life. The life of an innocent human being is simply inviolable, altogether immune from direct acts of suppression.[18]

Although he continued to hold to the conviction that human life is a gift from God and the basis and foundation for other goods and rights, he reached a slightly different conclusion a few years later about the moral implications of this conviction. Rather than say that the life of an innocent is simply inviolable, he would now say that life as a basic good "should be taken only when doing so is the lesser of two evils, and all things considered."[19] Furthermore, only human life "or its moral equivalent" can qualify as a lesser evil.

"Moral equivalent" refers to a good or value that is, in Christian assessment, comparable to life itself. This is the *substance* of the Christian tradition if our best casuistry in other areas (e.g., just warfare) is carefully weighed and sifted; for the permissible exceptions with regard life-taking (self-defense, just war, capital punishment, indirect killing) are all formulations and concretization of what is viewed in the situation as the lesser of two evils.[20]

Nonetheless, McCormick remains conscious of the difficulty and the danger of attempting to determine a moral equivalent to life. The difficulty arises because it is hard to compare basic human values. The danger is that such an exercise is vulnerable to cultural and personal biases and limitations.[21] Giving the presumption in favor of life, however, transfers the burden of proof to the one who would destroy human life in any form. Thus, it is clear that what must be established is not the basic inviolability of human life but the exceptional circumstance which would be deemed to weaken the demands of this imperative.

A second assumption in McCormick's moral position on abortion is that human life refers to "life from fertilization or at least from the time at or after which it is settled whether there will be one or two distinct human beings." Nonetheless, he recognizes that certain phenomena in the preimplantation period, such as twinning, the number of spontaneous abortions, the appearance of primary organizer, the possibility of recombination of two fertilized ova into one (chimera), and so forth, "generate evaluative doubts about the claims the fetus at this stage makes, at least in some cases."[22] The doubts about the status of the preimplanted embryo cannot be resolved scientifically. Therefore the evaluation of the status of human life at this stage is more a philosophical and religious question than a scientific one.

Although theologians have based their discussion of abortion on one theory of animation or another, McCormick believes that the Church's refusal to take a definitive position on the exact time of ensoulment is a correct approach.[23] The Church's position on abortion is based on the practical assumption that, from the moment of conception, the embryo is a human person. For McCormick, this implies that "the presence of the rational soul is attributable to a creative act of God" and is not open to direct human enquiry as to the time of its occurrence.[24] In his view, such position protects better the interest of the fetus than do theories of abortion which are based on nonconclusive presuppositions of the time of animation.

> If there is a human being, in the fullest sense, present from the moment of conception, directly destructive actions based on an opposite assumption will be in violation of his inviolable rights. The practical conclusion, therefore, is that there is a human being— because no other conclusion protects sufficiently the most voiceless, helpless, unorganized minority possible.[25]

McCormick, nonetheless, considers that nascent life at this stage does not make the same demands for protection as it does later.[26] Even so, he rules out a simple pro-choice position on abortion because it is incompatible with the Christian faith.[27] Abortion is a "life issue" and not a "women's issue." Therefore, a

> "prochoice" moral position abandons this structure and the arduous wrestling involved in determining if and when it is tragically justifiable to end fetal life. In so doing, it trivializes the moral problem.[28]

It is McCormick's understanding that the Church's teaching on abortion does not imply lack of sympathy in the face of women's suffering. However, that sympathy runs "far beyond mere tears and sentiment" and is founded on the conviction that the fate of the fetus comes before non–life threatening burdens of the mother. That sympathy cannot be in doubt given that "the Church has always been at the front ranks of charitable endeavors such as orphanages, adoptive agencies, marriage counselling, relief works."[29] It is the intention of the Church, through its teaching on abortion, to secure the optimum opportunity for full human life for everyone, including the woman. Also, in full agreement with tradition and Roman Catholic Church teaching, McCormick allows abortion only in situations where the life of the mother cannot be saved otherwise.[30] He justifies this stand on the ground that in such conflict situations it is better to save one than to lose two.[31]

Pastoral Position

McCormick has also enunciated a pastoral position on abor- . tion. While a moral position looks at what ought to be, the pastoral view considers what is possible to do. "Pastoral care deals with an individual where that person is in terms of his perceptions and strengths."[32] In this sense a pastoral approach to abortion is a recognition of the limits of the individual *qua* individual and is meant to acknowledge the individual differences which exist on abortion due to no fault of the agent's.

For this reason a pastoral position on abortion must grapple with structures that do not support or aid women with unwanted pregnancies. It must also consider the issue of structural poverty and injustice and be prepared to deal with "subtle escalating pressures against childbearing" in most modern societies of the West.[33] A pastoral position on abortion must also consider the differences in the perception of fetal life.

> Since the sum total of these influences, then, is an attitude that increasingly tends to frame the moral question almost exclusively in terms of the sufferings resultant on a prohibitive moral position, it is important to distinguish two things: (a) whether a moral position is right and truly embodies a good; (b) whether standing by it and proposing it as object of inspiration, both personal and societal, entails hardships and difficulties. In a highly pragmatic, technologically sophisticated, and thoroughly pampered culture the latter point (certainly a fact) could lead many to conclude that the moral position is erroneous. This must be taken into account in any sound pastoral procedure.[34]

While seeking to treat the agent with genuine compassion and understanding, pastoral care should also invite the person to "a better humanity" through consideration of abortion as an act of killing whose certain outcome (even if justified) is the death of the fetus.[35] A pastoral position on abortion does not excuse abortions. It tries to address the situations which give rise to or make it easy to foster an abortion mentality and to provide alternatives to abortion through social, psychological, medical, financial, and religious help which would encourage the woman to carry her pregnancy to term, if she so desires.[36] It is McCormick's conviction that the motivations behind most abortions are social and economic. If these social and economic conditions are modified, he believes the motivations behind most abortions will disappear.[37]

John Mahoney deplores the distinction between morality and pastoral care. It not only smacks of "pastoral paternalism" but is also "tantamount to disqualifying pastoral situations from participating in identifying and purifying" the general rules of morality. Furthermore, it lays too much emphasis on the general "to the exclusion of the particular, where reality is located." On these grounds, Mahoney accuses McCormick of perpetrating and widening "the gulf between objective morality and subjective morality" which he (Mahoney) believes should be done away with.

> No doubt as McCormick writes, "one of the most important functions of morality is to provide to a culture the ongoing possibility of transcending itself and its limitations."[38] But not at the possible cost of multiplying unjustifiable burdens and of engendering or reinforcing an unwanted sense of moral delinquency and moral failure.[39]

Mahoney's critique highlights the fact that the pastoral position McCormick enunciated plays no significant role in his moral assessment of abortion. Abortion is wrong except in the tragic cases where the life of the mother and her conceptus will be lost, but where one (usually the mother) could be saved if there is intervention from outside. Although he would not draw that conclusion, it seems to me that a complete participation of the pastoral in "purifying the general rules of morality" in this case would appear to Mahoney to allow some form of abortion and thus ease "the unjustifiable burdens . . . and unwarranted sense of moral delinquency and moral failure" he believes McCormick's position promotes.

William P. George has also commented on the moral/pastoral distinction in McCormick's work. Although he acknowledges its usefulness as a rudder for steering between several extreme positions, he believes, like Mahoney, that it is also extremely problematic.[40]

> Maintaining the distinction as he does may: (1) support a construal of pastoral care as less than fully moral, or only derivatively moral;

(2) too readily enshrine generalized principles and norms rather than, say, virtue or discernment as the privileged meaning of morality; (3) sustain and possibly entail an ecclesiology that is problematically hierarchical; (4) stifle the experiential input of certain persons and groups that might challenge norms that prevail in a moral community (such as the Roman Catholic Church); and (5) in subtle ways render such persons as less than full human members in that community.[41]

George argues with specific reference to homosexuality and remarriage after divorce in the Catholic Church that this distinction, as McCormick uses it, stifles the experiential input of homosexual and divorced Catholics in the formulation of norms on these issues. As on abortion, McCormick's positions on homosexuality and marriage are constructed around a moral (normative) position and a pastoral one. Here, for example, is how he states his views on homosexuality:

> I accept the heterosexual orientation and heterosexual genital expression as normative. . . . The covenanted friendship of marriage offers us the best opportunity to humanize our sexuality and our selves. Therefore we all *ought* (normative) to strive to structure our sexuality in this way.[42]

Although he maintains that all men and women are invited by the Church "to reach for this ideal,"[43] he also states that if an individual "is irreversibly homosexual" and "is not called to celibacy for the Kingdom," the community of faith has certain pastoral responsibilities toward him or her.

> In this instance, both the Church and her ministers will be a liberating presence to the homosexual: (a) by inviting him to approximate the qualities of the covenanted man-woman relationship through fidelity and exclusiveness; (b) by aiding the individual to develop those healthy, outgoing attitudes and emotional responses that make this possible; (c) by extending the full sacramental and social supports of the Church to his striving; (d) by condemning and combatting all social, legal and ecclesial discrimination against and oppression of the homosexual.[44]

George argues that behind this pastoral position is the view that homosexuality is flawed and disordered and in need of justification.[45] More important, a pastoral position as distinct from a moral one impedes "the very sort of generalization that McCormick views as a key task of moral theology." Furthermore, the distinction makes it virtually impossible for "what happens 'pastorally' " to have influence on normative ethics.[46] Besides, persons who are deemed defective and thus subjects of pastoral attention "may subtly be deemed defective in a manner that prevents their full inclusion in the Church as a moral community."[47]

There is no doubt that the distinction between moral theology as a study of the "general rules" and pastoral theology as "the art of the possible" can lead to a dualistic perception of the moral order which presupposes a disjunction between the objective and subjective moral order. Contemporary moral theological reflection (including McCormick's) has called this into serious question.[48] I do not think, however, that McCormick's distinction between the pastoral and moral aspects of the discussion on abortion is guilty of this disjunction. McCormick has been consistent in his conviction that abortion is wrong except in the situation I have already mentioned. He cannot justify it on any other ground because he cannot imagine any other moral equivalent to life. Similarly for homosexuality. He cannot justify it as normative, not only because scriptural data and the tradition forbid him to, but also because of the disagreement within the scientific community on whether it is a reversible or irreversible state.

As far as I can see, abortion is one of three instances where pastoral considerations must give way to other factors most of the time due to McCormick's strict definition of what constitutes a conflict situation which can warrant the procedure. Others are artificial insemination by donor and homosexuality. In abortion, every other factor is secondary to life. In artificial insemination by donor, the unitive good of marriage is not open to compromise. In homosexuality, the norm is heterosexual relationship. In all these cases, pastoral solicitude offers some form of inclusion to everyone involved by seeking to treat all persons respectfully while at the same time maintaining the Church's normative stand on particular issues which it perceives to be beyond its competence to tamper with. The last statement raises the question of the nature of those norms and of all norms in general. Short of sanctioning same-sex relationships the best one can do is to articulate a pastoral position which will treat everyone, the homosexual included, with equal dignity and respect as a son or daughter of God.

The Legal Regulation

Like pastoral care, law is interested not just in the good but in the good that is "possible and feasible in a particular society at a particular time." However, like pastoral practice, it must not settle for the merely possible and feasible. "Simple accommodation to cultural 'realities' not only forfeits altogether the educative function of law, but also could leave an enormous number of people without protection."[49]

Although McCormick is convinced of the necessity for an adequate public policy on abortion, he is aware of the difficulties in this regard. One of these difficulties is due to the differences in the moral assessment of fetal life.[50] One characteristic of a good law is that it must be feasible. McCormick argues, however, that in regard to abortion, it is difficult to apply the feasibility test because the good itself which the law seeks to protect is an object of doubt. Such a situation makes both a stringently prohibitive law socially costly and a permissive law socially divisive and confusing. Furthermore, a permissive law can lead to a further erosion of respect for human life.

For McCormick, laws or policies which do not limit or apply some control to the procurement of abortion would be immoral and unacceptable because they forfeit the notion of the sanctity of life for the unborn. Also, any law which gives the woman alone the right to determine the fate of the fetus in every circumstance is a bad law because it deprives the fetus of any legal and social status. Abortion cannot be considered to be a purely private affair because it also affects other people than the woman involved. "It affects husbands, families, nurses, physicians, politicians, and society in general."[51] An adequate abortion law "must contain provisions that attack the problems that tempt to abortion."[52] In other words, it must address the issues of structural poverty, oppression, injustice, and social prejudices, which do not encourage women to bring their pregnancies to term.

Ultimately, the search for an adequate abortion law is a choice between two evils. Although it is impossible to satisfy everyone and all interests, the attempt would be to choose the lesser of the two evils. McCormick is aware, however, of the difficulty in deciding which is the lesser of the two evils in the circumstance. Such a decision would depend on many factors, including fetal life. It cannot, however, prohibit or criminalize all abortions.

> Given the moral position I find persuasive, I believe that the most equitable law should be one that protects fetal life but exempts abortion done in certain specified conflict situations from legal sanctions. In other words, I believe that the social disvalues associated with such a law (a degree of unenforceability, clandestine abortions, less than total control over fertility) are lesser evils than the enormous bloodletting both allowed and, in some real and destructive sense, inescapably encouraged (*teste experientia*), by excessively permissive laws.[53]

The preceding section identified the various methodological changes in McCormick's discussion on abortion. It also identified the assumptions in his moral position on abortion. These are that life is the most basic of all human goods on which depend the enjoyment of all other goods; that human life starts at conception; and that for an act to be life serving or life saving, to be the lesser of two evils, "there must be at stake human life or its moral equivalent."[54] McCormick considers abortion a sanctity-of-life question. As was pointed out in the previous section, he also assumes that Christian belief in the sacredness of life is a logical consequence of Christian convictions about God and the good life. "If all persons are equally the creatures of the one God, then none of these creatures is authorized to play God toward any other."[55]

TO SAVE OR LET DIE

Another species of the sanctity of life questions is the problem of saving and letting die. The issue here has to do with the right to decide what quality of life is tolerable. Connected with this are questions regarding who has the competence to make such a decision and what criteria are to be employed. These problems all came together in the case of Baby Boy Houle, who was born severely deformed.[56] Baby Boy Houle's condition deteriorated with time as pneumonia set in and further complications were detected. The question was whether the infant was entitled "to the fullest protection of the law," as a Superior Court in Maine had ruled, or whether he should be allowed to die, as his parents had requested.

There were two clear alternatives in this case. One was to continue to sustain the life of this infant at all costs—with life-support systems and life-saving and corrective surgeries, some of which are very precarious and might even cause further complications for the child. The other alternative was to stop further treatment and let the child die. For McCormick, the problem in this case is to find out which of these two options represents a less harmful way to promote the value in the situation. Fundamentally, there is also the question of deciding what the protectable (that is, desirable) value is in this case.

McCormick finds the traditional distinction between ordinary and extraordinary means to be a useful guideline in cases like that of Baby Boy Houle. Pope Pius XII had brought this distinction into prominence in 1957. He argued that although it is the right of everyone in serious illness to receive necessary and adequate treatment for the preservation of life and health,

> normally one is held to use only ordinary means—according to circumstances of persons, places, times, and culture—that is to say, means that do not involve any grave burden for oneself or another. A more strict obligation would be too burdensome for most men and women and would render the attainment of the higher, more important good too difficult. Life, health, all temporal activities are in fact subordinated to spiritual ends.[57]

McCormick believes that the pope's position here raises two important questions—one about the nature of the 'spiritual ends,' 'the higher, more important' goods—and the other about how the attainment of the spiritual ends is rendered more difficult by the use of extraordinary means.

In response to the first question, McCormick identifies the spiritual end to which other temporal ends and activities must be subordinated as love of God through love of neighbor, a love which finds expression in human relationships "and in the qualities of justice, respect, concern, compassion and support that surrounds them." In answer to the second question he maintains that it is the quality of life – life considered in all its spiritual and physical aspects and in the light of the goal of creation – which determines whether a means is ordinary or extraordinary. For example, a painful, poverty-stricken life, lived in an oppressive milieu without friends, without family, would be "an excessive hardship for the individual" and would "distort and jeopardize" the individual's grasp "on the over-all meaning of life."[58] To seek to prolong such a life at all cost may not be worth the while but may rather strain and threaten human relationships which are the very possibility of growth in love of God and neighbor. Moreover, life, a subordinate good and the condition of other values and achievements, would in such a case usurp the place of these other goods and become itself the ultimate value. When that happens, the value of human life has been distorted.[59]

The same consideration applies to the case of grossly deformed infants such as Baby Boy Houle. Sometimes such lives can constitute a negation of every truly human relational potential, which is the basic criterion for judging which lives to preserve or not to preserve. The question in such situation would be: Which lives do we not preserve? Answer: Those lives which have become submerged to the mere effort for survival. Such lives have achieved their potentiality; we should not seek to preserve them at all costs. Was Baby Boy Houle's life such a life? Did he lose every human relational potential? McCormick would not say so emphatically. However, he insists that the terms 'ordinary' and 'extraordinary' can be relative to individuals. Thus, trying to determine whether a grossly deformed child should live while another is left to die is a judgment which the parents should make in close consultation with the doctors. In such a situation McCormick believes it is better to err on the side of life.

Moreover, the issue is not to determine whether this or that life has value, but to determine whether "this undoubted value has any potential at all, in continuing physical survival, for attaining a share, even if reduced, in the 'higher, more important good.' "[60] This decision must be made not out of utilitarian considerations but based on the child's good alone. The Judeo-Christian tradition of defense and protection of the powerless, the unwanted, and the defenseless must inform each particular decision. "Any application of a general guideline that forgets this is but a racism of the adult world profoundly at odds with the gospel."[61]

Two further questions arise concerning means and relational potential in the case of Baby Boy Houle. First, would all the terrible mutilation (through surgery) which this infant would undergo be worth the life of dependency on machines and the pain he, his parents, and the entire community would have to endure all through his life? Second, has Baby Boy Houle the capacity *in any way* to relate to others? Although McCormick does not say whether he would or would not save Baby Boy Houle, we can infer his judgment from his words:

> There is a difference between having a terribly mutilated body as a result of surgery, and having a terribly mutilated body from birth. There is also a difference between a long, painful, oppressive convalescence resulting from surgery, and a life that is from birth a long, painful, oppressive convalescence.[62]

Furthermore, he insists that no life should be supported through means which are disproportionate. To do so would be to maintain the condition of the relationship rather than the relationship.

> Such a concentration easily becomes overconcentration and distorts one's pursuit of the very relational good that defines our growth and our flourishing. The importance of relationships gets lost in the struggle for survival.[63]

In another place McCormick describes such a situation as "a kind of medical idolatry" which ought not to be the case.[64] The commitment of the medical profession to curing disease and preserving life must instead be implemented within a healthy and realistic acknowledgment that we are mortal, and that though life is a basic good, it is not an absolute one to be maintained at all costs.[65]

In 1983 McCormick further specified what the capacity for human relationships would imply especially in regard to defective newborns. First, "life-saving interventions ought not be omitted for institutional or managerial reasons." This means that no one should be allowed to die simply because his or her family alone cannot bear the financial or emotional responsibility of keeping the person alive. Society, too, has certain responsibilities at this point. Second, life-sustaining interventions may not be omitted simply on the grounds of a child's retardation, though further complications associated with retardation may justify withholding life-sustaining treatment. Third, excessive hardship on the patient combined with poor prognosis could justify omission or withdrawal of life-sustaining treatment. Fourth, when it becomes clear that expected life can only be had "for relatively brief time and only with continued use of artificial feeding," life-sustaining interventions may also be omitted.[66]

Some Down's-syndrome cases[67] further highlighted the question concerning who has the competence to determine what would be more respectful of the incompetent patient in line with McCormick's insistence on respect for the person. In his response to those cases McCormick opted for a principle of family self-determination. He reaffirms this principle over the "medical-objectives policy" proposed by Paul Ramsey. This latter proposal would base its judgment whether to treat or terminate treatment of seriously ill patients on "objective standards" based on "scientific evidence" alone.[68] Ramsey put it this way:

> The tests for telling whether to discontinue treatments should be clinical or physiological ones (if these are the proper words for my meaning), not anyone's "values." They should not *in themselves*, with or without intention, build into the condition for allowing the dying to die a discriminatory definition of a life worth living. A fortiori, whoever decides these questions should not be able to give effect to his own "values" in this regard as if they were certainly the patient's own. In the absence of expressed predetermination . . . the only remaining objective standard is medical decision to cease to combat the dying of the dying.[69]

First of all, McCormick refutes Ramsey's suggestion that family self-determination is a subjective standard for determining whether to treat incompetents. Since the aim is to discover the "objectively valuable treatment" for a person in that condition,[70] the choice should be left to family members where possible. The presumption is that they are in a better position to know what the "best interest" as "objectively valuable by a reasonable person" would be for the patient.[71] McCormick is aware of possible violation of the rights of the patient even by family members, as in the Infant Doe case. In an article he wrote with Robert Veatch in 1980 he had called for state intervention to protect the rights of the patient when necessary.[72] Later he specified that this intervention could take the form of legislation to protect the patient, and in the case of children, a child-neglect hearing. The purpose of these would be "to guarantee that primary decision-makers act in a responsible way, one that should sustain public scrutiny."[73]

Furthermore, McCormick rejects Ramsey's "medical indications policy" on the ground that it is not as value-free as Ramsey believed. The choice to treat or not to treat is rooted in subjective and value reasons of one kind or another and, as such, amounts to acceptance of one value preference over another. Finally, a medical indications policy leads to the violation of the rights of incompetent, nondying patients by making "life-preserving treatment the only option regardless of the patient's condition."[74]

McCormick's use of the traditional teaching on the use of ordinary and extraordinary means has been questioned. John Connery charged that whereas this notion was used to establish a quality of treatment norm, McCormick has turned it into a quality-of-life norm, thus going far beyond what the tradition intended. The fear is that such quality-of-life norms easily could be employed to justify even third trimester abortions.[75] Moreover, the difficulty with McCormick's relational approach, said Connery, was that it is very difficult "to make a very precise judgment at the time of birth about the eventual capability – or lack of it – of a seriously defective infant for human function."[76] For, "cognition can be present without communication."[77]

McCormick's response is that quality-of-life considerations were always part of the traditional definition of burdensome means. Therefore, his extension of the distinction between ordinary and extraordinary treatment (if extension it is) is in line with the tradition. If such extensions, while seeking to extend the original formulations into new problem areas, remain true to the substantial value judgment of the tradition, they are a departure only in formulation.[78]

I believe McCormick's use of the principle of ordinary/extraordinary means constitutes an extension of that principle. The precept, especially as used by the pope, was concerned with means and ends. Insofar as it was interested in the sick person *qua* human person, its interest was in the spiritual goods of human life. This was understandable given the prevalent understanding of the principle of double effect at that time and the general bent of moral theology in this period. Connery is right in his assertion that McCormick has moved the principle beyond its use. This too is understandable, given the different moral theological climate within which McCormick is reading the principle.

The good of the human person integrally and adequately considered makes it necessary to reinterpret the principle of ordinary/extraordinary means as a quality-of-life principle. As in the case of abortion, the question is how to safeguard life or how to decide what lives to save or not to save in the tragic situations where such decisions have to be made. McCormick's common response would be to do what is the lesser evil based on the understanding that life is the most basic of all goods, although it is not an absolute good. However, the decision in each case is arrived at with the use of different methodological principles. In abortion, it is proportionate reasoning. In the quality-of-life case it is the distinction between ordinary and extraordinary means. Both principles are limited in their scope and only serve to determine what is the good of the human person adequately and integrally considered in the circumstances. The search for the goods which promote the welfare of the human person is also the motivation for McCormick's moral decision-making in matters pertaining to human sexuality and family.

THE MEANING OF SEXUALITY AND FAMILY

McCormick has grouped the issues in this area under two broad headings. One relates to the separation of sexual expression and procreation through contraception; the second relates to the achievement of procreation apart from sexual expression.

STERILIZATION AND CONTRACEPTION

Although McCormick has remained fairly constant in his position on the sanctity of life issues, his stand on birth control has undergone one of the most radical changes in his entire theology. I shall first of all present his earlier position on this issue and later present his views on the same issue since *Humanae Vitae*.

In 1962 McCormick condemned the use of contraceptive pills, which were then being marketed. The use of these drugs, whose immediate purpose was to induce temporary sterility by suppressing ovulation, constituted a violation of the fifth and sixth commandments and was therefore absolutely forbidden. Moreover, such use was tantamount to direct sterilization, which was equal to mutilation because it either suppressed an organic function or notably diminished the distinctive use of human reproductive organs. Direct sterilization whether temporary or permanent was illicit because it was an unwarranted mutilation.[79] This was so because,

> whereas the individual organs of the body are immediately ordained to the good of the whole person and so absorbed by the whole that they possess no finality independent of the person, the generative *function* has a primary finality of its own, the good of the species. Hence the principles governing its expression must take this teleology into account.[80]

Like the tradition, McCormick was at this time interested more in safeguarding the integrity of the sexual act and the finality of the sexual organs. In 1964 he acknowledged for the first time the "pockets of deep unrest in Catholic circles" concerning the Church's traditional position on the inseparability of the procreative and unitive aspects of sexual intercourse. He framed aspects of these objections in the following words:

> How can the marriage act be called procreative, it is asked, when in the vast majority of instances conception is not possible? Can it be called so if one partner is sterile, or if both are? And what if rhythm is practiced precisely to avoid conception?[81]

Although he still believed that the Church's theological tradition on contraception was correct, he was now convinced that the theological formulation of the question left much to be desired. He offered some reflections on conjugal morality "in the hope that they may help us better understand our own position and so better assess its

values and problems."[82] This search for a more adequate formulation of the traditional teaching on contraception marks the second
phase of McCormick's ethical reflection on the issue of contraception. This phase lasted until the publication of *Humanae Vitae* in
1968. McCormick's theological reformulation of the teaching on
contraception at this period was beginning to be influenced by the
Second Vatican Council, because it was based on the understanding
of marriage as a community of shared life and love. However, he
still retained the then-prevalent view of procreation as the primary
end of marriage. McCormick's writings at this time show the influence of the new theology of marriage, which had just emerged from
the Council, as well as that of traditional theology, which considered marriage in terms of its primary and secondary ends. Thus he
argues that viewed institutionally, that is, as an institution within
the totality of the human race, "the primary end of marriage and
marital union [is] parenthood." More than this, however, married
life "is a vocation of two people to Christian perfection through
growth in love for each other." It is a relationship of total dedication
in which two people merge their lives and grow in likeness to God.
Conjugal intimacy is the symbol of this total relationship.

> The most important thing, then, about sexual intercourse is that it is
> a communication between persons, expressing and strengthening
> the complete self-giving, the unreserved self-commitment of love,
> that is their vocation. Acts that do not preserve a completeness of
> donation (e.g., condomistic intercourse and *coitus interruptus* or
> withdrawal) fail to express the relationship of total oblation. By more
> or less detracting from the total self-gift, such acts do not create unity
> in the flesh, and to that extent are separative.[83]

Thus, rather than continue his earlier insistence on the immorality of contraception merely on the basis that it does not allow
conception to occur, McCormick now regarded these acts as immoral on the grounds that they infringe on the total self-giving
which is the only adequate expression of the marital relationship.
Contraceptive intercourse was not an act of love since it was not a
communion of "loving personal exchange."[84] Such acts mar rather
than promote self-giving. McCormick defended himself against the
charge of biologism by arguing that to choose the procreative capa-

bility of the sexual act as a criterion for determining the meaning of self-giving in sexual intercourse

> is to recognize in a single essential aspect of sexuality a practical criterion for the safeguard of the completeness of self-giving. It is to ensure the integrity of the expression of love and union in one flesh by proscribing possible counterfeits.[85]

Traditional Catholic teaching on contraception, he said, was an indication that human sexuality and sexual union have a basically reproductive character. In a statement straight from Pius XI, he insisted that the contribution of the human effort in this totality is to provide the conditions required for the meeting of ovum and sperm. Insofar as sexual intercourse accomplishes this, "it preserves one of its basic inner meanings within this totality."[86]

The unity of the procreative and unitive aspects in the sexual union is suggestive of the real depth of conjugal love and morality in several ways:

> It suggests that marital . . . love cannot be conceived independently of personal relationships and conjugal love or parenthood. It also permits the use of the procreative aspect as a practical criterion of complete self-giving and suggests that we should consider the close connection between continuity of the race and conjugal love in the divine plan.[87]

As was said earlier, McCormick's effort was really nothing more than a rephrasing of traditional material. He still insisted on the inseparability of the procreative and unitive aspect of human sexuality and on the primarily procreative nature of human sexuality. However, he fell short, especially in the years immediately preceding *Humanae Vitae*, of outright condemnation of every use of contraception as evil. This perhaps may be explained by the fact that he was beginning to have doubts over the traditional teaching.[88]

The third and current phase of McCormick's reflection on the ethics of contraception dates from the publication of *Humanae Vitae*. I have already indicated his change of mind on the issue of contraception at this time and how that change occurred.[89] Although I have also done so before, I will again indicate, briefly, why

McCormick had problems with the central thesis of that encyclical. This will help us present a more coherent picture of the issues under discussion.

As McCormick puts it,

> The problem prior to *Humanae Vitae* was whether the positive doubts surrounding traditional teaching had encountered a true teaching statement. . . . The problem after *Humanae Vitae* is the extent to which this document, obviously a teaching statement, has truly solved the doubts.[90]

McCormick now objects to the encyclical's central thesis that it is intrinsically evil to engage in contraception on the following grounds. First is his belief that this teaching rests on the "unsupportable" supposition that "every act of coitus has and therefore must retain a per se aptitude for procreation."[91] Second, he considers the document inconsistent because it teaches that every sexual act must be destined for procreation yet allows intercourse during infertile periods. For McCormick, this seems nothing but "a factual separation of the unitive and procreative aspects of individual coital acts during the infertile period."[92] Third, the document measures the meaning of human acts on physiological grounds alone, thus going contrary to the teaching of Vatican II that the moral aspect of any procedure must be determined by objective standards based on the nature of the person and the person's acts. "Significance does not refer to mere physical acts; rather it is an assessment of an action's relation to the order of persons, to the hierarchy of values."[93] Therefore, in regard to contraception or sterilization the appropriate question would be whether contraception or sterilization would help or hinder the total relationship that is marriage.[94] Actions, he says, are morally right "not because they correspond to the nature of the agent, but because they respond properly to the ethical importance of the agent."[95]

Furthermore, McCormick objects to the central thesis of *Humanae Vitae* because he believes it exposes an inconsistency in methodology in Catholic moral teaching. He notes that in most areas of morality the Catholic tradition accepts that physical objects as such have no relation to the moral order. Thus, "taking another's property" is only a physical act; it is not yet a moral object. The same applies to uttering an untruth. However, if taking another's property contains an attack on persons or person, it contains the malice of theft. If uttering an untruth "jeopardizes man's life in community, it contains the malice of a lie." He believes these examples show that the tradition believes it is "the total good of the person which has determined which physical acts are theft, which are not. The same might be said of speech." The same should be said of contraception. Its moral significance must be determined, as in other cases, "by relating the physical object to the order of persons and by seeing it as an intersubjective reality." Nonetheless, McCormick shows some ambivalence in regard to the morality of contraception. Unlike some other theologians he does not embrace the view which would justify contraception as being of no moral significance.

> Of course, sexuality is founded on biological realities, and just as obviously sexual intercourse, materially considered, has some orientation toward fecundation. We are not calling these "thresholds of objectivity" into question here. We are only suggesting that the meaning of sexual activity cannot be defined narrowly from biological materialities; for this does not take account of the full range and meaning of human sexuality. It is not the sexual organs which are the source of life but the person.[96]

Finally, McCormick believes the issue of the morality of individual acts of contraception pertains to the area of the practical application of natural law which "does not belong to the Church's competence in the same way as the *depositum Fidei.*"[97] While this does not mean that the Church has no guidance to offer in regard to the practical application of natural law, McCormick contends that it "suggests appropriate caution and tentativeness" on matters related to the horizontal aspect of human existence.

REPRODUCTIVE TECHNOLOGIES

Another set of contemporary biological achievements that have challenged the meaning of sexuality and marriage are those which have achieved procreation apart from sexual expression: *in vitro* fertilization (IVF), artificial insemination by husband or by donor (AIH and AID), cloning, and surrogate motherhood. Like many other contemporary ethicists, McCormick's understanding of the meaning of marriage and sexuality has evolved in response to various challenges posed by developments in reproductive technologies. The challenge as he has come to define it is to determine which of these developments is promotive or destructive of the good of the human person integrally and adequately considered.

Two values emerge as important in McCormick's treatment of the morality of reproductive technologies: the exclusivity of marriage, and the necessity to hold together the unitive and procreative aspects of marriage. His understanding of the meaning of inseparability of the unitive and procreative aspects of marriage has undergone considerable evolution over the years and is evident in his reactions over several years to the challenges posed by the various reproductive technologies.

Artificial Insemination

Since Pius XII official Catholic teaching has objected to all forms of artificial insemination. Pius XII himself insisted on the total elimination of AIH because it is not procreation according to "the will and plan of the creator," is not in harmony with the dignity of the marriage partners, and threatens "to convert the domestic hearth, sanctuary of the family, into nothing more than a biological laboratory." The child so born is not the fruit of an act which is an expression of personal love.[98] More recently, the Vatican document on reproductive technologies has taken up the same line of reasoning. In connection with heterologous artificial fertilization, the document maintains that truly responsible procreation demands that the child be the fruit of marriage and the sign of the mutual self-giving of the spouses, of their love, and of their fidelity. The devotion of the spouses to each other in the unity of marriage involves reciprocal respect of their rights to become father and mother only through each other. Thus the document concludes:

> Heterologous artificial fertilization violates the rights of the child; it deprives him of his filial relationship with his parental origins and can hinder the maturing of his personal identity. Furthermore, it offends the common vocation of the spouses who are called to fatherhood and motherhood: it objectively deprives conjugal fruitfulness

of its unity and integrity; it brings about and manifests a rupture between genetic parenthood, gestational parenthood and responsibility for upbringing. Such damage to the personal relationships within the family has repercussions on civil society: what threatens the unity and stability of the family is a source of dissension, disorder and injustice in the whole of social life.[99]

Thus, fertilization of a married woman with sperm from a donor is wrong. The same applies to a widow or an unmarried woman who wishes to be artificially inseminated. AIH is also wrong because it sunders the unitive and procreative aspects of marriage and encourages or condones masturbation. Like AID and IVF, it is not a true expression of the self-giving which should characterize marital relationships.[100]

Methodological Considerations

McCormick has given considerable thought to the question of how to arrive at an adequate moral evaluation of the various reproductive technologies and has steadily demonstrated the difficulty of coming to a consensus on these questions even when the ethicists involved work from the same faith perspective.[101] In 1972 he devoted an entire edition of the "Notes" to a consideration of the methodological approaches which are discernible in the literature on genetic engineering.[102] He showed that there were three such approaches: a consequentialist approach, a deontological approach, and a 'mediating' approach. The consequentialist approach is based on the belief that "the rightness or wrongness of an action is ultimately based upon the quality of the consequences produced by it."[103] A representative of this approach would be Joseph Fletcher, who claims that "results are what count and results are good when they contribute to human well-being." Fletcher would support any genetic intervention "if the greatest good of the greatest number were served by it."[104] He would "reason from the data of each actual case or problem and then choose the course that offers an optimum or maximum of desirable consequences."[105] Thus, for example, he would approve cloning and bioengineering of parahumans if this would serve the greatest good of the greatest number. We ought not to fear the consequences of human genetic intervention, he says, for "to be men we must be in control. This is the first and last ethical word."[106]

Besides chiding Fletcher for proposing to do theology "by setting up dubious polarities, promulgating unexamined premises, and flourishing rhetorical *non sequiturs*."[107] McCormick also maintained that Fletcher's ethical methodology constituted an unexamined premise.

> (1) Have we not repeatedly experienced the fact that the greatest good of the greatest number, unassailable as it might be as a theoretical criterion, is practically the warrant for present policies which all but guarantee that this greatest good will not be served? (2) How is the social good to be spelled out even if we accept it as a goal? Who makes the determination? On what basis? (3) How would laboratory reproduction, cloning, etc. serve it? True, Fletcher has said "if," but his failure to confront the serious, indeed decisive, problems buried in this "if" means that for him proportionate good too easily translates "anything to get the job done."[108]

Having dismissed Fletcher as a bad consequentialist,[109] McCormick turned to an examination of the deontological approaches represented by Paul Ramsey and Leon Kass. Both ethicists considered certain human actions to be intrinsically evil. Unlike Fletcher's, Ramsey's position, built on the inseparability of the procreative and marital love and on the belief that we ought not to submit another human being "to experimental procedures to which he cannot consent when these procedures have no relation to his own treatment," led him to reject many genetic interventions.[110] Ramsey believed that we may not split what God had put together in creation. On this basis, he rejected AID, IVF, and cloning, because they are contrary to the nature of "human parenthood," which demands the inseparability of procreation and marital love. However, he approved AIH in sterile marriage on the grounds that the response of the couple to what God has joined together "would be expressed by their resolve to hold acts of procreation . . . within the spheres of acts of conjugal love, within the covenant of marriage."[111]

McCormick believed that Ramsey's position was ultimately consequentialist because his rejection of these procedures ultimately lies on consequences and not in spite of them. "The dominating effect or consequence is the depersonalization of man, and this simply overrides any long-term eugenic goals." Therefore he contended that Ramsey should not speak of his principle as valid independently of consequences.[112] However, McCormick maintained that to attribute a depersonalizing effect to any procedure "demands, of course, both some notion of the *humanum* and the predictable effects on the humanum of prospective procedures."[113] Two attitudes could emerge from this unpredictability and lack of knowledge of the humanum. One would be to reject all forms of genetic intervention as unwarranted intrusion into and possible distortion of the *humanum*, whatever it is. The other would be to proceed with caution and trepidation through the institution of appropriate checks as we proceed. McCormick endorses the second. That is why in his celebrated debate with Ramsey on experimentation involving children, he opts for such procedure provided the risk to the child is minimal and appropriate steps are taken to spare the child all undue discomfort. Parental consent for some form of experimentation on their children would neither dehumanize nor depersonalize the child. Contrary to Ramsey's position, such consent on behalf of the child can be an affirmation of the child's solidarity with and concern for others.

The 'mediating approach' is typified, McCormick said, by the works of James M. Gustafson[114] and Charles E. Curran.[115] Gustafson's concern was whether "*rights* of individuals" or *benefits* to persons and society should determine the concrete moral issues of both procedures and uses of research pertaining to genetic intervention.[116] He notes that there are more than just two options in the matter:

(a) The rights of individuals are sacred and primary, and therefore under no circumstances are they to be violated in favor of benefits to others that might be gained from their violation. (b) Anticipated consequences judged in terms of the "good" that will be achieved, or the "evil" that will be avoided, ought to determine policy and action, regardless of the restrictions on individual rights that this might require. (c) Propositions *a* and *b* are both one-sided. Decisions require consideration both of individual rights and of benefits to others. Thus one of the two can be the base line, and the other can function as the principle which justifies the restrictions on, or the exceptions to, the base line.[117]

Gustafson opted for the third alternative, because he believed that, generally speaking, it might be more responsible in some circumstances to make the thrust of individual rights the base line and to opt for the accounting of benefits in other circumstances.[118] Gustafson is thus trying to hold two very different moral alternatives in balance.

Although McCormick regarded Gustafson's work as "subtle, sensitive [and] sophisticated," he believed it was dissatisfying in some respects. He criticized Gustafson for, on the one hand, insisting on primacy of the right to physical life and, on the other, insisting that other values and rights can override this primacy, and yet failing to provide precise guidance to the particular values and rights which can override the right to life.

> To say that there are overriding values *without stating what they might be*, to state that there are circumstances in which the base-line priority shifts *without stating what they might be*, is to do two things: (1) to empty the notions of "primary" and "baseline" of most of their significance for decision-making; (2) to suggest that these overriding rules can only be discovered in individual decision. I do not think that these are true. What Gustafson wants (and rightly) to say is that rational moral discourse is limited, that there comes a point when the complexity of reality leads us beyond the formulation of traditional wisdom. That, I think, is true. And I believe that we have always known it, even though we have not always admitted it.[119]

In concluding his reflection on the literature on genetic engineering, McCormick put forward his own views. Like Ramsey and Leon Kass, he too considered the production and destruction of embryos in *in vitro* fertilization "a serious issue," but unlike them he fell short of condemning the procedure as morally wrong. Like these authors, however, he maintained that in view of the immediate and foreseeable effects of these procedures on marriage and family, "we should not take such steps (nor allow them to be taken, since a public good of the first order is involved) unless a value the equivalent of survival demands it."[120] He also believed, like Ramsey and Kass, that *in vitro* fertilization is depersonalizing and dehumanizing. First, the removal of the origin of the child from the sphere of specifically marital (bodily, sexual) love, redefines that love "in a way which deflates the sexual and bodily and its pertinence to human love, and therefore to the human itself." Although it remains true in some sense to say that the child born of *in vitro* fertilization is "the product of marital love," yet the term "marital" in this case has been "debiologized" and "debodified." Secondly, IVF weakens the family because it undermines the justification and support which biological parenthood gives to the family.

> The family as we know it is basically (not exclusively or eminently) a biological unit. To weaken the biological link is to untie the family at its root and therefore to undermine it. The family . . . embodies the ordinary conditions wherein [parents, children, and others] learn to become persons. In the stable, permanent man-woman relationship we possess the chance to bring libido and eros to the maturity of *philia*-friendship. Through monogamous marriage we experience the basic (not the only) form of human love and caring, and learn to take gradual possession of our own capacity to relate in love.[121]

In a review of the discussion which followed the birth in 1978 of Louise Brown, the first "test tube" baby, McCormick began to modify his view on *in vitro* fertilization. For the first time, he acknowledged the difficulty in rejecting *in vitro* fertilization with embryo transfer "on the sole ground of artificiality" or of the separation of the unitive from the procreative aspect of the reproductive process "unless one accepts this physical separation as an inviolable value."[122] Furthermore, he argued that the discussion on the spare zygote which had been fertilized *in vitro* should not center around the personhood of the fertilized ovum, since this is an evaluative question on which there are several positions. Nor must the loss of a high percentage of these zygotes be termed 'abortions' if these losses occur in the attempt to achieve a pregnancy. Such loss would be no worse than what occurs naturally in normal sexual relations. Although he rejected the production of zygotes for experimental use,[123] he supported certain types of *in vitro* fertilization:

> At the level of the individual couples's decision, there seems to be no argument that shows with clarity and certainty that *in vitro* procedures using their own sperm and ovum are necessarily and

inherently wrong, if abortion of a possibly deformed child is excluded and the risks are acceptably low.[124]

He was aware of the problems and dangers posed by *in vitro* fertilization. For this reason he argued that there should be no government support for research alone in this area, *in the present circumstances*. The reasons he adduced are respect for germinating life, the danger of "going beyond marriage," the cost, "the almost unavoidable dangers of proceeding to independent zygote research and the manipulation of the implanted fetus," and so on.[125]

In 1985 McCormick turned his attention to the issue of the physical union of the procreative and unitive aspect of procreation in relation to IVF. Again he made a subtle but significant change in his position on IVF. This time he shifted significantly in his understanding of the inseparability of the unitive and procreative elements in marriage.[126] Although McCormick had previously considered IVF as a debiologization, debodification, and dehumanization of human origins,[127] he now argued that to reject any of these genetic procedures or contraception on this view is to apply a very narrow reading of the meaning of the unitive and the procreative in human sexuality.

> Must these two be held together in every *act* (thus no contraception or I.V.F.), or is it sufficient that the *spheres* be held together, so that there is no procreation apart from marriage, and no full sexual intimacy apart from a context of responsibility for procreation?[128]

Thus, even though he continued to hold to the inseparability of the procreative and unitive dimensions of marriage and sexuality, he now moved from what he considered to be "an act analysis of this inseparability" to a person-centered understanding of the principle. In his judgment, the act-centered understanding of the principle had become an obstacle to the promotion of the human person integrally and adequately considered. Consequently it had lost its (generally operative) normative force because it had ceased to be "subject to, and judged by, the broader criterion."[129]

Although McCormick was clearly prepared to redefine his understanding of the principle of inseparability of the unitive and procreative elements in marriage in view of the principle of integral personalism, he was not prepared to compromise on the exclusivity of marital relationships. This position leads him to reject AID and some forms of IVF such as those which take donor sperm, donor eggs, donor embryos, or donor wombs. Although "each has distinctive dimensions and problems that cannot be summarily reduced and overlooked," they all infringe on conjugal exclusivity which, he says, "should include the genetic, gestational and rearing dimensions of parenthood." Separating these dimensions (except through rescue, as in adoption) too easily contains "a subtle diminishment of a certain aspect of the human person."[130] Arguing consequentially, McCormick states that relaxation of marital exclusivity would involve incalculable risks and potential harms. Deontologically speaking, he notes that third-party involvement is a violation of the marriage covenant.

CONCLUSION

Our principal aim in this chapter has been to examine the way McCormick engages in moral decision-making. Evidently his approach to moral decision-making reflects the tension in our continuous effort to know and to do what is right. It also indicates his willingness to offer his opinion on an issue which is of interest to him, as well as his preparedness to modify his views if he comes across more compelling argument.

McCormick is clearly not a situationist, because he considers norms very important, although he is prepared to change or modify them where necessary. The pastoral position he enunciates on several issues is meant to ease the harshness of some of these norms (on certain groups of people) in circumstances where he does not, at the moment, see the possibility of change in the normative position. Although we can criticize this attitude to norms, it strikes me as honest and consistent.

Clearly, two principles, to a lesser and greater degree (proportionate reason and integral personalism), form the hinges on which McCormick builds his casuistry. Removal of a nonviable fetus is morally wrong except when it is chosen as the lesser of two evils in situations of conflict. Contraception and sterilization can be morally right, if there is proportionate reason. The search for an

abortion law is nothing but a choice between two evils. The importance of proportionate reason is evident even when McCormick
ostensibly employs another principle to resolve an issue. This is the
case both in the case of deformed neonates and the terminally ill.
Ultimately, proportionate reasoning is only a tool for establishing
what is promotive or destructive of the good of the human person,
adequately considered. Thus, every genetic intervention must take
account of the familial, social, religious, and other characteristics of
the individual, that is, with proper and equal attention to all that it
means to be human.[131]

To qualify to be regarded as promotive rather than destructive
of the human good a genetic intervention must respect the sacredness of life. Such respect for life would imply the following: avoiding undue risks, and especially discriminatory distribution of risks;
and protecting the human rights of all, especially the least privileged and those least able to defend themselves. It must also issue in
respect for the interconnection of life systems and in respect for
human individuality and diversity, both as indispensable aspects of
the human condition.[132] Finally, respect for life would also imply
that research priorities must be set and the allocation of funds for
research must be made with the needs of every segment of society in
mind and not just in the interest of groups who influence politics.
The same goes for the enjoyment of the benefits of genetic research.

As McCormick suggests, the ultimate questions raised by
genetic technology are theological: Who is the human person?
What is his or her final destiny or future? What, therefore, is truly
beneficial to the human person? These are difficult questions with
no easy answers. Therefore, McCormick is correct to insist on a
collaborative approach to these questions. He is also right to assume
that the Church has a lot of wisdom to offer on these issues. As he
frequently points out, however, wisdom is not only a gift; it is above
all a responsibility to learn and to be in discussion with other
relevant and interested parties. Therefore,

> to absent itself from these discussions, to enter them ill-informed, to
> share in them from a position of authoritative arrogance as if the
> Church were in prior possession of concrete answers–all such ap-
> proaches would dim the "new light" and almost assuredly compro-
> mise 'solutions which are human.'[133]

One of aims of this chapter has been to see what important insights McCormick has contributed to Catholic moral thought in the course of making moral decisions. One of these insights is that attention to human experience can and often does lead to a reformulation of norms on certain issues. Furthermore, pluralism of opinion on ethical issues is not necessarily an indication of chaos; it can sometimes be the result of the complexity and fluidity of the point at stake.[134] McCormick has shown that moral norms for that reason are inherently reformable and revisable, because they are only approximations of truth based on our limited insights and judgment.

7

RICHARD A. McCORMICK AND
THE RENEWAL OF MORAL THEOLOGY

As I mentioned in the introduction, Roman Catholic moral theology has been experiencing an epistemological crisis since Vatican II. According to Alasdair MacIntyre, any solution to an epistemological crisis must fulfill three requirements. First, it must provide a systematic and coherent solution to the problems which had hitherto proved intractable. Second, it must be able to show what had gone wrong with the tradition in its previous form. Third, the two tasks above must maintain some fundamental continuity between the shared beliefs which had characterized the tradition of enquiry up to this point and the new theory.[1] We have so far analyzed McCormick's work as a moral theologian from the end of his study in Rome to date. Interest in McCormick's work is justified by two things; namely, the conciliar directive for the renewal of moral theology, and McCormick's expressed interest in working to correct or modify some of the weaknesses which were apparent in the manualist tradition in which he was brought up.[2]

We have been able to isolate the major difficulties that, according to McCormick, needed to be overcome. These difficulties relate to the nature of Christian ethics; the role of authority, community, and the individual in moral determination; and moral methodology. My intention in this chapter is to assess the solutions McCormick offered to the crisis in moral theology; and to find out whether they are coherent and systematic, and in fundamental continuity with previous (traditional) positions. To achieve these objectives I will first summarize the major findings in this work as well as identify and reflect on the major influences that shaped McCormick's agenda and achievement in moral theology. It will also be necessary to state what some of these achievements are and to reflect on their importance.

SUMMARY

In the first chapter we surveyed the ecclesial, social, and political contexts of McCormick's background and training. Through an appraisal of his doctoral dissertation we established the impact of this cultural context on his theological formation. It was also established that although McCormick was steeped in the manualist tradition, he was, by the end of his days as a student in Rome, starting to show discontent with aspects of its methodology. McCormick's interest in the renewal of moral theology was therefore much evident early in his career through his stated intention in his doctoral dissertation to revise and expand the meaning and range of some hallowed principles and dicta in the discipline. We also saw that his use of proportionate reasoning to resolve the dilemma over the removal of the probably dead fetus was a departure from the usual approach to such problems in the manuals. More important, his interpretation of various elements in the principle of double effect was, in many respects, an anticipation of Peter Knauer's work eight years later and, indeed, of the whole revision of that principle after Vatican II.

Chapter 2 established McCormick's understanding of Christian ethics. It noted the Trinitarian foundation of his views on the nature of Christian ethics. The basis of Christian ethics lies in God's saving grace made manifest in Jesus Christ. This "engendering deed" evokes a response, the highest expression of which is love or commitment to the good of the neighbor in the world. The Christian response, however, is not a legalistic response but an interior motivation, which is urged and assisted by the Holy Spirit. McCormick has retained the traditional Catholic conviction in the ability of human reason, unaided by faith, to come to knowledge about right and wrong. Scripture and the teaching of the Church can assist but not supplant reason in discovering what is normatively human. Although this confidence in human reason allows the faith community to address social problems in modern pluralistic societies based on the level of our common humanity, it raises two important problems: the relationship of reason to revelation, and the normative role of scriptures.

It was also established that even though McCormick maintains that faith has a transforming influence on the agent's view of the person and provides the agent with motivation for following Christ and with "a style of performing the moral tasks common to persons,"[3] he also believes it does not provide arcane insights into the material content of morality. Thus, there is an identity between Christian and natural morality in content but not in motivations, attitudes, or dispositions. This approach to the issue of the distinctiveness of Christian ethics has given McCormick the ability to incorporate the best of two worlds, so to speak. He is able genuinely to maintain the autonomy of the natural moral order while avoiding denial of the influence of faith on morality. Scripture cannot be used merely as proof-text or as an arcane source for determining issues at the material concrete level of morality; however, it can provide paranesis, motivation, and identity.

McCormick's view on the influence of faith on the moral agent is an acknowledgment of the shared public world, which pre-exists both the individual and his thought. This public world not only shapes the individual's thought, but also provides the shared resources of knowledge and the terms on which that knowledge is examined, tested, and transmitted.[4] Thus, the self finds its identity—moral or otherwise—through membership in a family, city, neighborhood, religion, and so forth. However, the question is whether an individual whose world is already so shaped by a tradition can be regarded as a free moral agent. Furthermore, does the acknowledgment of the contextual basis of our knowledge allow for cross-cultural understanding? Is it possible for persons brought up within or trained in these various worlds of meaning to understand one another or to acknowledge some common basis for rationality and moral action?

McCormick has tried to answer these questions not by denying the particularity which membership in human traditions can impose on the agent but by maintaining the belief in the ability of human reason 'unaided by faith' to come to sound moral judgment. This is a common tenet of natural law. Consequently, knowledge of the moral law is neither based directly on any faith nor limited to any one religious tradition, because it is disclosed through the order of creation which reflects the reason of God. The point, then, is that although the various traditions to which we belong shape our perceptions of the world and of the moral order, they neither have exclusive hold on our reasoning nor offer exclusive insights into normal moral dilemmas and problems. The corollary is, of course, that the notion of a moral order must always be tempered by the understanding that 'objectivity' in this sense does not mean "something out there" to which we must all conform irrespective of our particularities. It is an objectivity that is structured but not held captive by our subjectivities. The moral law does not exist independent of who we are, and yet it is logically prior to us, to our traditions, and to our caprices and whims.

The tension between particularity and universality and between the individual and community of faith is very much evident in chapter 3, which deals with the role of the Church as moral teacher. In this chapter we traced the evolution of McCormick's thought on the question of ecclesial competence in morality. It was shown that several factors, especially Vatican II and the birth-control debate, considerably shaped his views on this issue. This influence was salutary, because it led McCormick into consideration of many wider issues such as the proper meaning of natural law and the Church's competence in various aspects of it. However, it seems to have left noticeable scars on McCormick's views on the role of the Church as moral teacher. For one thing, it put McCormick in a somewhat polemic mode on this issue. The effects are evident in his ecclesiology, which is more interested in establishing the limits of hierarchical power than in exploring the influence of the Church as bearer of moral tradition. This also explains the great attention which McCormick pays to dissent as well as the stress, in later years, on the moral rightness/moral goodness issue.

I argued in this chapter also that although the moral rightness/moral goodness distinction has brought a much needed clarity into moral reasoning in Christian ethics, it also could lead to a dualist appreciation of Christian moral experience. The problem is how to establish a balance between the natural and supernatural order as well as how to maintain the validity of the authority of the Church as moral teacher without implying that such authority is sufficient validation for every moral teaching. This represents an unfinished issue in McCormick's agenda.

The chapter on anthropology reviewed McCormick's understanding of the human person as a being and as moral agent. It showed that his definition of person presupposes creatureliness. Creaturehood confers worth, equality, and sociality on the human person. Human personhood also implies finitude, genetic and developmental individuality, existence in history, and a gradual and communal approach to knowledge. McCormick's anthropology is closely connected with, even if not dependent on, the anthropologies of Rahner, Janssens, and Fuchs. Beginning with his belief of a fundamental faith dimension of moral agency, which expresses itself in moral action, he proceeds to argue, in line with Rahner, that the moral agent articulates a fundamental option for or against God through categorial acts of conscious choice. The Christian 'story' provides both the perspective from which such choices can be made and the confirmatory warrant for testing their validity, in broad terms at least.

Chapter 5 outlined McCormick's discussion on proportionate reason. The continuity between McCormick's view on proportionate reasoning in his doctoral dissertation and in his later writings was indicated. It was also shown that although McCormick had already begun to reinterpret the principle of double effect, he could not embark on the 'revolution' that Knauer later initiated, because he was not prepared to forgo the notion of intrinsic evil which he sensed to be part of a total embrace of a teleological methodology. McCormick's change of heart was helped by the person-centered thinking of Vatican II. Although this conversion began slowly, it was accelerated by the publication of *Humanae Vitae*.

The purpose of chapter 6 was to examine McCormick's application of moral theory to concrete issues. I showed how the various changes in his conception of the central elements in proportionate reasoning were manifested in his casuistry, notably on the question of abortion. The issue of proportionality was also shown to be central to his treatment of other sanctity-of-life questions, notably those pertaining to deformed neonates. In these, as in other cases, proportionate reasoning was used to determine what action would best promote the good of the human person integrally and adequately considered in the circumstances.

The interest in searching for the good of the human person integrally and adequately considered is described by modern theologians as personalism. The alternative is sometimes referred to as physicalism. While physicalism is characterized as the direct derivation of moral norms "from certain structures of nature, in particular, the structure of faculties and acts,"[5] personalism is the derivation of moral norms not only on the structure of human faculties and acts but on the basis of the entire human reality. Although personalism has become a staple of Catholic moral tradition since Vatican II, it has been interpreted variously. Brian Johnstone identifies three senses in which the term is used in recent Catholic moral thought. First, there is "ontological, complementary personalism," in which "the account of the human reality is extended by including certain aspects of the person, in such a way that there is a wide range of objective features available for consideration by moral reason."[6] However, although moral reason now goes beyond biology to include the full reality of the human person, it does not admit of any changes to moral norms. Thus, "where a norm was once defended because it derived from the structure of biology, the same norm is now upheld because it derives from the structure of the person."[7] Ontological, complementary personalism is a feature of many Roman documents.

A second form of personalism is "the personalism of the dignity of conscience." Like the first type, this form of personalism includes a wide range of factors. The emphasis here, however, is on freedom and conscience as the basis of human dignity.

> A particularly significant statement for this style of thinking is the teaching of *Gaudium et Spes* that "Conscience frequently errs from invincible ignorance without losing its dignity" (GS #16). This model, in particular, would stress the element of creativity and freedom in the contemporary idea of the person, and entertain favorably the notion of "creative conscience." The criterion of moral truth is not the conformity of the act to an abstract norm, but correspondence to the personal relation to God. Here, as a consequences of these changes, some modifications of previously accepted norms may be justified.[8]

The third model has been labelled totalist, revisionist personalism. In this model, the person in his or her entirety functions as basis for moral determination and there may be revision of previously accepted norms. One important characteristic of this model is the discernment of right and wrong by the use of proportionate reason. McCormick is squarely located within this model. To him, proportionate reason is only a tool for discerning what is promotive of the good of the human person. Therefore, it is not the central element of his moral theory. The center of that theory is the belief that moral norms ought to be derived from a theory of the human person. I buttressed this point in the chapter on casuistry.

It has been asked if the catalogue of the anthropological constants is intended as "a descriptive phenomenology, or an ontology or a hierarchical list of values."[9] For McCormick, it is a bit of all of these. They describe phenomenologically the various dimensions of being human. These dimensions together provide a transcendent grounding for human being and value. However, as individual values they are not, as in Grisez's theory, all at par with each other all the time. In other words, there is a hierarchy in the order of values. McCormick's casuistry is, in a way, a constant search for the order in this value system. This search is conducted, not in spite of, but in accord with human experience.

INFLUENCES

As Bernard Lonergan said, theology "is a product not only of the religion it investigates and expounds but also of the cultural ideals and norms that set its problems and direct its solution."[10] The cultural ideals, norms, and problems in question originate within what David Tracy has described as the three 'publics' of theology— the wider society, the academy, and the Church.[11] To understand any theologian one has therefore to investigate the level of interaction between the various publics and the theologian in question. There are two sides to such investigation. One is the search for the extent and manner the theologian has explicated or furthered discussion on the problems of the tradition. The other is to show what influences have been brought to bear from the various publics by different events, persons, or groups of persons and ideas on the theologian's work.

McCormick has written about the events, persons, and ideas that have considerably affected moral theology during the past forty years. He lists these as the Second Vatican Council, Karl Rahner and fundamental freedom, the discussion on moral norms and the revision of method, the birth control debate and the publication of *Humanae Vitae*, the emergence of feminism, the maturation of bioethics, liberation theology, the person as criterion of moral rightness and wrongness, the Curran affair, and "the attempt to 'tighten up' things in the Church, especially by authoritative interventions into theological work considered suspect or dangerous."[12] Some of these factors have particularly influenced McCormick's work. I have noted the various ways the birth-control debate and the publication of the encyclical on that subject influenced his thinking. I have as well pointed out individual authors whose influence have been crucial to his theological development. To conclude, I want to present McCormick's own views on the influence of three theologians on his work.

THEOLOGIANS

McCormick acknowledges the influence of three theologians on his theological development. The most important is Bruno Schüller.

> I watched and reported Schüller's development over the years, in the "Moral Notes." I found him challenging some basic concepts in fundamental moral theology, in a way which I find intellectually satisfying. Analytically satisfying. Schüller is a very careful and precise thinker. He enlightened me a great deal on the meaning of norms, on fundamental freedom, the magisterium, and things like that. He was saying things that made a lot of sense. And he had good grounds for saying them. He also said them carefully and analytically. I think he is the most careful analytic theologian in the Catholic realm in Europe. I found him very helpful.[13]

The second theologian is Josef Fuchs. McCormick believes that Fuchs influenced him as his professor mostly by openness to new ideas and by communicating to his students in those days that "things were not as neat and tidy as certain Catholic theologians would lead you to believe and that it was perfectly legitimate to question them, and in fact, it was healthy to do so."[14]

The third theologian whose influence McCormick readily acknowledges is Germain Grisez.

> I learned personally from Germain Grisez, whom I think, has many good things to say. I like his views on the development of moral obligation–his understanding and interpretation of St. Thomas, the basic inclinations toward certain basic goods. I found that as satisfying as anything else I have ever encountered. However, I do not think his applications of his moral theory are persuasive. "You never turn against a basic good." What does that mean? I think that doesn't make sense. All the same, I find his basic understanding of moral obligation very helpful and enlightening. I have learned a lot from him as a philosopher. He has a more sustainable understanding of St. Thomas than you would find in Thomas himself.[15]

McCormick also notes that Paul Ramsey and James Gustafson have been good friends and dialogue partners. However, he does not seem to believe that their work left any important marks on his.[16]

EVENTS

The Second Vatican Council and the birth-control debate, including the publication of *Humanae Vitae*, were the two events which had the greatest effect on his theology. I found three areas where this influence has been decisive. The first of these is his ecclesiology. McCormick has repeatedly acknowledged the dramatic effect of the Council on his vision of the Church. The various metaphors employed by the Council to explain the nature of the Church have affected his theology.[17] Of special importance has been the Council's understanding of the Church as people of God. He believes that this implies that the hierarchy alone does not constitute the Church. He further believes that "this has immediate implications for the elaboration and development of moral doctrine, for consultative processes and for the free flow of ideas."[18] The influence of the notion of Church as People of God is evident in McCormick's position on the nature of the teaching function in the Church and the question of the use and limit of authority in the moral sphere within the ecclesial community.

A second important influence of Vatican II on McCormick's theology is evident in his belief in the centrality of the person in moral thought. He points out the difference this has made in moral methodology:

> In an earlier period, significance was often drawn from an analysis of faculties and finalities. Thus the faculty of speech was given to us for the purpose of communicating true information. To use it in a way contradictory of this purpose (*locutio contra mentem*) was morally wrong. If, however, we view speech in broader perspective and see it not simply as an informative power, but as an endowment meant to promote the overall good of persons in community, we have altered the basis for our definition of a lie. This emphasis was explicitly introduced by Vatican II. *Gaudium et Spes* asserted that "the moral aspect of any procedure . . . must be determined by objective standards which are based on the nature of the person and person's acts."[19]

Like many other contemporary theologians, the root of much of his attempt to base the derivation of moral norms on the basis of the entire human reality lies in what he believes to be a conciliar directive.

A third major impact of the Council on McCormick's work is shown in the acceptance of tentativeness in moral judgments. McCormick believes he is justified in his attitude by Pope John XXIII's statement (also incorporated into Vatican II documents) that "the deposit of faith or revealed truths are one thing; the manner in which they are formulated without violence to their meaning is another."[20] McCormick believes that this statement calls for a careful distinction between formulation and substance as well as between the areas of "concrete moral statements that do not pertain to the deposit of faith"[21] and those statements which are not contingent and pertain to the deposit of faith. He interprets the conciliar statement to mean that truth is not something 'out there', "existing apart from its possession by anyone, apart from history."[22]

His belief in the tentativeness of moral judgments is founded therefore on historical consciousness.

> To me "historical consciousness" means taking our culture seriously as the soil for the "signs of the time," as framer of our self-awareness.

That means a fresh look at how Christian perspectives ought to be read in the modern world so that our practices are the best possible mediation of gospel values in the contemporary world. Fresh looks often lead to new emphases and a modification of more ancient formulations–formulations appropriate to one point in history but not necessarily to all.[23]

McCormick also believes that the Council encourages not only tentativeness in moral judgments but also leaves room for dissent, when necessary.

We have Vatican II underlining the rapidly changing times, the novelty of the problems cast up by these changes, the many competencies needed to face them adequately, the independence of the sciences and the openness required to face our problems, the freedom of inquiry and expression necessary, the incompleteness of the Church's competence, deficiencies in past effort to grapple with problems, the fact and need of development, the legitimacy of differences of opinion among believers, the fact of variation in Church discipline. If such considerations do not explain, and even foster and validate the notion of dissent in the Church, then I would like to know why not.[24]

The second major influence on McCormick's theological development and agenda is *Humanae Vitae*. I have already treated the influence of the encyclical on aspects of McCormick's theology. In McCormick's own words this influence is summarized as follows:

It was at this time [after the publication of the encyclical] that I realized more clearly than ever the dependence of the magisterium on theological work, and therefore the absolutely essential *critical* role of theology. This opened many other doors. For instance, it became clear to me that the proper response to authoritative teaching is not precisely obedience (we obey orders, not teachers), but a docile personal attempt to assimilate the teaching. If that attempt fails–as it has for so many–then the personal reflections of those who have so failed must be seen as a source of new reflections on the matter.[25]

It is clear that the impact of this document on McCormick was immediate and severe. He has often told how he ended up in the hospital as a result of the agony he went through in responding to the encyclical.[26] Yet the encyclical seems to have accelerated his passage on the path on which he had embarked as a result of the Council. This seems especially true in ecclesiology. In any case, the influence of Vatican II and the publication of the encyclical on birth control on the theology of Richard McCormick cannot be over-stated.

No theologian works in isolation from the faith-community or from other theologians. The theologian, like anyone else, speaks out of many memories, to paraphrase Paul Ricoeur. This is not different in the case of Richard McCormick. Consequently, no theologian can exclusively own 'discoveries'. Nonetheless, some stand out in the theological and ecclesial community for the quality of their insight and the value of their contribution to theological discourse; Richard A. McCormick is one of these, as his achievements witness.

THE ACHIEVEMENT OF RICHARD MCCORMICK

An assessment of Richard McCormick's achievement must be done primarily against the tradition and theology of the manuals for two reasons: He received his education in that tradition, and more important, the conciliar directive for renewal of moral theology was issued in view of its perceived defects.

I have already given an outline of the theology of the manuals.[27] One of the prominent characteristics of the manuals was their tendency to legalism, which was in turn brought to bear on everything, including their interpretation of natural law and the Church's teaching. Employing a deductive approach, they were so obsessed with searching for "immutable essences" that they often lost sight of the human subject as both the subject and the object of moral deliberation. As McCormick states, the manuals were "one-sidedly confession oriented, magisterium dominated, canon law-related, sin-centered, and seminary-controlled."[28]

In view of the defects of the neo-scholastic manuals of moral theology, what are the achievements of Richard McCormick? On the basis of our analysis of his work his achievements can be listed as follows.

RETRIEVING THE CRITICAL COMPONENT OF MORAL THEOLOGY

McCormick's characterization of pre–Vatican II moral theology as magisterium-dominated explains his effort to uphold the critical function of theology in the Church.

> The task of theologians is not to repeat formulations of the magisterium. It is rather to question, probe, hypothesize, analyze, in a effort to aid the magisterium in keeping its formulations not only consistent with substantial traditional values but also accurate and persuasive in a constantly changing world.[29]

Theology, for him, seems to be a third-order proposition, which starts when the faith begins to reflect on itself. Its place is behind faith and doctrine. Its role is to keep doctrine faithful to faith, as it were. This essentially critical role of theology stems from the very nature of the Church itself, which as a limited community on pilgrimage in the world needs to constantly re-appraise its understanding of its faith and revise its doctrinal and moral formulations in the light of insights gained from such reflections.

Moral and doctrinal teachings in the Church, being the products of limited human minds, insights, concepts, and language, are conditioned by their history and affected, like every other thing, by the presuppositions, concerns, and vocabulary of the times. This is McCormick's reason for insisting that we must constantly remember that there is a distinction between the substance and formulation of teaching in the Church, or as the Council said, echoing Pope John XXIII, "The deposit of faith or revealed truths are one thing; the manner in which they are formulated without violence to their meaning and significance is another."[30]

McCormick considers it the task of theology to be in constant search for new ways to articulate the deposit of faith. Theology as a critical discipline takes a distance from past formulations and tries to propose new and more adequate ones; that is, ones that are adequate to the insights and circumstances of the time. "This distancing and reformulation can be called critical evaluation or dissent." Without it there can be no doctrinal development. Without it the community stagnates and becomes "ripe for picking by any ideologies–fascists, communists, left-wingers, right-wingers, nationalists and, let it be said softly, curialists."[31] To prevent such stagnation and appropriation by one ideology or another, theology must resist every attempt to be 'privatized'. It must remain open because the faith itself is public by nature.

In reaction to a perceived attempt in the document of the Congregation for the Doctrine of the Faith on the vocation of the theologian to muzzle theological research and to privatize theology,[32] he stated that the public nature of theology arises also from the fact that it is at the service of the entire faith community, not just of the magisterium, and indeed of the whole humanity.

> The proposal, even by implication, that the theologian is only a behind-the-scenes adviser to the hierarchy (the pope, the other bishops and the curia) by serving always and under their mandate and at their pleasure, is to suggest that the other members of the Church (the vast majority) have no direct personal or communal interest in the process by which their own faith is examined and explained, nor in the practical outcomes of those deliberations. Such a proposal, even if only implicit, suggests that those outside the hierarchy have no capacity–intellectual, moral or spiritual–to grasp the theological process or its outcome.[33]

The debate over dissent will certainly continue, for good reasons. However, through the efforts of McCormick and other theologians in recent times, theology is reclaiming its place in the academy as a partner in the dialogue for the human good. Moral theology has set its sight beyond the confessional. It is making more effort to listen not only to the magisterium but also to other voices inside and outside the Church. It is also trying to interact not only with canon law but with other theological disciplines as well as other areas of culture and science. McCormick has been an important voice in this transformation. The perennial problem is how to move beyond criticism to construction and how to ensure that critics recognizes themselves for what they are–critics. The temptation sometimes is for the critic to pretend he or she is the sole possessor of truth. This could lead to arrogance or to some form of theological trade unionism, as we have seen in the last couple of years. For this reason, it did not damage McCormick's credibility that he did not sign the Washington declaration or any other forms of organized dissent.

The remarks above pertain to McCormick's theological efforts within one of Tracy's three publics–the ecclesia. Within this context it seems to me that McCormick's understanding of the role of theology as a critical function limits theology to "putting out fires," ecclesial fire, that is. He has not articulated a constructive role for theology, beyond the dispute over doctrinal formulations and magisterial competence over moral norms. Moreover, his efforts to appraise the Church's language and actions for their success or failure in adhering to the founding vision of Christianity in the gospel and in tradition is slanted. He needs to articulate, in a non-polemical way, an understanding of the behavioral implications of faith in Jesus Christ, within the Church itself. He seems to me to have been much more successful in doing this vis-à-vis the other public of theology–the wider society.

ENTERING INTO CRITICAL DIALOGUE WITH CULTURE

In McCormick's work one easily discerns an effort to establish continuous dialogue between the faith and its host culture and at the same time to construct a theology which is truly Christian and truly American. Lisa Cahill expresses the same view in the following words:

> [McCormick] sees moral theology as a crucial mediator between Church and culture, bringing to the Church a renewed foundation of human life and community, and to the culture a heightened sense of the dignity and worth of all persons, and the right of all to participate in the common good.[34]

McCormick himself characterizes his work in similar words:

> Since the Council, I have been conscious of the need to be in contact with those elements in the culture which are significant sources of information and formation within society. I mean, with the professions, the scientific community, and so on.[35]

McCormick's work is informed by the conviction that even though Christian faith is not an arcane source of moral judgments, it has a good deal to contribute to the formation of human attitudes and dispositions. His constant invitation to the culture to rise beyond the functional view of the person[36] and to maintain a realistic attitude to life and death is based on the Christian conviction that life is a basic but nonabsolute value. He has also indicated other ways the faith can challenge the culture to respectful treatment of persons. For example, his rejection of donor insemination is a summons to both the scientific and popular culture to respect the unitive aspect of marriage, which, in his view, does not allow for third-party involvement. He has also challenged the scientific and medical communities to accord special respect to nascent life. Although he would not take an extreme pro-life stand, which bans all abortions, he has also insisted that a simple pro-choice stance is incompatible with the Christian faith. In short, the faith of the Church must continue to act as check on and challenge to the human tendency "to make choices in light of cultural enthusiasms which sink into and take possession of our unwitting, pre-ethical selves."[37]

Martin Marty describes McCormick's work in the area of theology and society as "opening up the Catholic treasury, trying out its artifacts and achievements in the contemporary world, risking its values in a world that might need them more than it knows."[38] Such effort presupposes a thorough knowledge of the tradition as well as a belief in its basic soundness. As Walter J. Burghardt points out, McCormick's knowledge of the Catholic moral tradition is phenomenal.

> Richard McCormick knows the Catholic moral *tradition* – and much of our broader theological tradition – from scripture through medieval scholasticism to the twentieth century. From long experience and contemplation it is resident in his bones and blood. I trust he will be a living reproach to a generation of scholars who know Augustine only as a born-again Catholic who foist on the western world a hellish doctrine of original sin and a pessimistic view of marriage; who cannot spell Chalcedon, even though a quarter century ago Harvey Cox argued that apart from Chalcedon technopolis is unintelligible; who can anathematize Aquinas and scuttle scholasticism without

ever having read a word thereof; who sneer at the mere mention of "medieval," as if the middle ages were darker than our own; who could not care less about a papal pronouncement, much less peruse it.[39]

What McCormick himself said in the preface to one of his books stands as a testimony to his belief in the soundness of the Catholic moral tradition: "I write as a Catholic moral theologian, proud of the richness of the tradition in which I have been privileged to share."[40] As we have seen, this does not mean he accepts everything that has been handed down as part of the deposit of this tradition. This is why he has committed himself to correcting or modifying the tradition where necessary and to sharing with other persons the fruits of his efforts.

McCormick believes also that the challenges between the Christian faith and the wider human culture are mutual. The Church can also learn a lot from contemporary culture; for example, about "democratic" or "due process."

> When I say "the Church" I am talking about the administrative central body of the Church. I think they are basically unaware of the need for democratic processes within the Church as part of human dignity. What due process is in the Roman mind, in the Roman mentality, is what Rome thinks is due. That's totally unacceptable. This concept of due process is medieval compared to what exists in the ordinary processes in the United States. We can make a contribution there.[41]

Beside the mutual challenges there are also areas of mutual cooperation such as genetics. McCormick insists that because knowledge in this area is at its infancy, the Church can speak to the issues better if it does not isolate itself but enters into a collaborative learning process with the rest of humanity. The very future of humanity is at stake in these issues and ecclesial isolation from discussions about them would "dim the 'new light' and almost assuredly compromise 'solutions which are fully human.'"[42]

McCormick has also been exemplary in setting up dialogue between the faith and human culture by his memberships in numerous scientific and medical societies. His extensive literature on issues in bioethics and social ethics speaks even more eloquently of his commitment to dialogue between theology and society. McCormick's attitude to the wider culture lifts moral theology out of the ghetto in which it found itself as a result of the moral rationalism of the manuals. John Langan has adequately described the features of this moral rationalism.[43] As I showed in the first chapter, the isolation of moral theology from participation in public discourse was part of the fruits of *Aterni Patris* and *Pascendi* combined. In America, the situation was compounded by *Testem Benevolentiae*. McCormick's work is remarkable as among the first and sustained efforts within the American moral theological community to address the concerns of the culture and to initiate dialogue with it.

ACCELERATION OF THEOLOGICAL DIALOGUE

As author of the "Notes" McCormick mediated developments in moral theology after the Council to people in various parts of the world to a point where "the discipline of moral theology could no longer be provincial."[44] Charles E. Curran describes McCormick's contribution in the following way:

> As author of the "Notes" from 1965 to 1984 McCormick chronicled, discerned trends, and gave some direction to the tremendous changes that were taking place in Catholic moral theology. By carefully selecting, summarizing, and responding to the most important aspects of the current literature, he helped set the agenda for Catholic moral theology in one of the most tumultuous periods of its development. At times authors of outstanding books can make very original and pace-setting contributions to a particular field, but such works, by definition, cannot touch the *whole* field. Richard McCormick, through this genre, helped to shape and direct the entire field of moral theology.[45]

A perusal of the "Notes" will reveal the process of selection that Curran describes here. This process is heavily tilted in favor of issues related to authority, sexuality, norms, the nature of moral theology, and bioethics, all of which are traditional issues for moral theology. Thus it is not unusual in the "Notes" to come across the author's regrets that he has had to bypass a great deal of current literature on moral issues. A closer look at some of the literature reveals that much of the material left undigested pertains to issues outside of the traditional interests.[46]

While the choice of material is certainly dictated by volume and topicality, it also reflects the limitations of McCormick's world-view. The interest in fundamental moral theology and in bioethics reflected in his doctoral dissertation is further strengthened by the developments after the Council and especially after *Humanae Vitae*. This same interest is carried over to the authorship of the "Notes." The results are a thorough, objective, and fair assessment of the work of other authors on the traditional issues and a scant attention to or total silence on other equally important issues. Thus, as one critic puts it, the reader of the "Notes" might get the impression that "the ethical quandaries in the relations between male and female are principally those that arise in choices about sexual conduct."[47]

It is not correct to blame McCormick for the direction which moral theology took after the Council. The point is that whether for good or for bad (mostly for the former) he made a valuable contribution by judiciously using the pages of the prestigious and widely read *Theological Studies* as forum for advancing dialogue, calling attention to issues, molding theological opinion, and advancing new insights. His attention to theologians from all other Christian Churches not only brought these writers to the attention of the Catholic audience but also furthered the cause of ecumenical dialogue.

THE REDISCOVERY OF CASUISTRY

Another important achievement of Richard McCormick is his contribution to the revival of casuistry. Albert Jonsen and Stephen Toulmin mention Paul Ramsey's works and those of James Childress and Michael Walzer as examples of a contemporary revival for casuistry.[48] That list is incomplete without Richard McCormick. The desire to share the riches of the Catholic moral tradition with a larger audience, "to re-examine some traditional formulations that were authoritatively proposed to the Catholic community," and to contribute constructively to current debates on matters of concern to contemporary society have motivated his casuistry.[49] This casuistry is a search for what constitutes the good of the human person integrally and adequately considered. McCormick has conducted this search in most cases using proportionate reasoning as tool. Therefore it is not totally correct to say that a major characteristic of his work is to find ways "to avoid sinful acts" while taking into account human values which are worthy of realization.[50] The notion of sin, as far as McCormick is concerned, is a moral goodness question. His interest is mainly with the category of moral wrongness and rightness.

This concern gives his casuistry a different slant from that of the manuals and also from Protestant understanding of the purpose of casuistry. For the latter, casuistry is necessitated by the tension which arises from the 'high' demands of God and "man's low performance." Edward Long argues that in casuistry, "conscience is forced to compromise in order to act by choosing actions that are less than perfect expressions of the standard to which it gives full devotion."[51]

McCormick believes that conscience is a discerning guide, which has the ability to limit what is right or wrong in any given situation. Conscience is limited in its vision and scope because it is a human faculty. For this reason every decision it makes is a sacrifice. This sacrifice is not a compromise for "the less than perfect expression of the standard to which it gives full devotion." Rather, it amounts to an acceptance of reality as it is. Compromise is therefore not chosen but discovered, not created but accepted as the limits of one's possibilities in the situation.

McCormick is of course aware of sin. He believes, however, that sin is not the only cause of ambiguity in human choice. Ambiguity is primarily a result of the human condition, a result of human creaturehood and finitude. To argue otherwise would be to imply that sin is the cause of human finitude and creaturehood and to suggest that but for sin, all constraints to human knowing and doing would be nonexistent. McCormick does not subscribe to such a view. Because he acknowledges ambiguity he also acknowledges conflicts in moral decision-making. The awareness of conflict arising from limited possibilities enables him to search not for compromises but for moral truth. This moral truth is not bipolar, consisting of an objective order described by rules and a subjective world of one's conscience, as the manuals taught. In other words, there is only one moral order and truth is not something 'out there' but something to be discovered in one's consciousness.

McCormick's casuistry also involves the reinterpretation, extension, and revision of important theological principles. That has been amply demonstrated in the exposé of his doctoral dissertation, in the entire discussion on proportionate reasoning, in his use of the concept of ordinary and extraordinary means, and so on. One thread which runs through all these revisions is a deep reverence for the tradition as well as the belief in its capacity for expansion and growth. Some would argue that the end result of this process of revision can no longer be considered Catholic, because it takes the principles or themes far beyond what is acceptable.[52] However, McCormick has continued to present a vision of the Catholic moral tradition that he considers to be an authentic one.

Beside the fact that such debates for the proper understanding of what constitutes the good of the tradition are indicative of a living tradition, they also raise questions about the primary analogue itself. In this regard, it seems to me that the debate over proportionate reasoning represents more than a misreading of Aquinas's moral theory by participants in the discussion, as has been suggested.[53] This particular debate is conducted in the understanding that the structure of moral obligation as traditionally understood, even in Aquinas, is flawed. As McCormick puts it, the tradition has "enjoyed its share of distorted perspectives."[54] It is this view of the weakness in the tradition which sustains the drive for renewal. Only those, like McCormick, who are closely attuned to the tradition may understand where revision and reinterpretation is called for–proportionate reasoning, natural law, the concept of ordinary and extraordinary means–or where the tradition simply has to change course entirely–the deductive method of the past, sexism, anthropomorphism, and so forth.[55]

Closeness to the tradition ensures that one's theological agenda is dictated by developments within it. The advantages of this are obvious. For example, it establishes the person in the tradition and keeps him or her aware of the concerns of the community. However, it can also blind one to some obvious deficiencies of the tradition. Therefore, like the tradition, McCormick has been hardly interested in the discussion on the formation of the character of the agent or in what has come to be known as 'virtue ethics.' Like the tradition he has shown little awareness of the variations in cultures which characterize the Church. Although he has spoken on the issue of women in the Church,[56] the question of homosexuality,[57] and a host of social issues, he has hardly shown awareness of the issue of racism and oppression of minorities even in the United States. This is even more remarkable considering that he authored the "Notes" in the era of the Civil Rights Movement in the United States. The point is that he is tied too closely to the tradition and is too engrossed in reacting to its concerns to be a trend setter. Since the Catholic moral tradition has been interested almost exclusively in the problems of white Europe and America, McCormick could also not be expected to show any awareness of the moral issues of people beyond these groups.

Recently, McCormick has called for a universalist moral theology.

> I dream of a presentation of the moral life that will be appealing and make sense to Christians of many cultures. The Church is, as Karl Rahner noted, a world Church. I will refer to this characteristic of Christian morality as its "universalizing feature." I mean to underline the idea that Christian morality, while being theological to the core, must not be isolationist or sectarian.[58]

This search for a universal viewpoint for moral theology stems from the belief that there is a core at which point human divisions into cultural, racial, or personal groupings disappear. It is thus the work of moral theology to speak to this core or to draw from it in order to appeal to the human. The benefits of the recognition of a common core of humanity (humanness) has important implications for human rights and racial respect. I am not sure, though, that it can adequately respect the line between universality and particularity. For those of us who are still counting the cost of colonialism, this demarcation is an important issue. Therefore, the issue of maintaining "the universalizing feature" of moral theology and respecting behavioral patterns which are sanctioned by authentic cultural variations must continue to be debated.

A RENEWED MORAL THEOLOGY?

Are these achievements reliable indications of a renewed moral theology, or are they merely cosmetic and without any real significance to the life of the discipline? Several authors suggest, for different reasons, that moral theology is dead. Enda McDonagh attributes this 'death' to moral theology's "obsession" with "a limited" range of issues.

> It is not frivolous to suggest an end to moral theology and moral theologizing, even in the renewed forms in which it has been practiced from the 1950s through the 1970s. There are of course too few moral theologians, too few perhaps to keep it alive. And the interests of that few are still limited to formal questions of Christian autonomy and heteronomy, of specificity, of consequentialism and its alternatives, or to substantive questions which range little beyond sexuality, bioethics and a little touch of war. With such limited obsessions the verdict might well be suicide; moral theology dying at the hands of its own practitioners.[59]

There are a few important assumptions in this passage. One of them is that moral theology cannot be renewed. The discipline might not survive on its own because its concerns with questions of method, sexuality, bioethics, and war are too limited to cover the range of human issues which should be the concern of theology. McDonagh suggests, instead, an integrated theology which would take the demands of Christian discipleship seriously.

> The end of moral theology, provided it is accompanied by the end of the self-enclosed dogmatic theology, could prepare the way for rebirth of an integrated theology that will still permit and demand various emphases, even specializations. In the other sense of end as purpose, the end of moral theology and of the moral theologian must be to provoke and promote such conscientization among theologians in general and provide some guidance to how a new integrated theology of Christian truth and life might emerge.[60]

McDonagh also seems to assume that there has been little real renewal in moral theology because it is still concerned with issues in bioethics, sexuality, war, and peace. Notwithstanding McDonagh's argument, in my opinion moral theology has indeed been renewed and Richard McCormick has contributed immensely to its renewal— albeit from a North American perspective.

I believe McCormick has amply demonstrated the possibility of renewing moral theology by showing that discussions on questions related to "private morality" are as important and sometimes even more so than those concerned with so-called social ethics. In other words, how we treat the zygote is as relevant a moral issue as the way we treat the migrant worker; the ethical implications of contraception are not diminished by racism or sexism; and the growing possibility of a nuclear holocaust does not render discussion on ecclesiastical teaching authority irrelevant.

I also believe, as McCormick's involvement in issues pertaining to private morality shows, that these are foundational issues which have personal and public policy (therefore social) implications. Abortion, as he says, touches us all in various ways. Genetic engineering touches our future as a species. So do war and peace. Contraception is more than an issue of private sexual practice; it involves the question of the individual and society as partners in moral deliberation. Furthermore, although McCormick has certainly given much more attention to issues of private morality, he has not totally ignored other issues. A reviewer of the "Notes" makes the point this way:

> It should be insisted upon again that the "Notes" have not been totally fixated on private morality and Catholic ecclesiastical concerns. From M.'s first piece in 1965 there is concern with public morality. He ably draws solid evangelical messages from "liberation theology" and argues that "the Church does indeed have a proper mission in the social, political, and economic areas." From the beginning, too, M. has been in broad ecumenical dialogue. The "Notes" in his hands have never indulged in a sectarian Catholicism, though they have given special care to Catholic problems.[61]

McCormick could have done much more. He could have shown more interest than he did in the arms race and the nuclear build-up. He could, perhaps, have spoken more forcefully on the issues of race and gender relations, ecology, third-world debt, underdevelopment, advocacy advertising,and so on.[62] Nonetheless, no one scholar can creditably attend to every issue. McCormick himself believes that spreading oneself thin in this way is not only impossible but also injurious to the cause of theology.

Our theology will not influence medicine unless our theologians are medically knowledgeable and sophisticated. Much the same is true of law, business and economics and other areas of human life. What this means seems obvious to me: a severe limitation on what any one theologian undertakes to do or be. Daniel Callahan is what he is today in the world of bioethics because he limited himself and became creditably capable of challenging people on their own turf and therefore of enlivening a whole discipline. The same is true of the Rev. Bryan Hehir in foreign and strategic affairs.[63]

The next question is this: In what ways has McCormick contributed to the renewal of moral theology? This question has to be answered briefly under two headings: methodological and theological.

METHODOLOGY

McCormick's contribution to the fine points of the methodological discussions in moral theology are themselves major accomplishments. More than the details of these discussions his insistence, since his student days, on the importance of a continual methodological discussion in moral theology is itself a remarkable contribution to the renewal in moral theology, especially when it is placed against the manualist tradition in which he was trained. Despite the attention which they devoted to casuistry, the manuals hardly engaged in discussions on how moral judgments are made. On the contrary, McCormick's dissertation was centered on the conviction that it was important to inquire about the way to come to a right decision concerning the removal of the probably dead fetus. It was a search for the principles to use to judge the morality of the act. From that point the thesis was a remarkable achievement, more so than the resolution of the case on the basis of proportionate reason, contrary to established views.

Later, in the conclusion to his review of Joseph Fletcher's book on situation ethics, McCormick again underscored the point about the primacy of method. After arguing that Fletcher had not made up his mind on how moral judgments are made, he added that "as long as this remains unclear, he can squeeze out of any epistemological corner, because he has none he calls his own. And as long as he has none he calls his own, one can only say that he has adopted a method (and its content-conclusion) without first solving the problem of methodology."[64]

In the first installment of the "Notes" McCormick stressed the necessity of "open inquiry" as the basis of methodological discussions in ethics.[65] Beside being 'open', such discussion must also be person-centered. McCormick writes:

> St Thomas once wrote that "we do not wrong God unless we wrong our own good." His "our own good' is identical with the "person adequately considered." This matter is of major methodological importance, because there are still many theologians who acknowledge this theory but whose analyses and conclusions reveal different perspectives at work.[66]

A person-centered approach to the discussion of moral methodology must take into account the evidence of the sciences about the human person. In this regard McCormick believes "we have not successfully grappled with the task of integrating scientific studies into our moral assessment" of human conduct.[67] Finally, discussion of method in conflict situation must grapple with how to determine what in that particular situation is the lesser of the evils as well as how to come about that determination.

It is obvious, therefore, that by keeping alive the discussion on method, putting together some elements of a methodological construction, and bringing the human person into focus as the subject of moral decisions and as agent, McCormick has helped move moral theology far beyond its original location. Although Daniel Maguire was right to suggest that moral theology would benefit tremendously from "a full statement" of method from McCormick,[68] it must be pointed out that the sketch for such a statement is already present in McCormick's work. It would include the appreciation that the human person adequately considered is the center of moral choices and decisions. It would consider the diverse sources of moral norms and the need to understand the function and meaning of norms. Other elements of such a statement on method, in McCormick's view, would include the need to understand the proper relation between public policy and morality as well as the relation of faith to morality. Such a statement would take into account the influence of culture and the sciences in creating cultural awareness.[69]

Another important contribution of McCormick to the renewal of moral theology is in the conception of the role of moral theology itself. Whereas the moral theology of the manuals considered it necessary for moral theology to provide answers even to complex moral problems, McCormick considers the role of faith and theology to be that of value-raising.

> The Christian tradition only illumines human values, supports them, provides a context for their reading at given points in history. It aids us in staying human by underlining the truly human against all cultural attempts to distort the human.[70]

Although this does not excuse us from turning to the tradition for help in finding solutions, it forces us to value rigorous analyses of moral problems. This reasoning is informed by faith which acts as "a continuing check on and challenge to our tendency to make choices in the light of cultural enthusiasms which sink into and take possession of our unwitting, pre-ethical selves."[71] Therefore, the search for the influence of the faith on morality has, as William C. Spohn puts it, shifted "from the foreground of moral norms to the background of motivations, commitments and dispositions that shape the moral agent."[72]

This is a major shift. It is definitely a move away from a moral theology which was not only confident of its methods and conclusions[73] but also harbored the evangelical aspiration to 'impregnate' modern human sciences with "solidly certain principles of moral theology, derived from reason and revelation."[74] This move from certitude to tentativeness or, as McCormick has put it, from the understanding of moral theology as theology from an answer-giver to a value-raiser is perhaps the most profound change in all of moral theology since the Council. No matter how one explains it, it has sentenced the discipline to an endless quest for method and for content.

Furthermore, the discussion of the role of faith in ethics is an indication of a renewed moral theology. It moves the discipline away from an excessive influence of moral philosophy into closer contact with scripture and dogmatic theology, as the Council had directed. The use he makes of the work of systematic theologians like Yves Congar, Richard McBrien, and Francis Sullivan, to mention a few, has helped rescue moral theology from its former splendid isolation from other branches of theology.

In conclusion, McCormick's influence on moral theology has been tremendous. It has even been suggested that his work, as well as that of some other theologians, has carried moral theology beyond its original intent and scope and consequently led to its abolition.

> "Moral Theology" is, I believe, no longer a helpful term with which to categorize the work of Curran, Schüller, McCormick, Fuchs, Häring or other revisionist theologians. Their theological positions and moral theories are simply too distinct from the prime analogue. It creates more confusion than precision to attempt to join such plurality of positions under a common name. Further, the work of these theologians should no longer be understood as a revision of the past, be that past neo-Thomism, neo-scholasticism, or the writings of Aquinas himself, but rather as new expressions of a living tradition.[75]

There is no doubt, as this work has shown, that McCormick has created new paradigms. Nonetheless, these paradigms must continue to be seen as "new expressions of a living tradition." As such, they are not really distinct from the prime analogue, as Gallagher suggests. If they were, they would not be "new expressions of a living tradition." They would be a new tradition altogether. What McCormick and other revisionist theologians have tried to do is to bring moral theology up to date. Such an exercise involves correction, reinterpretation of old paradigms and the establishment of some new ones, and the expansion of the concerns and scope of the discipline. What emerges might be very distinct from the prime analogue, but it is not understandable without it, just as Einstein's physics, though it employs a very distinct paradigm, is incomprehensible without Newtonian physics.

I think McCormick is correct in his conviction about the basic soundness of the Catholic moral tradition. He is also right that the tradition needed correction and modification.[76] One might disagree with some points in his theology. However, no one can doubt the overall significance of his contribution to the renewal of moral theology in the post-Vatican II Church.

ABBREVIATIONS

The following list contains some of the sources frequently cited in this work.

A. *Works by Richard A. McCormick*

NMT1   *Notes on Moral Theology: 1965 through 1980.* Lanham, Md.: University Press of America, 1980.

NMT2   *Notes on Moral Theology: 1981 through 1984.* Lanham, Md.: University Press of America, 1984.

HMCT   *Health and Medicine in the Catholic Tradition.* New York: Crossroad, 1984.

HBNW   *How Brave a New World?: Dilemmas in Bioethics.* Garden City, N.Y.: Doubleday, 1981.

TCC   *The Critical Calling: Moral Dilemmas since Vatican II.* Washington, D.C.: Georgetown University Press, 1989.

HSCS   "Human Significance and Christian Significance." In *Norm and Context in Christian Ethics*, pp. 26–37. Edited by Gene Outka and Paul Ramsey. New York: Charles Scribner's Sons, 1968.

B. *McCormick with Others*

DEAG   *Doing Evil to Achieve Good: Moral Choice in Conflict Situations.* Edited with Paul Ramsey. Chicago: Loyola University Press, 1978.

RMT1   *Readings in Moral Theology No. 1: Moral Norms and Catholic Tradition.* Edited with Charles E. Curran. Mahwah, N.J.: Paulist Press, 1979.

RMT2   *Readings in Moral Theology No. 2: The Distinctiveness of Christian Ethics.* Edited with Charles E. Curran. Mahwah: Paulist Press, 1980.

TS   *Theological Studies*

NOTES

INTRODUCTION

1. "Nul ne parle de nulle part." See M. Ngindu, "Preface," in *Combats pour un christianisme africain: Melangés en l'honneur du Professeur V. Mulago*, edited by M. Ngindu et al. (Kinshasa: Faculté de Théologie Catholique, 1981), p. 15.

2. Alasdair MacIntyre, *Whose Justice? Which Rationality?* (Notre Dame, Ind.: University of Notre Dame Press, 1988), p. 350.

3. This assertion is true especially from point of view of emphasis. For, after all, gender inequality, the wider ecumenism, inculturation, and so on, are all 'universal' and 'perennial' issues, to a point.

4. Richard A. McCormick, S.J., "Moral Theology 1940–1989: An Overview," *Theological Studies* (hereafter *TS*) 50 (1989), p. 4.

5. See Alasdair MacIntyre, *Whose Justice? Which Rationality?* pp. 349–388, for a detailed discussion of an epistemological crisis.

6. Bernard J. F. Lonergan, *Method in Theology* (Minneapolis: Seabury Press, 1972), p. 130.

7. Alasdair MacIntyre, "Epistemological Crisis, Narrative, and Philosophy of Science," in *Why Narrative? Readings in Narrative Theology*, edited by Stanley Hauerwas and L. Gregory Jones (Grand Rapids, Mich.: Eerdmans, 1989), pp. 140–141.

8. John Langan, "Catholic Moral Rationalism and the Philosophical Bases of Moral Theology," *TS* 50 (1989), pp. 25–43.

9. For example, Cardinal Joseph Ratzinger points to the disagreement over several central moral teachings of the Church as an indication of the confusion that exists within the discipline. "Today the sphere of moral theology has become the main locus of the tension between magisterium and theologians, especially because here the consequences are most immediately perceptible. I should like to cite some trends: at times premarital relations, at least under certain conditions, are justified. Masterbation is presented as a normal phenemenon of adolescence. Admission of

remarried divorced couples to the sacraments is constantly demanded. Radical feminism—especially in women's religious orders—also seems to be gaining ground noticeably in the Church" (Joseph Cardinal Ratzinger with Vitterio Messori, *The Ratzinger Report: An Exclusive Interview on teh State of the Church* [San Francisco: Ignatius Press, 1985], p. 87). The cardinal also spoke of the gradual tolerance of homosexuals in various ways in some parts of the contemporary Church as well as the open and widespread rejection of the central message of *Humanae Vitae* against contraception. These trends, among others, Ratzinger says, represent a dominant mentality that "attacks the very foundations of the morality of the Church" (p. 86).

10. Richard A. McCormick, "Moral Theology since Vatican II: Clarity or Chaos?" *The Critical Calling: Moral Dilemmas since Vatican II* (hereafter *TCC*), p. 9.

11. Richard A. McCormick, "Dissent in the Church: Loyalty or Liability?" *TCC*, p. 23.

12. Alasdair MacIntyre, *Whose Justice? Which Rationality?* p. 222.

13. Richard A. McCormick, *TCC*, p. 23.

14. "Optatam Totius," in *The Documents of Vatican II*, edited by W. M. Abbott, S. J. (London: Geoffrey Chapman, 1966), pp. 451–452.

15. Josef Fuchs, "Moral Theology According to Vatican II," in *Human Values and Christian Morality* (Dublin: Gill & Macmillan, 1970), p. 1.

16. Richard A. McCormick, "Introduction," *How Brave a New World?* (hereafter *HBNW*), p. x.

17. Martin E. Marty, "Foreword" to Richard A. McCormick, *Health and Medicine in the Catholic Tradition* (hereafter *HMCT*), p. xi.

CHAPTER 1

1. Bernard F. Lonergan, "Theology in Its New Context," in *A Second Collection: Papers by Bernard J.F. Lonergan, S.J.*, edited by William F. J. Ryan and Bernard J. Tyrell (London: Darton, Longman and Todd, 1970), p. 58.

2. It is not my intention to write a history of moral theology prior to Vatican II or even of the entire movement for the renewal of moral theology around this time. Much work has been done in this area already. See, for example, Vincent MacNamara, *Faith And Ethics: Recent Roman Catholicism* (Dublin: Gill & Macmillan, Washington: Georgetown University Press, 1985). Also, John Mahoney, *The Making of Moral Theology: A Study of the Roman Catholic Tradition* (Oxford: Clarendon Press, 1987); John A.

Gallagher, *Time Past, Time Future: An Historical Study of Catholic Moral Theology* (New York, Paulist Press, 1990). I shall go into areas already covered by these authors only to the extent it is necessary for my effort to situate Richard McCormick in the tradition.

3. I refer to Father Howard Grey, S.J., who, until December 1990, was the Provincial Superior of the Detroit Province of the Society of Jesus, which is McCormick's home province. Grey knew McCormick as a senior at St. Ignatius High School. Says Grey, "The year 1947–48 was my first year as a student, and it was Dick's first year of the three-year regency period. He taught me Greek." Later, Grey became McCormick's student at West Baden, when McCormick returned from Rome after the completion of his doctoral studies.

4. Howard Grey and Walter Farrell speak of a deep esprit de corps among Jesuit moral theologians in the United States before and after Vatican II. (Farrell, a very good friend of Richard McCormick, was a professor of philosophy at West Baden in 1953, when McCormick was in his third year of theology and was ordained a priest. Farrell was rector of West Baden College from 1958 to 1965. McCormick was by this time a professor of moral theology at the college.) Says Grey, "They got together for drinks and for sharing of thoughts. They had a sense of being on the cutting edge. They really became a guild." McCormick was about the youngest member of this "guild." Farrell points out that the discussion in these circles "had a considerable impact on Dick as he went along." Grey describes what went on there as "a passing on of wisdom and approach" to the younger members of the group. This generated very deep bonds between McCormick and the older members of the group. Grey adds that "in Dick, there is a lot of pietas. This is why the break with John Connery and John Ford was very hard on him." These two men were his mentors. The break Grey mentions was caused by disagreements concerning the debate on proportionate reason.

5. Walter Farrell describes the community at the college as "an old monastic style community." There was a timetable for the entire day. The classes were large and teaching was done in Latin. The community usually ranged from 200 to 275 people, comprising about 100 theologians and 100 philosophers. The others were either faculty or ancillary staff.

6. See Richard A. McCormick, *Notes on Moral Theology: 1981 through 1984* (hereafter *NMT2*), p. 181.

7. Richard McCormick acknowledges the considerable influence Josef Fuchs has had on him. In an interview I had with him on April 22, 1992, at the University of Notre Dame, he recounted in some detail the origin and extent of this relationship. "I had Josef Fuchs as a professor at the Gregorian. He was perhaps the first experience I had of someone who

did not fit the model of the manuals. He was a very open man. I would go up to him after class and I would question him. I would say, 'I have this problem,' and he'd say, 'Its a very good question, let me think it over.' Later, we would get together and discuss the issue. Fuchs had a way of reinforcing one's own sense of confidence in one's intellectual ability. He made you much more willing to examine things analytically and to trust your senses, your intuitions. And it is very important, I think, at some point in one's development to get a sense that what one is thinking is not a screwball idea, that if one has a genuine difficulty seeing the point, maybe there is a difficulty in the point itself."

8. In the interview I had with him at the Jesuit residence, University of Detroit/Mercy in May 1991, Howard Grey had this to say about McCormick's pedagogical style: "Dick McCormick employed the case method. We had written cases. He would take a case and ask, 'What principles are at stake in this case? How do you approach this case? What resolution do you think you can bring to it?' He taught us methodology. He was a vivacious pedagogue; he was very lively."

9. Richard A. McCormick, *TCC*, p. x.

10. John A. Gallagher, *Time Past, Time Future*, p. 185.

11. Ibid., p. 186.

12. Jay P. Dolan, *The American Catholic Experience: A History from Colonial Times to the Present* (Garden City, N.Y.: Image Books, 1986), p. 108. The man behind this movement was John Carroll, who became the first American Catholic bishop in 1789. Carroll's dream and conviction was that "Catholicism in the United States was to be both American and independent." He insisted that the only relation which the American Church should have with Rome was a purely spiritual one which acknowledged the pope's "spiritual supremacy" and the importance of the see of St. Peter as "the center of ecclesiastical unity." This kind of ecclesiastical liberty was demanded by the temperament of the American people and the spirit of the times, and by national pride, he argued. It must be recalled that America had only recently secured its independence from Britain, and a tremendous feeling of national pride and desire for independence from "all foreign jurisdiction" was evident in every section of the population. "Like most Americans, Catholics were caught up in the enthusiasm of the birth of a nation. They were Americans, and they wanted their Church to reflect the spirit of the new nation, rather than mirror the ethos of a foreign country" (p. 107). To accomplish this, a clergy in tune with "the American way of life" was indispensable. This dream also included the desire for an episcopal hierarchy chosen by the people of the United States and appointed by Rome. This body of bishops, and the "permanent body of national clergy" working with them "should not be missioners working under the

control of Rome's missionary arm, the Congregation for the Propagation of the Faith, but a stable group of priests belonging to the Church in the United States." Moreover, the American Church should be headed by "an ordinary national bishop," not an Apostolic Vicar, a delegate of the pope. Cf. James Hennesey, S.J., *American Catholics: A History of the Roman Catholic Community in the United States* (Oxford, New York, Toronto, Melbourne: Oxford University Press, 1981), p. 84. Unlike some Europeans, Carroll and most American Catholics were, however, opposed to state intervention in religious matters as a guarantee against coercion in matters of worship.

13. John A. Gallagher, *Time Past, Time Future*, p. 189. Jay P. Dolan points out that it took the intervention of Cardinal Gibbons of Baltimore to get Rome to allow Catholic membership in the Knights of Labor. While in Rome to receive the cardinal's red hat in February 1887, Gibbons argued forcefully before Vatican officials that to allow Catholic participation in these movements would be to recognize the right of the worker to fight "the social evils, public injustices . . . and heartless avarice" which plagued the nation. To organize into one labor movement was the only hope the working class in America had to redress these injustices. The Church would be seen to be against these unjust conditions if it sanctioned organized labor among Catholics. Otherwise, the working class, as in Europe, would become estranged from the Church, "souls would surely be lost, the revenues of the Church would suffer immensely (the effect of which would be felt in Rome), and the Holy See would be looked upon 'as a harsh and unjust power.' " The Vatican endorsed Catholic presence in the general labor movement, and the Roman Catholic Church in America for the first time made a commitment for labor. Cf. Jay P. Dolan, *The American Catholic Experience*, p. 333.

14. Jay P. Dolan, *The American Catholic Experience*, p. 313. The following passage from a sermon preached in 1894 by a Protestant minister in Rochester, New York, succinctly captures the heart and meaning of this controversy: "There are two distinct and hostile parties in the Roman Catholic Church in America. One is led by Archbishop Ireland. It stands for Americanism and a larger independence. It is sympathetic with modern thought. It believes the Roman Catholic Church should take its place in all great moral reforms. It is small, but progressive, vigorous and brave. The other party is led by the overwhelming majority of the hierarchy. It is conservative, out of touch with American or modern ideas. It is the old medieval European Church, transplanted into the nineteenth century and this country of freedom, interesting as an antiquity and curiosity, but fast losing its power and consequently, growing in bitterness." Quoted in Jay P. Dolan, *The American Catholic Experience*, pp. 313–314.

15. The book in question was *The Life of Isaac Thomas Hecker*, co-founder of the Paulists and an influential writer in the mid-nineteenth century. Like John Ireland and others in this era, Hecker worked for a Church which took modern trends seriously.

16. Pope Leo XII, "True and False Americanism in Religion," in *The Great Encyclical Letters of Pope Leo XIII* (New York, Cincinnati, Chicago: Benzinger Brothers, 1903), p. 442. This letter is also known as *Testem Benevolentiae*.

17. Ibid., p. 443.

18. Jay P. Dolan, *The American Catholic Experience*, p. 316.

19. Ibid.

20. It is one of those ironies of history that an entire ecumenical council was convoked some decades later precisely to address the need for the gospel to be in dialogue with the "signs of the times." The debate concerning the relationship between Christianity and the world around is an ongoing fact of contemporary Christianity in every part of the Christian world.

21. The term 'modernism' was used in the sixteenth century to characterize "the tendency to esteem the modern age more highly than antiquity." Some Protestants in the nineteenth century used it in a religious sense to characterize "the anti-Christian tendencies of the modern world and also the radicalism of liberal theology." Starting in Italy in the last century, some Catholics applied the term to the movement in the Church which urged reform of the Church and its doctrine by adapting them to modern needs. Pius X took up this term in his encyclical *Pascendi*. "Here it means a complex of clearly defined heresies which form the logical conclusion of the heterodox trends within the movement in question, which took in fact many forms and was in many respects legitimate, but which was also simply imprudent and given to wild exaggeration. In connection with modernism and the reaction to it, the term was often applied without distinction to all who refused to adopt a strictly conservative standpoint." Roger Aubert, "Modernism," in *Encyclopedia of Theology: The Concise Sacramentum Mundi*, edited by Karl Rahner (New York: Crossroad, 1986), p. 969.

22. The encyclical letter Leo XIII published in 1879 to promote the study of the work of the Scholastics, especially Thomas Aquinas.

23. John P. Boyle, "The American Experience in Moral Theology," *CTSA Proceedings* 41 (1986), p. 36.

24. Gerald P. Fogarty, *The Vatican and the American Catholic Hierarchy from 1870 to 1965* (Wilmington, Del.: Michael Glazier, 1985), p. 193.

25. William M. Halsey, *The Survival of American Innocence: Catholicism in an Era of Disillusionment, 1920–1940* (Notre Dame, Ind.: Univer-

sity of Notre Dame Press, 1980), p. 38. Cf. also Jay P. Dolan, *The American Catholic Experience*, p. 319.

26. Leo XIII was convinced that a great number of the societal ills of his day could be traced back to bad philosophical influence. The only philosophy founded on true and solid principles and thus capable of bringing "a vast amount of benefit for the public and private good" was the philosophy of Thomas Aquinas. Therefore, in order to arrest "the tempest that is upon us" by which "the Christian faith is being constantly assailed by the machinations and craft of a certain false wisdom," Leo XIII called for the restoration and spread of the golden wisdom of St. Thomas "for the defense and beauty of the Catholic faith, for the good of society, and for the advantage of all the sciences. Pope Leo XIII, "Aeterni Patris," in *The Great Encyclical Letters of Pope Leo XIII*, p. 35 and p. 56. For a detailed account of the intellectual output engendered by *Aeterni Patris*, see Alasdair MacIntyre, *Three Rival Versions of Moral Enquiry: Encyclopaedia, Genealogy, and Tradition* (Notre Dame, Ind.: University of Notre Dame Press, 1990). Leo's Thomistic revival was not universally well received. Some European theologians, especially in Germany and France, were convinced that Thomistic theology and philosophy could not meet the challenges posed by communism and existentialism after the two world wars. In addition, the changed intellectual climate in Europe at this time brought about an acute tension between Scholastic theologians and Catholic exegetes. The point at issue concerned "the ability of a non-historical discipline like Scholastic theology to provide an accurate interpretation of Scripture's meaning" (Gerald McCool, "Twentieth Century Scholasticism," *Journal of Religion* 58 [1978 Supplement], p. S216. In spite of this opposition, the movement bore fruit in many ways. Cf. James Hennesey, "Leo XIII's Thomistic Revival: A Political and Philosophical Event," *The Journal of Religion* 58 (1978, Supplement), p. S193.

27. Richard A. McCormick, interview with the author, University of Notre Dame, April 22, 1992.

28. See L. Vereecke, "History of Moral Theology: 700 to Vatican I," in *The New Catholic Encyclopedia*, vol. 9 (San Francisco, Toronto, Sydney, London: Catholic University Press, 1967), p. 1121. See also, John A. Gallagher, *Time Past, Time Future*, p. 29; Bernard Häring, "Moral Theology: Catholic," in *Encyclopedia of Theology*, p. 988.

29. Henry Davis, S.J., *Moral and Pastoral Theology* (London: Sheed and Ward, 1945), p. vii.

30. M.-D. Chenu, "The Plan of St. Thomas' Summa Theologiae," *Cross Currents* 2 (1952), p. 72.

31. Gerald McCool, *Catholic Theology in the Nineteenth Century* (New York: Seabury Press, 1987), p. 196. See also Enda McDonagh,

"Teaching Moral Theology Today," *Irish Theological Quarterly* 32 (1966), p. 199.

32. Henry Davis, *Moral and Pastoral Theology*, vol. 1, p. 1. "Theologia moralis est scientia activitatis humanae, prout ad Deum finem ultimum supernaturalem dirigitur" (H. Noldin, A. Schmitt, G. Heinzel, *Summa Theologiae Moralis*, vol. 1, editio 33 [Innsbrück: Felizian Rauch, 1960], p. 1. Dominicus Prümmer has virtually the same definition: "Theologia moralis est scientiae theologiae illa pars, quae diiudicat atque dirigit actus humanos in ordine ad finem supernaturalem" (Prümmer, *Manuale Theologiae Moralis*, vol. 1 [Barcelona: Editorial Herder, 1946], p. 2.

33. Thomas Slater, *A Manual of Moral Theology*, vol. 1, 5th edition (New York, Cincinnati: Benzinger Brothers, 1931), p. 1.

34. Again, the same view is held by Prümmer: "Deus est finis ultimis hominis eiusque actum, ita ut homo teneatur tendere ad Deum eumque glorificare" (*Manuale Theologiae Moralis*, p. 20).

35. "La grandeur de l'acte humain consiste précisément à dépasser le moment même où il se pose pour engager tout l'orientation d'une vie, pour l'amener à prendre position vis-à-vis de l'absolu. C'est vrai déjà de l'activité quotidienne: à combien plus forte raison d'un acte qui engage, avec l'amour réciproque des époux, leur avenir et celui descendance" (*AAS* [1951], May 19, 1956, p. 470).

36. Among the laws Thomas considered as participations in the eternal are positive law and ecclesiastical law.

37. "Sic igitur aeternus divinae legis conceptus habet rationem legis aeternae, secundum quod a Deo ordinatur ad gubernationem rerum ab ipso praecogitarum" (*Summa Theologiae*, Ia-IIae, q.91, a.2).

38. *Summa Theologiae*, Ia-IIae, q.94, a.2.

39. Germain G. Grisez, "The First Principle of Practical Reason: A Commentary on the *Summa Theologiae* 1-2, Question 94, Article 2," *Natural Law Forum* 10 (1965), p. 177.

40. Arthur Vermeersch, *Theologia Moralis*, vol. 1 (Bruges, 1922), pp. 137ff.

41. Thomas Slater, *A Manual of Moral Theology*, p. 24.

42. *Summa Theologiae*, I-IIae, q.7, art.1. See also, q.18, art.10.

43. Vincent McNamara, "Religion and Morality II," *The Irish Theological Quarterly* 44 (1977), p. 180.

44. Ibid., p. 181.

45. Slater, *A Manual of Moral Theology*, p. 60.

46. Ibid., p. 29.

47. "Peccatum est dictum vel factum vel concupitum contra legem Dei aeternam" (Prümmer, *Summa Theologiae Moralis*, p. 241).

48. Henry Davis, *Moral and Pastoral Theology*, p. 253.

49. Thomas Slater, *A Manual of Moral Theology*, p. 28.

50. Ibid., p. 29. See also, Noldin and Schmitt, *Summa Theologiae Moralis*, p. 92.

51. Thomas Slater, *A Manual of Moral Theology*, p. 29.

52. Henry Davis, *Moral and Pastoral Theology*, p. 48.

53. This is what Prümmer has under this condition. *Status Viator*: Post mortem enim homo nequit mereri, ita volente Deo, iuxta verbi Christi in sensu spirituali intellecta: "venit nox [ie. mors], quando nemo potest operari [scil. meritorie]."

54. Henry Davis, *Moral and Pastoral Theology*, p. 50.

55. John Mahoney, *The Making of Moral Theology: A Study of the Roman Catholic Tradition* (Oxford: Clarendon Press, 1987), pp. 73–115.

56. Ibid., pp. 97-98.

57. Ibid., p. 97.

58. Catholic moral tradition understands the word 'probable' in a variety of ways. An opinion is termed probable "if one has good and solid reasons for thinking that a certain line of action is morally correct." This is so even if one is aware at the same time that there are "better, sounder, and more cogent reasons for thinking that it is not." 'Probable' in McCormick's thesis (unlike in English usage) is not the same as "more likely." It could in fact refer to the least likely. Casuists in the course of the centuries have added what are now known as "qualifying notes." Thus, depending on the degree of probability of the conclusions reached, a case or an opinion may be "more / less probable," "thinly / hardly probable," and so on (Henry Davis, *Moral and Pastoral Theology*, p. 78).

59. Richard A. McCormick, "The Removal of a Fetus Probably Dead to Save the Life of the Mother" (unpublished STD dissertation, Rome: Pontifical Gregorian University, 1957), p. i.

60. Ibid., pp. 1-2.

61. "Recte vero excipit Sanchez (idque asserit ut commune apud omnes, contra paucos aliquos), si dubium adsit an fetus sit vel ne animatus: eo quod tunc intrinsice malum est, innocentem positive periculo exponere" (Alphonsus Liguori, *Theologia Moralis*, Rome [ed. Gaude], 1905, I, Lib. III, tract. IV, cap. I, n. 394. Cited in Richard A. McCormick, "The Removal of a Fetus," p. 4).

62. Richard A. McCormick, "The Removal of a Fetus," p. 196.

63. This can happen either because it is questionable whether the lawgiver wanted it to be used for that particular type of action – the Suarezian view, or because obedience to the law would not serve the reason for which it was introduced in the first place – the Thomistic view.

64. A virtual voluntary is an action willed not for itself but because it is known as a side effect, a circumstance, an inferior of the object actually

and expressly willed. "Thus, I am uncertain whether it is licit here and now to eat meat. If I eat the meat, my will has made a choice and the object is chosen precisely as known–sc., as a probably illicit act. This probable illiceity, since it is presented as a modification of the object of choice, vitiates the choice. The choice, it is true, is to eat meat; but it must be remembered, the act is chosen as I know it, sc., as probably illicit" (Richard A. McCormick, "The Removal of a Fetus," pp. 239–240). Hypothetical voluntareity refers to almost the same thing. More specifically, the agent does not really will the side effect. But all the same, he cares little whether there is an evil side effect or not. In effect the agent is prepared to accept the evil side effect as well as the good. Moralists in the past have argued that such an attitude manifests a disposition toward what is morally wrong or even sin.

65. Here is the axiom in Latin: Idem est in moralibus facere et exponere se periculo faciendi.

66. Richard A. McCormick, "The Removal of a Fetus," p. 483.

67. Ibid., p. 322.

68. Ibid., pp. 375–376.

69. Ibid., p. 376.

70. Ibid., p. 382.

71. Ibid.

72. Ibid., p. 383.

73. Ibid., p. 386.

74. Ibid.

75. Ibid., pp. 390–391.

76. Ibid., p. 397.

77. Carol Tauer has made a useful distinction between the notion of doubt of fact and what she calls theoretical doubt. She asserts that although the manualists never defined what they meant by fact, it is safe to assume that this referred to empirical and verifiable reality. She notes that the presence or absence of a fertilized egg in the fallopian tube is a matter of empirical verification. Tauer assumes that McCormick in his thesis accepts this notion of doubt as empirical and verifiable reality. That is why she could conclude that McCormick justified the problem of the removal of the probably dead fetus based on the probable opinion that the fetus was dead. See Carol Tauer, "The Tradition of Probabilism and the Moral Status of the Early Embryo," in *Abortion and Catholicism: The American Debate*, edited by Patricia Beattie Jung and Thomas A. Shannon (New York: Crossroad, 1988), pp. 54–84. This is not McCormick as I read him. As I state in the main body of this work, whether the fetus is alive or dead is of secondary consideration here. For McCormick, the important issue is that the situation is that of conflict (save the mother or lose both mother and child). In this case, however, the resolution of the conflict is made a little

easier by the fact of the uncertainty of the existence of the fetus. Therefore, considered according to the hierarchy of values, the uncertain life of a fetus takes a secondary position vis-à-vis that of a certainly living person (the mother). The decision is based on a proportionate reason rather than on the probable opinion that the fetus is inanimate. Thus I doubt that Tauer can, based on this dissertation, justifiably use McCormick to justify her stand that "there are 'good and solid reasons' for not including early human embryos under the full weight of the law against killing" (Ibid., p. 79).

78. Richard A. McCormick, "The Removal of a Fetus," p. 255.

79. See Peter Knauer, S.J., "The Hermeneutic Function of the Principle of Double Effect," *Readings in Moral Theology No. 1: Moral Norms and Catholic Tradition* (hereafter *RMT1*), pp. 1–39.

80. Richard A. McCormick, "The Removal of a Fetus," p. iii.

81. Ibid., p. 77.

82. Ibid., p. 94.

83. The Scholastic method was essentially a rational investigation of every relevant problem in several areas of learning. This is done "in order to reach an intelligent, scientific solution that would be consistent with accepted authorities, known facts, human reason, and Christian faith. Its ultimate goal was science (*scientia*), although frequently schoolmen had to be content with probable opinions and dialectical solutions (J. A. Weisheipl, "Scholastic Method," in *New Catholic Encyclopedia*, vol. 12 [New York, San Francisco, Toronto, Sydney: Catholic University Press, 1967], pp. 1145–1146).

84. McCormick himself acknowledges this point. "Because I have desired to challenge the use of some rather hallowed dicta with the hope of arriving at greater clarity of principle, the style adopted is occasionally deliberately personal. If this wording seems aggressive, it would be a misinterpretation to read into it the author's assurance of his position or of the absolute validity of his objections; rather, he hoped thereby more readily to stimulate confirmation (if the reflections seem reasonable) or denial and disproof (if they are incorrect). The spirit, then, in which this work was undertaken was one of enquiry-by-challenge; it was pursued in the hope that the digging and the delving would uncover, if not a complete solution, at least a more profound understanding of necessary principles" (Richard A. McCormick, "The Removal of a Fetus," p. iii).

85. I have already noted the tendency in McCormick to take proper note of other theological opinion on an issue. This attitude has stayed with McCormick into his later years as a mature theologian. He often proceeds to handle a problem by an extensive survey of theological opinion on the issue, and through what may be called a dialectical manner, eliminates from and

adds to these opinions. In the end what emerges is usually something new and different, a truly 'McCormickan' synthesis, so to speak.

86. Richard A. McCormick, "The Removal of a Fetus," p. 96.

87. Although the exaggeration in this is obvious, it is correct to a large extent.

88. Dionigi Tettamanzi, "Is There a Christian Ethics?" *Readings in Moral Theology 2: The Distinctiveness of Christian Ethics* (hereafter *RMT2*), pp. 20–25.

89. Richard A. McCormick and Charles E. Curran, *RMT2*, pp. 1–2.

CHAPTER 2

1. Richard A. McCormick, "Human Significance and Christian Significance," (hereafter *HSCS*), pp. 233–261.

2. Richard A. McCormick, "Theology and Biomedical Ethics," *Église et Théologie* 13 (1982), p. 315.

3. Richard A. McCormick, *HMCT*, p. 31. See also, "Theology and Bioethics," *Hastings Center Report* (March/April 1989), p. 6.

4. Richard A. McCormick, "The Primacy of Charity," *Perspectives* (August/September 1959), p. 21. This work is heavily dependent on Gérard Gilleman, *The Primacy of Charity in Moral Theology* (Westminster, Md.: The Newman Press, 1959).

5. Richard A. McCormick, *HSCS*, p. 235.

6. Ibid., p. 236.

7. Lisa Sowle Cahill, "On Richard McCormick: Reason and Faith in Post–Vatican II Catholic Ethics," *Second Opinion* 9 (November 1988), p. 111.

8. Richard A. McCormick, "Practical and Theoretical Considerations," in *The Problem of Population: Vol. 3 Educational Considerations* (Notre Dame, Ind.: University of Notre Dame Press, 1965), p. 61.

9. John L. McKenzie, "Natural Law in the New Testament," *Biblical Research* 9 (1964), pp. 1–11.

10. Richard A. McCormick, *Notes on Moral Theology: 1965 through 1980* (hereafter *NMT1*), pp. 14–15.

11. Ibid., p. 16.

12. Richard A. McCormick, *HSCS*, p. 240.

13. Ibid., p. 241.

14. Ibid.

15. Richard A. McCormick, "Moral Theology 1940–1989: An Overview," p. 8.

16. Karl Rahner, "Anonymous Christians," *Theological Investigations*, vol. 6 (London: Darton, Longman, and Todd, 1969), p. 391.

17. Karl Rahner, "History of the World and Salvation History," in *Theological Investigation*, vol. 5 (London: Darton, Longman, and Todd, 1966), p. 98.

18. Karl Rahner, "Anonymous Christians," pp. 391-392.

19. Juan Alfaro, "Nature and Grace," in *Encyclopedia of Theology: The Concise Sacramentum Mundi*, pp. 1033-1034.

20. John Mahoney, *The Making of Moral Theology*, p. 99.

21. Karl Rahner, "Anonymous and Explicit Faith," in *Theological Investigations*, vol. 16 (London: Darton, Longman, and Todd, 1979), p. 53.

22. McCormick himself has not only noted the "enormous repercussions" of Rahner's anthropology "on some basic concepts of moral theology," but also that this anthropology was "domesticated in moral theology largely through the writings of Josef Fuchs, S.J., and his disciple Bruno Schüller, S.J." (Richard A. McCormick, "Moral Theology 1940-1989," p. 8).

23. Vincent MacNamara, *Faith and Ethics: Recent Roman Catholicism*, p. 38.

24. Josef Fuchs, "Is There a Distinctively Christian Morality?," in *Personal Responsibility and Christian Morality* (Dublin: Gill & Macmillan; Washington, D.C.: Georgetown University Press, 1983), p. 53. This article was first published as "Gibt est eine spezifisch Moral?" *Stimmen der Zeit* 185 (1970), pp. 99-112.

25. Ibid., p. 53.

26. Charles E. Curran, "Is There a Distinctively Christian Social Ethic?" *Metropolis: Christian Presence and Responsibility* (Notre Dame, Ind.: Fides, 1970).

27. Richard A. McCormick, *NMT1* (1971), p. 300.

28. Richard A. McCormick, "The Judeo-Christian Tradition and Bioethical Codes," *HBNW*, p. 4. This article first appeared in 1975 in *Human Rights and Psychological Research*, edited by Eugene C. Kennedy (New York: Crowell Publishers, 1975), pp. 23-36.

29. Nobert Rigali, "On Christian Ethics," *Chicago Studies* 10 (1971), pp. 227-247. McCormick acknowledges his indebtedness to Rigali on this point.

30. Richard A. McCormick, "Does Religious Faith Add to Ethical Perception?" *RMT2*, pp. 156-171. McCormick acknowledges his indebtedness to Rigali on this point.

31. Ibid., p. 158.

32. Ibid.

33. Richard A. McCormick, "Does Religious Faith Add to Ethical Perception?" pp. 156-161; also, *TCC*, pp. 191 ff; *HMCT*, pp. 48 ff.

34. Richard A. McCormick, "Theology in the Public Forum," *TCC*, p. 193.

35. "Does Religious Faith Add to Ethical Perception?" *RMT2*, p. 159. See also "Theology in the Public Forum," *TCC*, p. 196.

36. Richard A. McCormick, "Does Religious Faith Add to Ethical Perception?" p. 170.

37. Richard A. McCormick, "Theology and Biomedical Ethics," *Église et Théologie*, p. 316.

38. Richard A. McCormick, *HMCT*, pp. 59–60.

39. Richard A. McCormick, "Theology and Biomedical Ethics," *Église et Théologie*, p. 318.

40. Richard A. McCormick, "Theology and Biomedical Ethics," *Logos* 3 (1982), p. 31.

41. Richard A. McCormick, *TCC*, p. 204; also, *HMCT*, pp. 59–60.

42. Ibid., p. 196.

43. The address was delivered at the Hastings Center on the occasion of his reception of the Henry Knowles Beecher Award in June 1988. See "Theology and Bioethics," *The Hastings Center Report*, pp. 5–10.

44. Richard A. McCormick, "Theology and Bioethics: Christian Foundations," in *Theology and Bioethics: Exploring the Foundations and Frontiers*, edited by Earl E. Shelp (Dordrecht: D. Reidel Publishing Co., 1985), p. 97.

45. Richard A. McCormick, "Theology and Bioethics," *Église et Théologie*, pp. 321–322;

46. Ibid., p. 325.

47. Ibid., pp. 326–327.

48. Ibid., p. 328.

49. Richard A. McCormick, "Theology and Bioethics," *The Hastings Center Report*, p. 8.

50. Ibid., pp. 8–9.

51. Richard A. McCormick, "Theology and Biomedical Ethics," *Église et Théologie*, p. 330.

52. Richard A. McCormick, *TCC*, p. 204.

53. Stanley Hauerwas, "Nature, Reason, and the Task of Theological Ethics," *Readings in Moral Theology No. 7: Natural Law and Theology*, edited by Richard A. McCormick and Charles E. Curran (Mahwah, N.J.: Paulist Press, 1991), p. 52.

54. Ibid., p. 54.

55. David Hollenbach, "Fundamental Theology and the Christian Moral Life," in *Faithful Witness: Foundations of Theology for Today's Church*, edited by Leo J. O'Donovan and T. Howland Sanks (New York: Crossroad, 1989), p. 171.

56. Ibid., p. 173.
57. Ibid., p. 174.
58. George A. Lindbeck, *The Nature of Doctrine: Religion and Theology in a Postliberal Age* (Philadelphia: Westminster Press, 1984), esp. pp. 30–42.
59. Richard A. McCormick, *HSCS*, p. 224.
60. Richard A. McCormick, "The New Morality," *America* 118 (June 15, 1968), p. 771.
61. Ibid.
62. *Gaudium et Spes*, no. 51. *Schema Constitutionis Pastoralis de Ecclesia in Mundo huis Expensio Modorum Partis Secundae* (Vatican Polyglot, 1965), p. 37; also see Richard A. McCormick, "Moral Theology Since Vatican II: Clarity or Chaos?" *TCC*, p. 14.
63. Richard A. McCormick, *TCC*, p. 14.
64. Richard A. McCormick, *HSCS*, p. 249.
65. Richard A. McCormick, *TCC*, p. 18.
66. Richard A. McCormick, *HSCS*, p. 245.
67. Richard A. McCormick, *NMT1* (1975), p. 528.
68. Richard A. McCormick, *NMT1* (1976) , p. 579
69. Bernard Hoose has shown that the absence of this distinction in the earlier work of proportionalists (including McCormick) was a hindrance to clear thinking on their part as well as to the proper perception on the part of what they (proportionalists) were saying about norms. See Bernard Hoose, *Proportionalism: The American Debate and Its European Roots* (Washington, D.C.: Georgetown University Press, 1987), esp. pp. 41–67.
70. To try to explain the distinction between moral goodness and badness, moral rightness and wrongness, I will borrow two illustrations from Bruno Schüller. In one example a doctor who is motivated by purely selfish ambition develops a new therapeutic device that assists a number of people who are ill and suffering. On the surface this physician by the consequences of his act has acted in accordance with the requirements of the commandment of love. By definition, however, he does not act from his love for his neighbor. Schüller argues that, although only actions done out of love are morally good and those actions done from a purely selfish motive are morally bad, the physician in question has done what is morally right because his action was beneficial and helpful to other people. "Therefore, an action may be morally bad because performed from pure selfishness, but nonetheless, be morally right on account of its beneficial consequences" (Bruno Schüller, "The Double Effect in Catholic Thought: A Re-evaluation," in *Doing Evil to Achieve Good: Moral Choice in Conflict Situations* [hereafter *DEAG*], p. 83). In another work Schüller illustrates this point with an example about someone who, because of love, feels obliged to help a neighbor. But in the process of helping this

neighbor the person inadvertently causes harm, that is, "the opposite of what love demands in deeds." Although the pain that results in this case may be *pre-morally wrong*, nevertheless, this person's action is *morally good* because "it springs from the best intentions or inner disposition" (Bruno Schüller, "Various Types of Grounding for Ethical Norms," in *RMT1*, pp. 184–198. It is in this sense that McCormick and other proportionalists speak about ontic or pre-moral evil which means "any lack of perfection at which we aim, any lack of fulfillment which frustrates our natural urges and makes us suffer" (see Louis Janssens, "Ontic and Moral Evil," *RMT1*, p. 60). These include, for example, natural diseases, sicknesses, ignorance, death, and everything we experience as regretful and harmful to human growth and welfare. Thus not all evils are moral evils. Some acts are bad and some are merely wrong. The two examples above point to the discrepancies that arise in conflicts between the agent's intention and the consequences of his or her actions. The traditional safeguard, "the end does not justify the means," does not cover all aspects of these conflicts, as McCormick observes.

71. Richard A. McCormick, *NMT1*, p. 579. Also see *HSCS*, p. 245.

72. Richard A. McCormick, "Bishops as Teachers, Scholars as Listeners," *TCC*, p. 98. Also, Josef Fuchs, "Moral Truths–Truths of Salvation?" in *Christian Ethics in a Secular Arena*, p. 55 ff. "Bishops as Teachers, Scholars as Listeners" was first published as "Bishops as Teachers, Jesuits as Listerner," *Studies in the Spirituality of Jesuits* 18 (1986), pp. 1–22.

73. Richard A. McCormick, *TCC*, p. 98

74. Ibid.

75. Ibid.

76. Richard A. McCormick, *NMT1* (1967), p. 136.

77. Richard A. McCormick, *HSCS*, p. 235.

78. Kenneth R. Himes, "The Contribution of Theology to Catholic Moral Theology," in *Moral Theology: Challenges for the Future: Essays in Honor of Richard A. McCormick, S.J.*, edited by Charles Curran (New York: Paulist Press, 1990), p. 66.

79. William C. Spohn, *What Are They Saying about Scripture and Ethics* (New York: Paulist Press, 1983), pp. 13, 36–54.

CHAPTER 3

1. Richard A. McCormick, interview with the author, University of Notre Dame, April 22, 1992.

2. This is not a discussion on McCormick's judgment about the rightness or wrongness of this issue. That will take place later in the

chapter on casuistry. The focus here is the role of the discussion on birth control in the development of McCormick's thought on the Church as moral teacher.

3. See his review of Stanlislas de Lestapsis, *Family Planning and Modern Problems*, in *America* 106 (December 9, 1961), p. 370. Also see the following: "Anti-Fertility Pills," *Homiletic and Pastoral Review* 62 (May 1962), pp. 692–700; a review of *Our Crowded Planet*, edited by Fairfield Osborn, in *America* 107 (June 9, 1962), pp. 386–387; a review of George A. Kelly, *Birth Control and Catholics*, in *America* 109 (October 19, 1963), pp. 465–466; "Conjugal Love and Conjugal Morality," *America* 110 (January 11, 1964), pp. 38–42; "Whither the Pill?" *The Catholic World* 199 (July 1964), pp. 207–214; reviews of Louis Dupre, *Contraception and Catholics*, and *Contraception and Holiness* (no author given), in *America* 111 (November 14, 1964), pp. 628–629; "Family Size, Rhythm, and the Pill," in *The Problem of Population: Moral and Theological Considerations*, edited by Donald N. Barrett (Notre Dame, Ind.: University of Notre Dame Press, 1964–1965), pp. 58–84; a review of Germain G. Grisez, *Contraception and the Natural Law* in *The American Ecclesiastical Review* 153 (August 1965), pp. 119–125; "The Council on Contraception," *America* 114 (January 8, 1966), pp. 47–48; "The History of a Moral Problem," *America* 114 (January 29, 1966), pp. 174–178; "Conjugal Morality," in *Married Love and Children* (New York: America Press, 1966), pp. 24–32.

4. Richard A. McCormick, "Conjugal Love and Conjugal Morality," p. 39.

5. Louis Janssens, "Morale Conjugale et progestogènes," *Ephemerides Theologicae Lovanienses* 39 (1963), pp. 787–826. Also see Jacques Ferin and Louis Janssens, "Progestogènes et Morale Conjugale," *Bibliotheca Ephemeridum Theologicarum Lovaniensium* 22 (Louvain: Publications Universitaires; Gembloux: Duculot, 1963), pp. 9–48.

6. Richard A. McCormick, "Whither the Pill?" pp. 207–214.

7. Richard A. McCormick, "Book Review," *America* 111 (November 14, 1964), pp. 628–629.

8. Richard A. McCormick, "The Council on Contraception," p. 47.

9. See Robert Blair Kaiser, *The Politics of Sex and Religion* (Kansas City, Mo.: Leaven Press, 1985), pp. 55–56.

10. Richard A. McCormick, *NMT1* (1965), pp. 50–51.

11. Ibid.

12. Richard A. McCormick, *NMT1* (1966), p. 115.

13. Ibid.

14. Richard A. McCormick, *NMT1* (1966), p. 115. Charles E. Curran writes about McCormick's position here as follows: "Notice the move within one year from an omission by authority to the intrinsic evidence of the

arguments" (Charles E. Curran, "The Teaching Function of the Church in Morality," in *Moral Theology, Challenges for the Future*, p. 159.

I do not share Curran's suggestion here of a move from authority to intrinsic evidence. In fact, McCormick seemed to have suspended judgment on the matter for the time being until a few things became clearer. This is not uncharacteristic. He tended to cling to traditional positions until it became abundantly clear to him that the position in question was no longer tenable. Then he would change to a new and perhaps burgeoning position and become its champion and perfecter. This being so, it would not be surprising that, as Curran concludes, he could not at this time bring himself to conclude that "the arguments against the Church's teaching on contraception are now convincing" (ibid).

15. Richard A. McCormick, *NMT1* (1967), pp. 165–166.

16. This was just prior to the publication of *Humanae Vitae* in 1968. See John C. Ford and John J. Lynch, "Contraception: A Matter of Practical Doubt?" *Homiletic and Pastoral Review* 68 (1968), pp. 563–574.

17. Richard A. McCormick, *AAS* 558 (1966), pp. 218–224 at 219, quoted in *NMT1* (1968), p. 211.

18. Richard A. McCormick, *NMT1* (1968), p. 212.

19. The same sentiment was expressed by a group of theologians at Marquette University after the publication of the encyclical. The encyclical, they said, raised the following questions: (1) "In the areas of human understanding which are proper to human reasoning, such as natural law, what is the function of the Church as the authoritative teacher of revelation? (2) What are the sources for the formulation of binding moral doctrine within the Christian community? (3) What is the precise role of the pope as an authoritative teacher in those areas? (4) What is the role of the bishops, of the body of the faithful, and of the Church's theologians in formulating such moral teaching? (5) What qualifications may be attached to the individual Christian's assent to admittedly fallible statements of the merely authentic magisterium, especially when this involves practical judgments of grave consequence?" (*Our Sunday Visitor*, August 18, 1968. Also quoted by McCormick, *NMT1* [1968], p. 215).

20. Richard A. McCormick, "The Teaching Role of the Magisterium and of the Theologians," *CTSA Proceedings* (1969), pp. 239–254. McCormick uses the ideas in this article in a good number of places. See, for example, "A Moral Magisterium in Ecumenical Perspective," *Studies in Christian Ethics: Ethics and Ecumenism*, vol. 1, no. 1 (1988), p. 23; *HMCT*, pp. 62 ff.; *NMT1* (1969), pp. 262–263; *TCC*, pp. 38 ff.

21. Richard A. McCormick, "The Teaching Role of the Magisterium and of the Theologians," p. 240.

22. Ibid., p. 241.

23. Ibid., p. 242.

24. Richard A. McCormick, "Changing My Mind About the Changeable Church," in *How My Mind Has Changed*, edited by James Wall and David Heim (Grand Rapids, Mich.: Eerdmans, 1991), p. 64.

25. "The Pastoral Constitution of the Church in the Modern World" (*Gaudium et Spes*), in *Vatican Council II: The Conciliar and Post Conciliar Documents*, edited by Austin Flannery (Northport, N.Y.: Costello Publishing Co., 1984), no. 43.

26. Richard A. McCormick, "The Role of the Magisterium and of the Theologians," p. 243.

27. Ibid.

28. Ibid., p. 245.

29. Ibid., pp. 246–247.

30. Ibid., p. 247.

31. Ibid., pp. 247–248.

32. Richard A. McCormick, "The Teaching Office as guarantor of Unity in Morality," *Concilium* 150 (1981), p. 72.

33. Richard A. McCormick, interview with the author, University of Notre Dame, April 22, 1992.

34. Richard A. McCormick, "Practical and Theoretical Considerations," p. 65.

35. Ibid.

36. Ibid., p. 71.

37. Richard A. McCormick, *NMT1* (1965), p. 20.

38. This article was originally published as "Morality and Magisterium," *Cross Currents* 18 (Winter 1968), pp. 41–65. It has since been published in other places and sometimes under a slightly different title. See Daniel Maguire, *Moral Absolutes and the Magisterium* (Washington, D.C.; Cleveland: Corpus Papers, 1968). See also *Readings in Moral Theology No. 3: The Magisterium and Morality* (herafter *RMT3*), pp. 34–66.

39. Daniel Maguire, *RMT3*, p. 47.

40. Ibid., p. 48.

41. Richard A. McCormick, *NMT1* (1968), p. 199.

42. Richard A. McCormick, *NMT1* (1969), p. 240.

43. Richard A. McCormick, "Bishops as Teachers, Scholars as Listeners," p. 98.

44. Ibid., p. 100.

45. Richard A. McCormick, "Catholic Moral Theology: Is Pluralism Pathogenic?" *TCC*, p. 149.

46. This text is often quoted by McCormick. It is important for this reason to give its official Latin version: "Ecclesia, quae depositum verbi Dei custodit, ex quo principia in ordine religioso et morali hauriuntur,

quin semper de singulis quaestionibus responsum in promptu habeat, lumen revelationis cum omnium peritia coniungere cupit, ut iter illuminetur, quod humanitatis nuper ingressa" ("Concilium Vaticanum II–1962–1965: De ecclesia in mundo," in *Decrees of the Ecumenical Councils*, vol. 2: *Trent-Vatican II*, edited by Norman P. Tanner [London: Sheed and Ward; Washington, D.C.: Georgetown University Press, 1990], p. 1089).

47. "Interpretanda est igitur constitutio iuxta normans generales theologicae interpretationis, et quidem ratione habita, praesertim in secunda eius parte, adiunctorum mutabilium cum quibus res de quibus agitur natura sua connectuntur" (Norman Tanner, *Decrees of the Ecumenical Councils*, p. 1069).

48. Austin Flannery, *Vatican Council II: The Conciliar and Post Conciliar Documents*, p. 955. Here again is the Latin text of this passage which McCormick often refers to: "Moralis igitur indolens rationis agendi, ubi de componendo amore coniugali cum responsabili vitae transmissione agitur, non a sola sincere intentione et aestimatione motivorum pendet, sed obiectivis criteriis, ex personae eiusdemque actuum natura desumptis, determinari debet, quae integrum sensum mutuae donationis ac humanae procreationis in contextu veri amoris observant" (Norman P. Tanner, *Decrees of the Ecumenical Councils*, p. 1104).

49. Gaudium et Spes, no. 51. *Schema Constitutionis Pastoralis de Ecclesia*, p. 37, answer to *modi* 104: "Ex personae ejusdemque actuum natura desumptis; quibus verbis asseritur etiam actus diiudicandos esse non secundum aspectum merum biologicum, sed quatenus illi ad personam humanam integre et aedequate considerandam pertinent. Agitur de principio generali." See also Richard A. McCormick, *TCC*, p. 14.

50. Richard A. McCormick, *TCC*, p. 157.

51. Ibid., p. 159.

52. Richard A. McCormick, "Catholic Moral Theology: Is Pluralism Pathogenic?" p. 161.

53. Richard A. McCormick, "Matters of Free Theological Debate," *TCC*, p. 169.

54. John C. Ford and Germain Grisez, "Contraception and the Infallibility of the Ordinary Magisterium," *Theological Studies* 39 (1978), pp. 286–287.

55. Ibid., p. 272.

56. Ibid., p. 275.

57. Francis Sullivan argues that if Grisez's position were correct it would not have been necessary for either Vatican I or Vatican II to talk of infallibility in morals. The Councils could have said something like this instead: "Whenever the magisterium speaks in a definitive way it must be speaking infallibly, because the very fact that it speaks in a definitive way

would guarantee that what it speaks about would be a proper matter for infallible teaching" (Francis Sullivan, *Magisterium: Teaching Authority in the Catholic Church* [New York: Paulist Press, 1983], p. 145).

58. Ibid., p. 147.

59. Richard A. McCormick, *TCC*, pp. 82–83.

60. Richard A. McCormick, "The Search for Truth in the Catholic Context," *America* (November 8, 1986), p. 278.

61. Richard A. McCormick, interview with the author, University of Notre Dame, April 22, 1992.

62. Ibid.

63. Richard A. McCormick, *NMT1* (1965), p. 39.

64. Richard A. McCormick, *NMT1* (1968), pp. 205–206.

65. Ibid., pp. 207–208.

66. Ibid., p. 221.

67. Ibid., p. 222.

68. For example, Paul VI stated in *Humanae Vitae* (no. 28) that "the Pastors of the Church enjoy a special light of the Holy Spirit in teaching the truth." And this, rather than the arguments they put forward, is the reason the faithful are bound to obedience. What then is the meaning of "the assistance of the Holy Spirit"? See Austin Flannery, *Vatican Council II: The Conciliar and Post Conciliar Documents*, vol. 2, pp. 412–413.

69. Richard A. McCormick, *NMT1* (1969), pp. 261–262.

70. Ibid., pp. 262–263.

71. Ibid., pp. 264–265.

72. Ibid., p. 249.

73. Richard A. McCormick, "Loyalty and Dissent: The Magisterium–A New Model," *America* (June 27, 1970), p. 674.

74. Richard A. McCormick, *NMT1* (1969), p. 249.

75. Ibid., p. 250.

76. Richard McCormick, "L'Affaire Curran," *TCC*, p. 117. This article was first published in *America* (April 5, 1986). It has also been published in *Readings in Moral Theology No. 6: Dissent in the Church*, edited by Richard A. McCormick and Charles E. Curran (Mahwah, N.J.: Paulist Press, 1988), pp. 408–420.

77. Richard A. McCormick, *TCC*, p. 118.

78. Ibid., p. 119.

79. Ibid., pp. 128–129.

80. Ibid., p. 121.

81. Richard A. McCormick, "The Teaching Office as Guarantor of Unity in Morality," pp. 73–81.

82. Richard A. McCormick, *TCC*, pp. 29–39.

83. Richard A. McCormick, "The Teaching Office as Guarantor of Unity in Morality," p. 79.

84. Richard A. McCormick, "Moral Theology Since Vatican II: Clarity or Chaos?," *TCC*, p. 20.

85. Richard A. McCormick, "Matters of Free Theological Debate," p. 169.

86. Richard A. McCormick, *NMT1* (1977), p. 664.

87. Richard A. McCormick, *NMT1* (1968), p. 221.

88. Ibid.

89. Germain G. Grisez, *The Way of the Lord Jesus* (Chicago: Franciscan Herald Press, 1983), p. 879.

90. Ibid., p. 880.

91. Ibid., p. 883.

92. Ibid., p. 885.

93. Richard A. McCormick, *NMT1* (1977), p. 667.

94. Richard A. McCormick, "Personal Conscience," *Chicago Studies* 13 (Fall 1974), p. 241.

CHAPTER 4

1. See chapter 2.

2. The issue of dependence here raises a familiar problem in McCormick's work. He exhibits a tendency to downplay his own original contribution and to give credit to some other person whose work on the issue he believes to be more encompassing. Sometimes this obscures the fact that he may in fact have been the originator of the idea under discussion or at least that he himself had previously held the same or similar views. Therefore, on the issue of the definition of personhood, it is difficult to distinguish what McCormick appropriates from Louis Janssens from his own original insights.

Searching for the roots of dependency, one would be correct to wonder what influence Emmanuel Mounier's work had on Janssens's view of the human person. See Emmanuel Mounier, *Personalism* (London: Routledge and Kegan Paul, 1952). This work was originally published in France in 1950 as *Le Personnalisme*.

3. Edward Schillebeeckx, *Christ: The Experience of Jesus as Lord* (New York: Crossroad, 1986), pp. 733–734.

4. For Janssens, the human person is a subject, that is, a being who is called to consciousness, to live according to his or her conscience, and to live in freedom. As incarnate spirit, the human person is "a conscious interiority in corporeality" and part of the material world. Therefore, the

person is a being-in-the-world. As such, he or she is essentially directed to the other. Human persons are social beings not only because they are open to each other but also because they live in appropriate structures and institutions. As beings created in the image and likeness of God, they are called to know, worship, and glorify God in attitude and actions. They are historical beings who live through successive stages, each characterized by special possibilities. Finally, human persons are fundamentally equal, unique, and original (Louis Janssens, "Artificial Insemination: Ethical Considerations," *Louvain Studies* 8 [1980], p. 5).

5. Richard A. McCormick, *HMCT*, p. 106.

6. Ibid., p. 107

7. Joseph F. Rautenberg, "Abortion: Questions of Value and Procedure," in *Moral Theology: Challenges for the Future*, pp. 240–263.

8. Majorie Reiley Maguire, "Personhood, Covenant, and Abortion," in *Abortion and Catholicism: The American Debate*, p. 109.

9. Joseph Fletcher, "Four Indicators of Personhood–The Enquiry Matures," in *On Moral Medicine: Theological Perspectives in Medical Ethics*, edited by Stephen E. Lammers and Allen Verhey (Grand Rapids, Mich.: Eerdmans, 1987), p. 276.

10. Richard A. McCormick, "The Abortion Dossier," *HBNW*, p. 134. This article first appeared in *TS* 34 (1974), pp. 312–359.

11. Richard A. McCormick, *HBNW*, p. 148.

12. Richard A. McCormick, "The Ethics of Reproductive Technology," *TCC*, pp. 345–346.

13. Richard A. McCormick, "Theology in the Public Forum," p. 206.

14. Richard A. McCormick, "The Judeo-Christian Tradition and Bioethical Codes," pp. 10–11.

15. Richard A. McCormick, "Saving Defective Infants: Options for Life or Death," *HBNW*, p. 359.

16. Richard A. McCormick, *NMT2*, p. 49.

17. Richard A. McCormick, *HMCT*, p. 46.

18. Richard A. McCormick, *DEAG*, p. 49.

19. Richard A. McCormick, "The New Morality," p. 771.

20. Ibid.

21. Richard A. McCormick, "The Judeo-Christian Tradition and Bioethical Codes," p. 12.

22. Ibid., p. 13.

23. Ibid.

24. Richard A. McCormick, "Proxy Consent in the Experimentation Situation," *HBNW*, p. 62. This article first appeared in *Perspectives in Biology and Medicine* 18 (1974), pp. 2–20.

25. McCormick defines experimentation as "procedures involving no direct benefit to the person participating in the experiment" (*HBNW*, p. 51).

26. Ibid., p. 62.

27. Ibid., p. 61.

28. Ibid., p. 67.

29. See Paul Ramsey, "The Case of the Curious Exception," in *Norm and Context in Christian Ethics*, edited by Paul Ramsey and Gene Outka (New York: Charles Scribner's Sons, 1968).

30. Ibid., p. 126.

31. Ibid., p. 129.

32. Ibid., p. 131.

33. See Lisa Cahill, "Within Shouting Distance: Paul Ramsey and Richard McCormick on Method," *The Journal of Medicine and Philosophy* 4.4 (1979), p. 402.

34. Ibid., p. 403.

35. Richard A. McCormick, *HBNW*, p. 67.

36. Ibid., pp. 64–65.

37. This can happen when it is certain that use of dead animals and dead fetal tissue is not sufficient and that "proportionate benefits are reasonably anticipated." See Richard A. McCormick, "Public Policy and Fetal Research," *HBNW*, p.85.

38. "Actus humanus definiri potest: actus, qui procedit ex deliberata hominis voluntate, seu: qui procedit a ratione cognoscente et voluntate, seu cuius homo est dominus" (Prümmer, *Manuale Theologiae Moralis*, vol. 1, p. 26.

39. Richard McCormick, "Moral Theology since Vatican II: Clarity or Chaos?" p. 11.

40. Josef Fuchs, "Basic Freedom and Morality," in *Human Values and Christian Morality*, p. 93.

41. Richard A. McCormick, "The New Morality," p. 770.

42. Richard A. McCormick, *NMT1* (1971), pp. 304–305.

43. Ibid., p. 305.

44. Richard McCormick, *TCC*, p. 174.

45. Ibid., p. 175.

46. See Joseph Fuchs, "Basic Freedom and Morality," p. 107, McCormick, *TCC*, p. 175; Thomas Aquinas, *Summa Theologiae* I-II, q.112, 1.5c.

47. Richard A. McCormick, *TCC*, p. 175.

48. Germain Grisez, *The Way of the Lord Jesus*, vol. 1, pp. 382–390.

49. Richard A. McCormick, *TCC*, p. 186.

50. Ibid., p. 187.

51. Richard A. McCormick, *HBNW*, p. 4.

52. Richard A. McCormick, *DEAG*, p. 250.

53. James J. Walter, "The Foundation and Formulation of Norms," in *Moral Theology: Challenges for the Future*, p. 140.

54. Ibid.

55. Richard A. McCormick, *DEAG*, p. 251.

56. Ibid.

57. Richard A. McCormick, "The Judeo-Christian Tradition and Bioethical Codes," p. 13.

58. Richard A. McCormick, "Personal Conscience," p. 243.

59. Ibid.

60. Ibid., p. 247.

61. These are axioms meant to regulate human conduct. Their purpose is to help a person determine the moral character of an act. They do this in a general way by indicating the allowable limits of conduct. In this they differ from the remote principle of probabilism, which specifically states that, in conflict situations, it is lawful to follow a probable opinion, even if the opposite is more probable.

62. Richard A. McCormick, "Moral Theology since Vatican II: Clarity or Chaos?" p. 21.

63. "Pastoral Constitution on the Church in the World Today," in *Decrees of the Ecumenical Councils*, vol. 2, p. 1104.

64. *Gaudium et Spes*, no. 51. *Schema Constitutionis Pastoralis de Ecclesia*, p. 37.

65. Richard A. McCormick, "The Primacy of Charity," pp. 18–27.

66. Richard A. McCormick, "The New Morality," p. 771.

67. Richard A. McCormick, *HSCS*, p. 254.

68. Richard A. McCormick, *NMT2*, p. 51.

69. See pages 32–40 above.

CHAPTER 5

1. See chapter 1, pages 20–22

2. Peter Knauer, "La determination du bien et du mal moral par le principe du double effet" (*Nouvelle Revue Théologique* 87 [1965]: 356–376. A shortened version of this article was later published in English as "The Principle of Double Effect," *Theology Digest* 15 (1967): 100–104. An expanded and revised version of the article appeared in 1967 as "The Hermeneutic Function of the Principle of Double Effect," in *Natural Law Forum* 12 (1967). This same version is also found in *RMT1*, pp. 1–39.

3. Joseph A. Selling, "The Problem of Reinterpreting the Principle of Double Effect," *Louvain Studies* 8 (1980), p. 48.

4. Germain Grisez, *The Way of the Lord Jesus*, p. 308.

5. Peter Knauer, "The Hermeneutic Function of the Principle of Double Effect," *RMT1*, p. 1.

6. Ibid., p. 2.

7. Ibid.

8. Ibid., p. 4.

9. Ibid., p. 11.

10. Peter Knauer, "The Hermeneutic Function of the Principle of Double Effect," *RMT1*, p. 12.

11. bid., p. 14.

12. Ibid.

13. Ibid., p. 20.

14. Ibid., p. 19.

15. Ibid.

16. Peter Knauer, "A Good End Does Not Justify an Evil Means—Even in a Teleological Ethics," in *Personalist Morals: Essays in Honour of Professor Louis Janssens*, edited by Joseph A. Selling (Leuven: Leuven University Press, 1988), p. 81.

17. Ibid.

18. Richard A. McCormick, *NMT1* (1965), pp. 9–13.

19. Ibid., p. 11.

20. To prove this imprecision McCormick challenged Knauer's view that a medical operation in which an organ is removed to effect a cure was justified on grounds of proportionate reason since such an organ would only be considered an 'obstacle' whose removal must be seen as merely 'accidental' in the circumstances. In this case the removal of the organ as such is not willed directly because it is justified by proportionate reason. McCormick noted that a little change in the wording of this problem would make it sufficiently clear why Knauer's thesis must not be accepted. Let us imagine, for example, that the 'obstacle' in question is a living, nonviable fetus, or, in the case of a bombing mission in view of a nation's survival through deterrence, that this 'obstacle' which must be 'accidentally' removed is the population of another nation. In Knauer's view, as McCormick understood it at this time, the destruction of the nonviable fetus as well as the destruction of the enemy's noncombatant population are not directly willed and could not be considered moral evils because they are justified by proportionate reason. "One senses immediately that something is wrong here," said McCormick (*NMT1* [1965], p. 10).

21. Richard A. McCormick, *NMT1* (1965), p. 12.

22. Ibid., p. 10.

23. One of the initial contributors to the debate on proportionate reasoning was Bruno Schüller, "What Ethical Principles Are Universally Valid? *Theology Digest* 19 (1971), pp. 23-28. This article is an abridged version of the original German "Zur Problematik allegemein verbindlicher ethischer Grundsätze," *Theologie und Philosophie* 45 (1970), pp. 1-23. Besides Schüller there were other early contributors to the debate on method and norms in moral theology. One of these is Peter Chirico, "Tension, Morality, and Birth Control," *Theological Studies* 28 (1967), pp. 258-285. Chirico argued that due to concupiscence, the human person finds it difficult to relate to the other and to God, or even to keep these various strands of relationships in proper order. The duty of the Christian in this morally difficult situation is to affirm and to internalize all values present in the situation and to implement them externally, as far as possible. While commending Chirico for relating concrete norms to urgent problems, McCormick argued that Chirico's use of the terms 'moral' and 'immoral' seemed to suggest that external acts which do not achieve all possible values are morally wrong. The implication is that the moral quality of the act is ultimately to be measured by its relation to an individual value rather than to a relation to the whole hierarchy of values. McCormick's contention is that where an act observes the hierarchy of values there is no question of moral evil in the act as Chirico's paper supposes. See Richard A. McCormick, *NMT1* (1967), pp. 123-124.

24. Richard A. McCormick, *NMT1* (1968), pp. 219-220.

25. Ibid., p. 219.

26. Ibid., p. 220.

27. Ibid.

28. This lecture was originally published as *Ambiguity In Moral Choice* (Milwaukee: Marquette University Press, 1973). It was reprinted in 1978 with a number of critical essays and co-edited by Paul Ramsey and Richard A. McCormick as *Doing Evil to Achieve Good: Moral Choice in Conflict Situations* (*DEAG*).

29. Richard A. McCormick, *DEAG*, p. 11.

30. Richard A. McCormick, *DEAG*, p. 10.

31. Ibid., p. 11.

32. Ibid., pp. 11-12.

33. William Van der Marck, *Toward a Christian Ethic: A Renewal of Moral Theology*.

34. Cornelius J. Van der Poel, "The Principle of Double Effect," in *Absolutes in Moral Theology?* edited by Charles E. Curran (Washington, D.C.: Corpus Books, 1968), pp. 186-210.

35. Grisez lists eight categories of goods which present themselves as goods-to-be-realized. These include life, play, aesthetic experience, speculative knowledge, integrity, practical reasonableness, friendship, and religion. While the first four are purposes and/or goods which one can seek for their sake, without reference to any other purposes, the latter four are goods or purposes which can be sought for their own sake but whose meaning inherently implies human action. The meaning of the first four, on the contrary, is independent of human action. This moral theory is elaborated in many places in Grisez's writings. See especially Germain Grisez, *Abortion: The Myths, the Realities and the Arguments* (New York and Cleveland: Corpus Books, 1970), pp. 307–346. See also *The Way of the Lord Jesus*, vol. 1, and Germain Grisez and Russell Shaw, *Beyond the New Morality* (Notre Dame and London: University of Notre Dame Press, 1974).

36. Germain Grisez, *Abortion*, p. 315.

37. Ibid., p. 332.

38. Ibid., p. 333.

39. Ibid., p. 26.

40. Ibid., p. 28.

41. Richard A. McCormick, *DEAG*, p. 25.

42. Bruno Schüller, "Direct Killing, Indirect Killing," *RMT1*, pp. 138–157. See also Richard A. McCormick, DEAG, p. 29.

43. Bruno Schüller, "Direct Killing, Indirect Killing," p. 139.

44. Ibid., p. 141.

45. Ibid., p. 142.

46. Ibid., p. 143.

47. Ibid., p. 152.

48. Richard A. McCormick, *NMT1* (1972), p. 352.

49. Richard A. McCormick, *DEAG*, p. 31.

50. Ibid., p. 32.

51. Richard A. McCormick, *DEAG*, pp. 31–32.

52. Richard A. McCormick, "The Removal of a Fetus," p. 391.

53. Richard A. McCormick, *DEAG*, p. 37.

54. Bruno Schüller, "The Double Effect in Catholic Thought," p. 181.

55. Ibid., p. 188.

56. Richard A. McCormick, "Commentary on the Commentaries," *DEAG*, p. 257.

57. Richard A. McCormick, *DEAG*, p. 45.

58. Ibid., p. 46.

59. Ibid., p. 46.

60. Ibid.

61. Richard A. McCormick, *NMT2* (1981), p. 16.

62. Richard A. McCormick, *HBNW*, p. 350.

63. Ibid., p. 47.

64. We should, perhaps, recall the story of Maximilian Kolbe, the Polish priest who gave his life in exchange for that of another prisoner in the hands of the Nazis. To say that people who give their lives to save their neighbors do a proportionate thing is to say that they are aware that we live in a sinful world of conflicts where we are not yet mature in charity but often have to prevent an evil only by a corresponding or even greater loss.

65. Richard A. McCormick, *DEAG*, pp. 49–50.

66. John Connery, "Catholic Ethics: Has the Norm for Rule-Making Changed?" *TS* 42 (1981), p. 234.

67. Ibid., p. 235.

68. Richard A. McCormick, *NMT2*, p. 63.

69. Ibid., p. 64.

70. Ibid.

71. Lisa Sowle Cahill, "Teleology, Utilitarianism, and Christian Ethics," *TS* 42 (1981), p. 617.

72. John Connery, "Catholic Ethics," p. 248.

73. Richard A. McCormick, *NMT2* (1982), p. 66.

74. Lisa Sowle Cahill, "Teleology, Utilitarianism, and Christian Ethics," p. 617.

75. Ibid.

76. Richard A. McCormick, "The New Morality," p. 771.

77. John Finnis, *Moral Absolutes: Tradition, Revision, and Truth* (Washington, D.C.: Catholic University Press, 1991), p. 2.

78. Louis Janssens, "Ontic Evil and Moral Evil," p. 60.

79. Richard A. McCormick, *NMT1* (1971), p. 317.

80. Richard A. McCormick, "Commentary on the Commentaries," p. 232.

81. Richard A. McCormick, *DEAG*, p. 42.

82. Ibid., p. 44.

83. Richard A. McCormick, *NMT2* (1983), p. 118.

84. Ibid.

85. That is, "a law established on the presumption of common and universal danger" (Richard A. McCormick, *DEAG*, p. 44).

86. See William B. Smith, "The Revision of Moral Theology in Richard A. McCormick," *Homiletic and Pastoral Review* 81 (1981), pp. 8–28.

87. John Connery, "Morality of Consequences," *RMT1*, p. 245.

88. William Frankena, "McCormick and the Traditional Distinction," *DEAG*, p. 160.

89. Baruch Brody, "The Problem of Exceptions in Medical Ethics," *DEAG*, p. 56.

90. See Bartholomew M. Kiely, "The Impracticality of Proportionalism," *Gregorianum* 66 (1985), pp. 655–685.

91. John Connery, "Morality of Consequences," p. 245.

92. Ibid.

93. Ibid., p. 246.

94. Richard A. McCormick, *NMT1* (1975), p. 541.

95. Richard A. McCormick, *NMT1* (1978), p. 716.

96. Ibid., p. 717. Welfare values refer to those values such as health, life, pleasure, power, and so on, which help in the fulfillment of the person's potentials for action and enjoyment. Dignity values–fidelity, autonomy, self-respect, trust, integrity of life, justice, and so forth–have little to do with these things. "The values of dignity introduce a quasi-aesthetic dimension into morality. It is these values which cause us to speak of certain actions as fitting or unfitting, as decent or indecent" (Albert Di Ianni, "The Direct/Indirect Distinction in Morals," in *RMT1*, pp. 230–231).

97. Paul Ramsey, "Incommensurability and Indeterminacy in Moral Choice," *DEAG*, p. 90.

98. Ibid., p. 92.

99. Ibid., p. 93.

100. See also Germain Grisez, *The Way of the Lord Jesus*, pp. 56 ff.

101. Paul Ramsey, "Incommensurability and Indeterminacy in Moral Choice," p. 78. Also see, John Langan, "Direct and Indirect– Some Recent Exchanges Between Paul Ramsey and Richard McCormick," *Religious Studies Review* 5:2 (April 1979), p. 98; Sanford S. Levy, "Paul Ramsey and the Rule of Double Effect," *Journal of Religious Ethics* 15 (1987), p. 59.

102. Ramsey, "Incommensurability and Indeterminacy in Moral Choice," p. 79.

103. Ibid., p. 108.

104. Richard A. McCormick, "Commentary on the Commentaries," p. 213.

105. Ibid., p. 214.

106. Ibid., p. 217.

107. Ibid., p. 223.

108. Ibid., p. 224.

109. Ibid., p. 227.

110. Ibid., p. 228.

111. Ibid., p. 229. See also *NMT1* (1979), p. 720.

112. Richard A. McCormick *NMT1* (1969), p. 720.

113. Sanford S. Levy, "Richard McCormick and Proportionate Reason," *Journal of Religious Ethics 13* (1985), p. 259.

114. Ibid., p. 262.

115. Richard A. McCormick, "Commentary on the Commentaries," p. 236. See also NMT1 (1978), p. 720.

116. Richard McCormick, interview with the author, University of Notre Dame, April 22, 1992.

117. Richard A. McCormick, *NMT2* (1982), pp. 67–68.

118. Ibid.

119. Ibid.

CHAPTER 6

1. Casuistry refers to the practical applications of particular principles of a science to particular facts. In moral theology, it signifies that aspect of the discipline which treats of the application of moral principles to singular cases with a view to determining their morality. Casuistry thus includes the definition, interpretation, and application of principles of conduct to past or future action. More than this, its purpose extends also "to the discovery of sound methods along which those principles can truly be interpreted and applied as need arises, or along which conflict of principles can be solved; and in virtue of which the solutions proposed can be vindicated" (Kenneth E. Kirk, *Conscience and Its Problems: An Introduction to Casuistry* [London, New York, Toronto: Longman's Green and Co., 1927], p. 111). I have also extensively treated the notion and history of casuistry in an earlier work. See Paulinus I. Odozor, "Richard A. McCormick and Casuistry: Moral Decision-making in Conflict Situations" (Toronto: Th.M. thesis, 1989). See also E. Hamel, "Casuistry," in *The New Catholic Encyclopedia*, vol. 3 (San Francisco, Toronto, London, Sydney: Catholic University Press, 1967), p. 195.

2. Stephen Pope, "Book Discussion: Richard McCormick's *The Critical Calling*," *CTSA Proceedings* 46 (1991), p. 118.

3. See Paulinus I. Odozor, "Richard A. McCormick and Casuistry."

4. Concentration on bioethical issues means that we will leave out such vital issues as divorce and remarriage, the morality of war, the question of nuclear deterrence, and so on. There are several reasons for these omissions. The principal reason has to do with space and scope. Besides, some of these issues have been adequately handled by other authors. Moreover, their omission does not diminish our appreciation of

the contributions of Richard A. McCormick to the renewal of moral theology.

5. Beside the numerous studies of issues related to bioethics in the "Notes" as well as in many other journals, McCormick has published two books on bioethics: *How Brave a New World?* and *Health and Medicine in the Catholic Tradition.* Even *The Critical Calling* contains a substantial treatment of issues related to ethics and medicine.

6. Richard A. McCormick, "Abortion," *America* 112 (June 19, 1965), p. 878.

7. Richard A. McCormick, "Past Church Teaching on Abortion," *CTSA Proceedings* 23 (June 1968), p. 140.

8. Richard A. McCormick, "Abortion: Aspects of the Moral Question," *America* 117 (December 9, 1967), p. 718.

9. Ibid.

10. William Van der Marck, *Toward a Christian Ethic*, p. 57.

11. Ibid.

12. Richard A. McCormick, "Past Church Teaching on Abortion," p. 144.

13. Ibid., p. 45.

14. McCormick always held that although the direct killing of the innocent is forbidden, there can be circumstances such as cancer of the uterus which can excuse its removal and make the death of the fetus morally acceptable as an unintended side-effect of the life-saving action.

15. See Richard A. McCormick, *NMT1* (1979), p. 764.

16. Richard A. McCormick, "The Consistent Ethic of Life: Is There an Historical Soft Underbelly?" in Joseph Cardinal Bernadin, *Consistent Ethic of Life* (Kansas City, Mo.: Sheed and Ward, 1988), p. 115.

17. Ibid.

18. Richard A. McCormick, "Abortion," *America*, p. 877.

19. Richard A. McCormick, "The Abortion Dossier," *NMT1* (1974), p. 515.

20. Ibid.

21. Ibid., p. 516.

22. Richard A. McCormick, "Public Policy on Abortion," *HBNW*, p. 194.

23. Richard A. McCormick, "Abortion," *America*, p. 879.

24. Ibid.

25. Ibid., p. 879.

26. Richard A. McCormick, "The Ethics of Reproductive Technology," p. 344.

27. Richard A. McCormick, "Theology and Biomedicine," p. 325.

28. Richard A. McCormick, *NMT2* (1984), p. 185.

29. "Abortion," *America*, p. 879.

30. Richard A. McCormick, "Abortion: The Unexplored Middle Ground," *Second Opinion* 10 (March 1989), pp. 41–44.

31. Richard A. McCormick, *DEAG*, p. 28.

32. Richard A. McCormick, "The Abortion Dossier," *NMT1* (1974), p. 516.

33. Ibid.

34. Ibid., p. 517.

35. Richard A. McCormick, "Abortion: The Unexplored Middle Ground," pp. 41–44.

36. Ibid.

37. Richard A. McCormick, "The Abortion Dossier," *NMT1* (1974), p. 492.

38. See Richard A. McCormick, *NMT1*, p. 517.

39. John Mahoney, "McCormick on Medical Ethics," *The Month* (December 1981), p. 412.

40. William P. George, "Moral Statement and Pastoral Adaptation: A Problematic Distinction in McCormick's Theological Ethics," *Annual of Society of Christian Ethics* (1992), pp. 135–136.

41. Ibid., p. 136.

42. Richard A. McCormick, "Homosexuality as a Moral and Pastoral Problem," *TCC*, pp. 305–306.

43. Ibid., p. 308.

44. Ibid.

45. William P. George, "Moral Statement and Pastoral Adaptation," p. 140.

46. Ibid.

47. Ibid., p. 149.

48. Nobert Rigali, "The Unity of Moral and Pastoral Truth," *Chicago Studies* 25 (1986), pp. 224–232.

49. Richard A. McCormick, "The Abortion Dossier," *NMT1* (1974), p. 517.

50. Ibid., p. 518.

51. Richard A. McCormick, "Abortion: The Unexplored Middle Ground," p. 45.

52. Richard A. McCormick, *NMT1* (1974), p. 518.

53. Ibid.

54. Ibid., p. 515.

55. Richard A. McCormick, *HBNW*, p. 197.

56. Richard A. McCormick, "To Save or Let Die: The Dilemma of Modern Medicine," *HBNW*, p. 339.

57. Pope Pius XII, "The Prolongation of Life," an address to an International Congress of Anaesthesiologists, November 24, 1957, *The Pope Speaks* 4 (1957), pp. 395–396. See also *Acta Apostolicae Sedis* 49 (1957), pp. 1031–1032.

58. Richard A. McCormick, *HBNW*, p. 347.

59. Ibid., pp. 347–348.

60. Richard A. McCormick, *HBNW*, p. 350.

61. Ibid., p. 351.

62. Ibid., p. 348.

63. Ibid., p. 346.

64. Richard A. McCormick, "If I Had Ten Things to Share with Physicians," *TCC*, p. 366.

65. Ibid., p. 365.

66. John Paris and Richard A. McCormick, "Saving Defective Infants: Options for Life or Death," *America* (April 23, 1983), p. 316.

67. Two cases in particular captured McCormick's attention. One involved Infant Doe, "a Down's-syndrome baby with a tracheo-esophageal fistula who was left unfed and untreated in a Bloomington, Indiana, hospital for eight days until he expired of natural causes" on April 16, 1982. The second case, which happened in 1981, was that of a Down's-syndrome baby in Leicester, England, who had a stomach disorder and was left untreated. These cases stirred considerable debate concerning hospital policies and societal expectations pertaining to the treatment of severely defective newborns (see Paris and McCormick, "Saving Defective Infants," p. 313).

68. Paul Ramsey, "Two Step Fantastic: The Continuing Case of Brother Fox," *TS* 42 (1981), pp. 122–134.

69. Ibid., p. 133.

70. Richard A. McCormick, *NMT2* (1981), p. 35.

71. Ibid.

72. Robert Veatch and Richard A. McCormick, "The Preservation of Life and Self-Determination," *TS* 41 (1980).

73. John Paris and Richard A. McCormick, "Saving Defective Infants," p. 316.

74. Richard A. McCormick, *NMT2* (1981), p. 36.

75. John Connery, "Quality of Life," *Linacre Quarterly* (February 1986), pp. 27–32.

76. Ibid., p. 27.

77. Ibid., p. 28.

78. Richard A. McCormick, *NMT2* (1981), p. 32.

79. Richard A. McCormick, "Anti-Fertility Pills," p. 294.

80. Ibid.

81. Richard A. McCormick, "Conjugal Love and Conjugal Morality," p. 38.

82. Ibid.

83. Ibid., p. 39.

84. Ibid., p. 38.

85. Ibid.

86. Richard A. McCormick, "Conjugal Love and Conjugal Morality," p. 40.

87. Ibid.

88. See chapter 3.

89. Ibid.

90. Richard A. McCormick, *NMT1* (1968), p. 215.

91. He was convinced that this view, as well as the teaching of the encyclical that genital powers are intrinsically ordained toward procreation, starts from an obsolete biology and on this basis "attributes a meaning to all coitus on the basis of what happens with relative rarity" (ibid., p. 218).

92. Ibid.

93. Ibid., p. 220.

94. Richard A. McCormick, "Moral Theology since Vatican II: Clarity or Chaos?" p. 15.

95. Ibid.

96. Ibid., p. 220.

97. Richard A. McCormick, "Bishops as Teachers, Scholars as Listeners," p. 99.

98. Pope Pius Xll, "Apostolate of the Midwife: An Address by His Holiness to the Italian Catholic Union of Midwives, October 29, 1951," *Catholic Mind* 50 (1952), p. 61.

99. The Sacred Congregation of the Doctrine of the Faith, *Instruction on Respect for Human Life in Its Origin and on the Dignity of Procreation* (Vatican City: Vatican Polyglot Press, 1987), p. 24.

100. Ibid., p. 27.

101. Richard A. McCormick, *NMT1* (1969), pp. 280-290. With reference to *in vitro* fertilization, he showed how two Christian ethicists, Paul Ramsey and Michael Hamilton, both speaking from the Christian faith perspective, had arrived at different conclusions. See Paul Ramsey, "Moral and Religious Implications of Genetic Control," in papers given at Notre Dame conference on Genetics and the Future of Man, pp. 109-169; and Michael Hamilton, "New Life for Old: Genetic Decisions," *Christian Century* 86 (1969), pp. 741-744. McCormick believed that the challenge for theologians involved in these discussions is to show how they arrive at the normative position they take. He summarizes the methodological differ

ences between Hamilton and Ramsey in the following words: "Here we have two Christian thinkers in profound disagreement about the means of genetic control. When faced with the possibility of fecundation in vitro and AID, Hamilton states that he can find no a priori theological reason for excluding such things. Ramsey, on the other hand, had insisted that a contemporary Christian reflection on Scripture leads us to conclude to the inseparability of the spheres of procreation and conjugal love. He then used this norm to exclude certain forms of genetic control. In other words, he did find a priori theological reasons for excluding these things" (Richard A. McCormick, *NMT1* [1969], p. 290).

102. Richard A. McCormick, "Genetic Medicine: Notes on the Moral Literature," *NMT1* (1972), pp. 401–422.

103. Baruch Brody, "The Problem of Exceptions in Medical Ethics," p. 55.

104. Joseph Fletcher, "Ethical Aspects of Genetic Controls," *New England Journal of Medicine* 285 (1971), p. 779.

105. Ibid.

106. Ibid., p. 781.

107. Richard A. McCormick, *NMT1* (1972), pp. 403–404.

108. Ibid., p. 404.

109. Ibid., p. 405.

110. Paul Ramsey, *Fabricated Man* (New Haven: Yale University Press, 1970), p. 124.

111. Ibid., p. 36.

112. Richard A. McCormick, *NMT1* (1972), p. 409.

113. Richard A. McCormick, "Genetic Medicine," p. 409.

114. James M. Gustafson, "Basic Ethical Issues in the Biomedical Fields," *Soundings* 53 (1970), pp. 151–180.

115. Charles E. Curran, "Theology and Genetics: A Multi-faceted Dialogue," *Journal of Ecumenical Studies* 7 (1970), pp. 61–89.

116. James Gustafson, "Basic Ethical Issues in the Biomedical Fields," p. 173.

117. Ibid., pp. 173–174.

118. Ibid., pp. 174.

119. Richard A. McCormick, *NMT1* (1972), p. 418.

120. Ibid., p. 421.

121. Ibid., pp. 421–422.

122. Richard A. McCormick, *NMT1* (1979), p. 796.

123. Ibid., p. 797.

124. Ibid., pp. 798–799.

125. Ibid., p. 799.

126. McCormick has always been conscious of the fact that in regard to IVF we are dealing with a technology which touches on some basic human values: marriage and family, parenting, genealogy and self-identity, human sexual intimacy, and even the sanctity of life itself. Quoting George Annas (*The Washington Post*, April 14, 1985), he points out that it is now possible for a child to be born with five distinct parents: a genetic father, a rearing father, a mother who provides the egg, the woman in whose womb the egg gestates, the mother who rears the child. It is also possible to freeze the egg for a generation, then thaw it and transfer it to its now adult sister, thus making the newborn the daughter or son of its sister (Richard A. McCormick, "Therapy or Tampering? The Ethics of Reproductive Technology," *America* [December 7, 1985], p. 397).

127. See Richard A. McCormick, "Genetic Medicine," pp. 421–422.

128. Richard A. McCormick, "Therapy or Tampering?" p. 400.

129. Ibid.

130. Ibid., pp. 401–402.

131. Richard A. McCormick, "Genetic Technology and Our Common Future," *America* (April 27, 1985), p. 340.

132. Ibid., p. 341.

133. Ibid., p. 342.

134. See McCormick's report on the differing views of Karl Rahner and Pope John Paul II on questions pertaining to the moral status of the embryo (Richard A. McCormick, "Therapy or Tampering: The Ethics of Reproductive Technology," *TCC*, pp. 343–344).

CHAPTER 7

1. Alasdair MacIntyre, *Whose Justice? Which Rationality?* p. 362.

2. See Richard A. McCormick, "Self-Assessment and Self-Indictment," *Religious Studies Review* 13 (January 1987), p. 37. See also *HBNW*, p. x.

3. Richard A. McCormick, "Does Religious Faith Add to Ethical Perception?" p. 170.

4. Anthony Thiselton, "Knowledge, Myth and Corporate Memory," in *Believing in the Church: The Corporate Nature of Faith* (Toronto: Anglican Book Centre, 1982), p. 45.

5. Brian V. Johnstone, "From Physicalism To Personalism," *Studia Moralia* 30 (1992), p. 72.

6. Ibid., p. 81.

7. Ibid.

8. Ibid., p. 82.

9. Ibid., p. 86.

10. Bernard F. Lonergan, "Theology in Its New Context," p. 58.

11. David Tracy, *The Analogical Imagination: Christian Theology and the Culture of Pluralism* (New York: Crossroad, 1989), p. 5.

12. Richard A. McCormick, "Moral Theology 1940–1989: An Overview," pp. 6–18.

13. Richard A. McCormick, interview with the author, University of Notre Dame, April 22, 1992.

14. Ibid.

15. Ibid.

16. Ibid.

17. Although he had previously spoken of these realities in his way, McCormick has lately relied on Richard McBrien's articulation of these themes in the Council documents for his discussion of the ecclesiology of Vatican II.

18. Richard A. McCormick, "Changing my Mind about the Changeable Church," p. 65.

19. Richard A. McCormick, "Moral Theology since Vatican II: Clarity or Chaos?" p. 14.

20. *Gaudium et Spes*, no. 62, in *Vatican II: The Conciliar and Post Conciliar Documents*, p. 966.

21. Ibid., p. 83.

22. Walter J. Burghardt, "The Role of the Scholar in the Catholic Church," in *Moral Theology: Challenges for the Future*, p. 27.

23. Richard A. McCormick, *TCC*, p. 9.

24. Richard A. McCormick, "Dissent in the Church: Loyalty or Liability?" p. 34.

25. Richard A. McCormick, "Self-Assessment and Self Indictment," p. 38.

26. Ibid.

27. See above pages 7–15.

28. Richard A. McCormick, "Moral Theology 1940–1989: An Overview," p. 3.

29. Richard A. McCormick, *NMT1* (1976), p. 588.

30. *Gaudium et Spes*, no. 62, in *Vatican Council II: The Conciliar and Post Conciliar Documents*, p. 966.

See also Richard A. McCormick, "Moral Theology Since Vatican II: Clarity or Chaos?" p. 17. Also, *Critical Calling*, pp. 83, 137; *HBNW*, p. 182; *NMT1*, pp. 525, 744.

31. Richard A. McCormick, "The Search for Truth in the Catholic Context," pp. 279–280.

32. Congregation for the Doctrine of the Faith, "Instruction on the Ecclesial Vocation of the Theologian," *Origins* 28, no. 8 (July 5, 1990).

33. Richard A. McCormick and Richard P. McBrien, "Theology as a Public Responsibility," *America* 165:8 (September 28, 1991), p. 203.

34. Lisa Sowle Cahill, "On Richard McCormick: Reason and Faith in Post-Vatican II Catholic Ethics," p. 109.

35. Richard A. McCormick, interview with the author, University of Notre Dame, April 22, 1992.

36. See Richard A. McCormick, "To Save or Let Die: The Dilemma of Modern Medicine," pp. 339–352.

37. Richard A. McCormick, "Theology and Biomedical Ethics," *Église et Théologie*, p. 316.

38. Martin E. Marty, "Foreword," *HMCT*, p. xi.

39. Walter J. Burghardt, "The Role of the Scholar in the Catholic Church," p. 27.

40. Richard A. McCormick, "Preface," *HBNW*, p. ix.

41. Richard A. McCormick, interview with the author, University of Notre Dame, April 22, 1992. See also, Richard A. McCormick, "Moral Theological Agenda: An Overview," *Catholic New World* 226 (Jan./Feb. 1983), p. 6.

42. Richard A. McCormick, "Genetic Technology and Our Common Future," *TCC*, p. 271.

43. John Langan, "Catholic Moral Rationalism and the Philosophical Basis of Moral Theology," *TS* 50 (1989), pp. 25–43.

44. William C. Spohn, "Richard A. McCormick: Tradition in Transition," *Religious Studies Review* 13 (January 1987), p. 39.

45. Charles E. Curran, "Introduction: Why This Book?" in *Moral Theology: Challenges for the Future*, p. 7.

46. For example, see *NMT1* (1975), pp. 572–573; *NMT1* (1976), pp. 623–624; *NMT1* (1977), pp. 625–627.

47. James M. Gustafson, "The Focus and Its Limitations: Reflections on Catholic Moral Theology," in *Moral Theology: Challenges for the Future*, p. 182.

48. See Albert Jonsen and Stephen Toulmin, *The Abuse of Casuistry: A History of Moral Reasoning* (Berkeley, Los Angeles, London: University of California Press, 1988), pp. 304–306.

49. Richard A. McCormick, *HBNW*, p. x.

50. See James M. Gustafson, "The Focus and Its Limitations: Reflections on Catholic Moral Theology," p. 181.

51. Edward LeRoy Long, Jr., *Conscience and Compromise: An Approach to Protestant Casuistry* (Philadelphia: Westminster Press, 1954), p. 18.

52. William B. Smith, "The Revision of Moral Theology in Richard A. McCormick," pp. 8–28.

53. Jean Porter, "Moral Rules and Moral Actions: A Comparison of Aquinas and Modern Moral Theology," *Journal of Religious Ethics* 17 (Spring 1989), pp. 123–124.

54. Richard A. McCormick, *HBNW*, p. ix.

55. See Richard A. McCormick, "The Consistent Ethic of Life: Is There an Historical Underbelly?" pp. 104–108.

56. See Richard A. McCormick, *NMT1* (1972), p. 386. See also, *TS* 42 (1982), pp. 114–121.

57. See Richard A. McCormick, "Moral Theological Agenda," pp. 4–7; *NMT1* (1978), pp. 735–736; *TCC*, pp. 289–314.

58. Richard A. McCormick, "Moral Theology in the Year 2000: Tradition in Transition," *America* 166 (1992), p. 314.

59. Enda McDonagh, *The Making of Disciples: Tasks of Moral Theology* (Wilmington, Del.: Michael Glazier, 1982), p. 1.

60. Ibid., p. 2.

61. Daniel C. Maguire, "Review" of *NMT1*, *TS* 43 (March 1982), p. 166.

62. Ibid.

63. Richard A. McCormick, "Moral Theology in the Year 2000," p. 318.

64. Richard A. McCormick, *NMT1* (1966), p. 77.

65. Richard A. McCormick, *NMT1*, p. 41.

66. Richard A. McCormick, *NMT2* (1982), p. 51.

67. Ibid., p. 52.

68. Daniel Maguire, "Review" of *DEAG*, *Journal of Religion* 61 (1981), p. 117.

69. Richard A. McCormick, "Bioethics and Method: Where Do We Start?" *Theology Digest* 29 (1981), pp. 303–318.

70. Richard A. McCormick, "Theology and Biomedical Ethics," *Logos* 3 (1982), p. 31.

71. Ibid.

72. William C. Spohn, "Richard A. McCormick: Tradition in Transition," p. 40.

73. John Langan, "Catholic Moral Rationalism and the Philosophical Basis of Moral Theology," pp. 30–34.

74. William J. McCarry, "Recent Canon Law and Moral Theology: Some Important Items," *TS* 1 (1940), p. 418.

75. John A. Gallagher, *Time Past, Time Future*, p. 270.

76. Richard A. McCormick, *HBNW*, p. x.

BIBLIOGRAPHY

WORKS BY RICHARD A. McCORMICK

A. Books and Monographs

"The Removal of a Fetus Probably Dead to Save the Life of the Mother."
Unpublished STD dissertation. Rome: Pontifica Universitas Gre-
goriana, 1957.
Ambiguity in Moral Choice. Milwaukee: Marquette University Press, 1973.
Corrective Vision: Explorations in Moral Theology. Kansas City, Mo.: Sheed
and Ward, 1994.
The Critical Calling: Moral Dilemmas since Vatican II. Washington, D.C.:
Georgetown University Press, 1989.
Doing Evil to Achieve Good: Moral Choice in Conflict Situations. Edited
with Paul Ramsey. Chicago: Loyola University Press, 1978.
Health and Medicine in the Catholic Tradition. New York: Crossroad, 1984.
How Brave a New World? Dilemmas in Bioethics. Garden City, N.Y.:
Doubleday, 1981.
Notes on Moral Theology: 1965 through 1980. Lanham, Md.: University
Press of America, 1980.
Notes on Moral Theology: 1981 through 1984. Lanham, Md.: University
Press of America, 1984.
Readings in Moral Theology No. 1: Moral Norms and Catholic Tradition.
Edited with Charles E. Curran. Mahwah, N.J.: Paulist Press, 1979.
Readings in Moral Theology No. 2: The Distinctness of Christian Ethics.
Edited with Charles E. Curran. Mahwah, N.J.: Paulist Press, 1980.
Readings in Moral Theology No. 3: The Magisterium and Morality. Edited
with Charles E. Curran. Mahwah, N.J.: Paulist Press, 1982.
Readings in Moral Theology No. 4: The Use of Scripture in Moral Theology.
Edited with Charles E. Curran. Mahwah, N.J.: Paulist Press, 1984.
Readings in Moral Theology No. 5: Official Catholic Social Teaching. Edited
with Charles E. Curran. Mahwah, N.J.: Paulist Press, 1986.

224 Bibliography

Readings in Moral Theology No. 6: Dissent in the Church. Edited with Charles E. Curran. Mahwah, N.J.: Paulist Press, 1988.
Readings in Moral Theology No. 7: Natural Law and Theology. Edited with Charles E. Curran. Mahwah, N.J.: Paulist Press, 1991.

B. ARTICLES

"Abortion," *America* 112 (June 19, 1965): 877–881. [Reprinted, condensed form, *Family Digest* 112 (December 1965): 37–43.]
"Abortion: A Changing Morality and Policy," *Hospital Progress* 60 (February 1979): 36–44.
"Abortion and Moral Principles," *The Wrong of Abortion* (New York: American Press, 1966): 1–13.
"Abortion: Rules for Debate," *America* 139 (July 15–22, 1978): 26–30.
"The Abortion Ruling: Analysis and Prognosis Commentary: Fr. McCormick,"*Hospital Progress* 54 (March 1973): 85, 96.
"Abortion: The Unexplored Middle Ground," *Second Opinion* 10 (March 1989): 41–50.
"Adolescent Affection: Toward a Sound Sexuality," *Homiletic and Pastoral Review* 61 (December 1960): 244–261. [Reprinted in "Adolescent Love: Toward a Sound Sexuality" (Derby, N.Y.: St. Paul Publications).]
"Adolescent Masturbation: A Pastoral Problem," *Homiletic and Pastoral Review* 60 (March 1960): 527–540.
"AIDS: The Shape of the Ethical Challenge," *America* 158 (1988): 147–154.
"Anti-Fertility Pills," *Homiletic and Pastoral Review* 62 (May 1962): 692–700.
"Aspects of the Moral Question," *America* 117 (December 9, 1967): 716–719 (on abortion).
"Autonomy and Coercion: Moral Values in Medical Practice," *Linacre Quarterly* 39 (May 1972): 101–105. [Reprinted in *Catholic Mind* 71 (March 1973): 8–11.]
"Begotten, Not Made," *Notre Dame Magazine* 15 (1987): 22–25.
"The Best Interests of the Baby," *Second Opinion* 2 (1986): 18–25.
"Bioethical Issues and the Moral Matrix of U.S. Health Care," *Hospital Progress* 60 (May 1979): 42–45.
"Bioethics in the Public Forum," *Milbank Memorial Fund Quarterly* 61 (1983): 113–126.
"Biomedical Advances and the Catholic Perspective," *Contemporary Ethical Issues in the Jewish and Christian Traditions*, edited by Frederick Greenspan (Hoboken: Ktav Publishing House, 1986): 30–52.

"Bishops' AIDS Letter 'Splendid' Theology," *National Catholic Reporter* 24 (January 22, 1988): 1, 5-6.

"Bishops as Teachers and Jesuits as Listeners," *Studies in the Spirituality of Jesuits* 18 (1986): 1-22.

"Caring or Starving? The Case of Claire Conroy," *America* 152 (1985): 269-273.

"The Catholic Tradition on the Use of Nutrition and Fluids," with John Paris, S.J., *America* 156 (1987): 356-361.

"Changing My Mind about the Changeable Church." In *How My Mind Has Changed*, edited by James M. Wall and David Heim (Grand Rapids, Mich.: Wm B. Eerdmans Publishing Co., 1991).

"The Chill Factor: Recent Roman Interventions," *America* 150 (1984): 475-481.

"Christian Morals," *America* 122 (January 10, 1970): 5-6.

"Christianity and Morality," *Catholic Mind* 75 (October 1977): 17-29.

"The Concept of Authority: A Catholic View," *Seminar on Authority: The Proceedings of a Dialogue between Catholics and Baptists Sponsored by the Ecumenical Institute of Wake Forest University and Belmont Abbey College*, edited by J. William Angell (Winston-Salem: The Ecumenical Institute of Wake Forest University, 1974): 9-18.

"Conference without Consensus," *America* 117 (September 23, 1967): 320-321.

"Conjugal Love and Conjugal Morality," *America* 110 (January 11, 1964): 38-42.

"Conjugal Morality," *Married Love and Children* (New York: American Press, 1966): 24-32.

"The Contemporary Moral Magisterium," *Lectureship* (Mt. Angel Seminary, 1978): 48-60.

"The Cost-Factor in Health Care," *Notre Dame Journal of Law, Ethics and Public Policy* 3 (1988): 161-167.

"The Council on Contraception," *America* 114 (January 8, 1966): 47-48.

"Divorce and Remarriage," *Catholic Mind* 73 (November 1975): 42-57. [Reprinted as "Scheidung und Wiederverheiratung," *Theologie der Gegenwart* 18, no. 4 (1975): 210-220.]

"Document Is Unpersuasive," *Health Progress* 68 (July/August 1987): 53-55.

"Ethical Questions: A Look at the Issues," *Contemporary Ob/Gyn* 20 (November 1982): 227-232.

"The Ethics of In Utero Surgery," with William Barclay, et al., *Journal of the American Medical Association* 246 (October 2, 1981): 1550-1555.

"Ethics of Political Protest," *Catholic Mind* 68 (March 1970): 11-22.

"Ethics of Reproductive Technology: AFS Recommendations, Dissent," *Health Progress* 68 (March 1987): 33–37.

"Experimental Subjects: Who Should They Be?" *Journal of the American Medical Association* 235 (May 17, 1976): 2197.

"Experimentation in Children: Sharing in Sociality," *Hastings Center Report* 6 (December 1976): 41–46.

"Experimentation on the Fetus: Policy Proposals," *Appendix: Research on the Fetus* (Washington, D.C.: U.S. Department of Health, Education, and Welfare Publication, 1975): 5-1-5-11.

"Family Size, Rhythm, and the Pill," *The Problem of Population: Moral and Theological Considerations*, edited by Donald N. Barrett (Notre Dame, Ind.: University of Notre Dame Press, 1964): 58–84.

"Fetal Research, Morality, and Public Policy," *The Hastings Center Report* 5 (June 1975): 26–31.

"The Fifth Synod of Bishops," *Catholic Mind* 79 (September 1981): 46–57.

"Finality," "Double Effect," "Magisterium," in *Dictionary of Christian Ethics*, edited by James Childress and John Macquarrie (Philadelphia: Westminster Press, 1986).

"Foreword," in Philip S. Kaufman, *Why You Can Disagree and Remain a Faithful Catholic* (Bloomington: Meyer-Stone Books, 1989), pp. xi–xii.

"The Fox Case," *Journal of the American Medical Association* 244 (November 14, 1980): 2165–2166.

"Fr. Richard McCormick, S.J., on Pope Paul's Encyclical 'Humanae Vitae' and the Church's Magisterium," *The Catholic Leader* (September 22–September 28, 1974): 10–16.

"The Future of Chaplaincy: Bioethical Problems that Shape Ministry," *Charting the Future of Pastoral Care* (Special Publications of National Association of Catholic Chaplains, v. 4, Summer 1988): 24–39.

"*Gaudium et Spes* and the Bioethical Signs of the Times," *Questions of Special Urgency* (Washington, D.C.: Georgetown University Press, 1986): 79–95.

"General Confession," *Catholic Mind* 64 (May 1966): 10–12.

"Genetic Medicine: Notes on the Moral Literature," *Theological Studies* 33 (September 1972): 531–552. [Reprinted in *New Theology No. 10*, edited by Martin E. Marty and Dean G. Peerman (New York: The Macmillan Company, 1973): 55–84.]

"Genetic Technology and Our Common Future," *America* 152 (1985): 337–342.

"Ghosts in the Wings," *America* 86 (January 5, 1952): 377–379.

"Guidelines for the Treatment of the Mentally Retarded," *Catholic Mind* 79 (November 1981): 44–51.

"Gustafson's God: Who? What? Where? (etc.)," *Journal of Religious Ethics* 13 (1985): 53–70.

"Health and Medicine in the Catholic Tradition," *Ephemerides Theologicae Lovanienses* 62 (1986): 207–215.

"Heterosexual Relationships in Adolescence," *Review for Religious* 22 (January 1963): 75–92. [Reprinted as "Heterosexual Relationships in Adolescence: The Ideal and the Problem," in *Adolescence: Special Cases and Special Problems*, edited by Raymond J. Steimel (Washington, D.C.: The Catholic University of America Press, 1963): 42–65.]

"The History of a Moral Problem," *America* 114 (January 29, 1966): 174–178.

"Human Significance and Christian Significance," in Gene H. Outka and Paul Ramsey, eds., *Norm and Context in Christian Ethics* (New York: Charles Scribner's Sons, 1968): 233–261.

"H.V. in Perspective," *The Tablet* (London: The Tablet Publishing Co., Ltd., February 8, 1975): 126–128.

"The Importance of Naturalness and Conjugal Gametes," *In Vitro Fertilization and Other Assisted Reproduction* (Annals of the New York Academy of Sciences, v. 541) (1988): 664–667.

"Indissolubility and the Right to the Eucharist: Separate Issues or One?" *Canon Law Society of America Proceedings of the 37th Annual Convention* (October 6–9, 1975): 26–37.

"Infant Doe: Where to Draw the Line," *Washington Post* (July 27, 1982): A 15.

"The Insights of the Judeo-Christian Tradition and the Development of an Ethical Code," in *Human Rights and Psychological Research: A Debate on Psychology and Ethics*, edited by Eugene Kennedy (New York: Thomas Y. Crowell, 1975): 23–26.

"Is Professional Boxing Immoral?" *Sports Illustrated* 17 (November 5, 1962): 71–72, 74, 76, 78–80, 82. [Condensed reprint in *Catholic Digest* 27 (May 1963): 108–113.]

"Issue Areas for a Medical Ethics Program," in *The Teaching of Medical Ethics*, edited by Robert M. Veatch, Willard Gaylin, and Councilman Morgen (New York: Hastings Center Publication, 1973): 103–114.

"The Karen Ann Quinlan Case: Editorial," *Journal of the American Medical Association* 234 (December 8, 1975): 1057.

"Kernenergie und Kernwaffen," *Theologie der Gegenwart* 24 (1981): 147–156.

"L'Affaire Curran," *America* 154 (1986): 261–267.

"Lessions intensifs aux nouveau-nes handicapes," *Etudes* (November 1982): 493–502.

"Life/Death Decisions: An Interview with Moral Theologian Fr. Richard McCormick, S.J.," *St. Anthony Messenger* 83 (August 1975): 33–35.

"Life in the Test Tube," *New York Times* (August 8, 1978).

"Life-Saving and Life-Taking: A Comment," *Linacre Quarterly* 42 (May 1975).

"Living-Will Legislation, Reconsidered," *America* 145 (1981): 86–89.

"Loyalty and Dissent: The Magisterium–A New Model," *America* 122 (June 27, 1970): 674–676.

"The Magisterium," in *Authority, Community and Conflict*, edited by Madonna Kolbenschlag (Kansas City, Mo.: Sheed and Ward, 1986): 34–37.

"Maker of Heaven and Earth," in *Christian Theology: A Case Method Approach*, edited by Robert A. Evans and Thomas E. Parker (New York: Harper & Row, 1976): 88–93.

"Man's Moral Responsibility for Health," *Catholic Hospital* 5 (July-August 1977): 6–9.

"Marriage, Morality and Sex-Change Surgery: Four Traditions in Case Ethics," *Hastings Center Report* 11 (August 1981): 10–11.

"Medicaid and Abortion," *Theological Studies* 45 (1984): 715–721.

"Modern Morals in a Muddle," *America* 115 (July 30, 1966): 116.

"Moral Argument in Christian Ethics," *Journal of Contemporary Health Law and Policy* 1 (1985): 3–23.

" 'Moral Considerations' Ill Considered," *America* 166 (March 14, 1992): 210–214.

"Moral Considerations in Autopsy," *Linacre Quarterly* 28 (November 1961): 161–169. [Reprinted in *Hospital Progress* (April 1962): 102–108. Also in *Trustee* 15 (July 1962): 18–21.]

"A Moral Magisterium in Ecumenical Perspective?" *Studies in Christian Ethics* 1 (1988): 20–29.

"Moral Norms and Their Meaning," *Lectureship* (Mt. Angel Seminary, 1978): 31–47.

"The Moral Right of Privacy," *Hospital Progress* 57 (August 1976): 38–42.

"Moral Theology, 1940–1989: An Overview," *Theological Studies* 50 (1989): 3–24.

"Moral Theology in the Year 2000: Reverie or Reality?" (Regina: Campion College, 1989. The Nash Lecture, privately printed.)

"Moral Theology in the Year 2000: Tradition in Transition," *America* 166 (April 18, 1992): 312–318.

"The Moral Theology of Vatican II," in *The Future of Ethics and Moral Theology* (Chicago: Argus Communications, 1968): 7–18.

"A Moralist Reports," *America* 123 (July 11, 1970): 22–23.

"Morality of War," *New Catholic Encyclopedia* 14 (1976): 802–807.

"Neuere Uberlegungen zur Unveranderlichkeit sittlicher Normen," in *Sittliche Normen*, edited by Walter Kerber, S. J. (Dusseldorf: Patmos, 1982): 46–57.

"Neural Tube Defects," in *Maternal Serum Alpha-Fetoprotein: Issues in the Prenatal Screening and Diagnosis of Neural Tube Defects*, edited by Barbara Gastel, et al. (Washington, D.C.: Government Printing Office, 1980): 128-129.

"The New Directives and Institutional Medico-Moral Responsibility," *Chicago Studies* 11 (Fall 1972): 305-314.

"The New Medicine and Morality," *Theology Digest* 21 (Winter 1973): 308-321.

"The New Morality," *America* 118 (June 15, 1968): 769-772.

"1973-1983: Value Impacts of a Decade," *Hospital Progress* 63 (December 1982): 38-41.

"No Short Cuts to Making Public Policy on Abortion," *Washington Star* (March 23, 1981).

"Not What Catholic Hospitals Ordered," *America* 125 (December 11, 1971): 510-513. [Reprinted in *Linacre Quarterly* 39 (February 1972) 16-20.]

"Notes on Moral Theology," *Theological Studies* 16 (December 1965): 596-662.

"Notes on Moral Theology," *Theological Studies* 17 (December 1966): 607-654.

"Notes on Moral Theology: January-June, 1967," *Theological Studies* 28 (December 1967): 749-800.

"Notes on Moral Theology: January-June, 1968," *Theological Studies* 29 (December 1968): 679-741.

"Notes on Moral Theology: January-June, 1969," *Theological Studies* 30 (December 1969): 635-692.

"Notes on Moral Theology: April-September, 1970," *Theological Studies* 32 (March 1971): 66-122.

"Notes on Moral Theology: April-September, 1971," *Theological Studies* 33 (March 1972): 68-119.

"Notes on Moral Theology: April-September, 1972," *Theological Studies* 34 (March 1973): 53-102.

"Notes on Moral Theology: The Abortion Dossier," *Theological Studies* 35 (June 1974): 312-359.

"Notes on Moral Theology: April-September, 1974," *Theological Studies* 36 (March 1975): 77-129.

"Notes on Moral Theology: April-September, 1975," *Theological Studies* 37 (March 1976): 70-119.

"Notes on Moral Theology: 1976," *Theological Studies* 38 (March 1977): 57-114.

"Notes on Moral Theology: 1977," *Theological Studies* 39 (March 1978): 76-138.

"Notes on Moral Theology," *Theological Studies* 40 (1979): 59-112.

"Notes on Moral Theology," *Theological Studies* 42 (1981): 74-121.

"Notes on Moral Theology," *Theological Studies* 43 (1982): 69-124.

"Notes on Moral Theology," *Theological Studies* 44 (1983): 71-122.

"Notes on Moral Theology," *Theological Studies* 45 (1984): 80-138.

"Notes on Moral Theology: Moral Norms–An Update," *Theological Studies* 46 (1985): 50-64.

"Notes on Moral Theology," *Theological Studies* 47 (1986): 69-88.

"Notes on Moral Theology: Dissent in Moral Theology and Its Implications," *Theological Studies* 48 (1987): 87-105.

"Nuclear Deterrence and the Problem of Intention: A Review of the Positions," in *Catholics and Nuclear War*, edited by Philip Murnion (New York: Crossroad, 1983): 168-182.

"Panel Talk on Curriculum: Anti-Semitism and Christian Ethics," in *Judaism and the Christian Seminary Curriculum*, edited by J. Bruce Long (Chicago: Loyola University Press, 1966): 94-98.

"Past Church Teaching on Abortion," *CTSA Proceedings* 23 (June 17-20, 1968): 131-151.

"The Past, Present, and Future of Moral Theology," *Proceedings of 1984 Theological Symposium* (Villanova University, 1985).

"Pastoral Guidelines for Facing the Ambiguous Eighties," in *The Future of Ministry* (Milwaukee: St. Francis Seminary, 1982): 41-44.

"Personal Conscience," *Chicago Studies* 13 (Fall, 1974): 241-252. [Reprinted in *An American Catholic Catechism*, edited by George J. Dyer (New York: The Seabury Press, 1975): 181-193.]

"Pluralism within the Church," in *Catholic Perspectives on Medical Morals*, edited by Edmund D. Pellegrino, John P. Langan, John Collins Harvey (Dordrecht: Kluwer Academic Publishers, 1989): 147-167.

"The Polygraph in Business and Industry," *Theological Studies* 27 (September 1966): 421-433.

"Practical and Theoretical Considerations," in *The Problem of Population*, vol. 3: *Educational Considerations* (Notre Dame, Ind.: University of Notre Dame Press, 1965): 50-73.

"The Preservation of Life," *Linacre Quarterly* 43 (May 1976): 94-100.

"The Preservation of Life and Self-determination," *Theological Studies* 41 (1980): 390-396.

"Presidential Address," *CTSA Proceedings* 26 (June 14-17, 1971): 239-250. [Reprinted as "Leadership and Authority," *Catholic Mind* 70 (March 1972) 8-16. Also reprinted as "Leadership and Authority," in *Dimensions in Religious Education*, edited by John R. McCall (Haverton: CIM Books, 1973): 61-68.]

"The Priest and Teen-age Sexuality," *The Homiletic and Pastoral Review* 65 (February 1965): 379-387. Part 2 in vol. 65 (March 1965): 473-480. [Reprinted in *All Things to All Men*, edited by Joseph F.X. Cevettello (New York: Joseph F. Wagner, Inc., 1965): 362-381.

"The Primacy of Charity," *Perspectives* (August/September 1959): 18-27.

"The Principle of the Double Effect," *Concilium* 120 (December 1976): 105-120.

"The Problem of Motivation," in *The Population Crisis and Moral Responsibility*, edited by J. Philip Wogaman (Washington, D.C.: Public Affairs Press, 1973): 320-323.

"A Proposal for 'Quality of Life' Criteria for Sustaining Life," *Hospital Progress* 56 (September 1975): 76-79.

"Proxy Consent in the Experimentation Situation," *Perspectives in Biology and Medicine* 18 (Autumn 1974): 2-20. [Reprinted in *Love and Society: Essays in the Ethics of Paul Ramsey*, edited by James T. Johnson and David H. Smith (Missoula: Scholars Press, 1974), pp. 209-227.]

"Psychosexual Development in Religious Life," *Review for Religious* 23 (November 1964): 724-741.

"The Quality of Life, The Sanctity of Life," *Hastings Center Report* 8 (February 1978): 30-36.

"Reflections on Sunday Observance," *The American Ecclesiastical Review* 161 (July 1969): 55-61.

"Response to Professor Curran-II," *CTSA Proceedings* 29 (June 10-13, 1974): 161-164.

"Restatement on Tubal Ligation Confuses Policy with Normative Ethics," *Hospital Progress* 61 (September 1980): 40.

"Romische Erklarung zur Sexualethik," *Theologie der Gegenwart* 19, no. 2 (1976): 72-76.

"Saving Defective Infants: Options for Life or Death," with John Paris, S.J., *America* 148 (1983): 313-317.

"Scheidung und Wiederverheiratung als pastorales Problem," *Theologie der Gegenwart* 24 (1981): 21-32.

"The Search for Truth in the Catholic Context," *America* 155 (1986): 276-281.

"Searching for the Consistent Ethic of Life," in *Personalist Morals*, edited by J. A. Selling (Leuven: Leuven University Press, 1988): 135-146.

"Self-Assessment and Self-Indictment," *Religious Studies Review* 13 (1987): 37-39.

"Sexual Ethics-An Opinion," *National Catholic Reporter* 12 (January 30, 1976): 9.

"The Shape of Moral Evasion in Catholicism," *America* 159 (1988): 183–188.

"The Silence since *Humanae Vitae*," *America* 129 (July 21, 1973): 30–33. [Reprinted in *Linacre Quarterly* 41 (Fall 1974): 26–32.]

" 'Sleeper' on DNA," *National Catholic Reporter* (July 15, 1977): 9.

"The Social Responsibility of the Christian," *The Australian Catholic Record* 52 (July 1975): 253–263. [Digested in *Theology Digest* 24 (Spring 1976): 11–14.]

"Some Neglected Aspects of Responsibility for Health," *Perspectives in Biology and Medicine* 22 (1978): 31–43.

"Standards and the Stagirite," *America* 87 (May 3, 1952): 135–137.

"Sterilization and Theological Method," *Theological Studies* 37 (September 1977): 417–477.

"Sterilization: The Dilemma of Catholic Hospitals," with Corrine Bayley, *America* 143 (1980): 222–225.

"Sterilization: The Dilemma of Catholic Hospitals," in *History and Conscience*, edited by R. Gallagher and Brendan McConvery (Southampton: Camelot Press, 1989): 105–122.

"Sterilization und Theologische Methode," *Theologie der Gegenwart* 20 (1977): 110–114.

"Surrogate Motherhood: A Stillborn Idea," *Second Opinion* 5 (1987): 128–132.

"Symposium: Bioethical Issues in Organ Transplantation," *Southern Medical Journal* 79 (1986): 1471–1479.

"The Teaching of the Magisterium and Theologians," *CTSA Proceedings* 24 (June 16–19, 1969): 239–254.

"The Teaching Role of the Magisterium–and of the Theologians," *The Catholic Leader* (August 11–August 17, 1974): 7–8.

"Theologians View the Directives," *Hospital Progress* 53 (December 1972): 51, 53, 54, 68.

"Theologians View the Directives," *Hospital Progress* 54 (February 1973): 73–74.

"Theological Dimensions of Bioethics," *Logos* 3 (1982): 25–46.

"Theology and Bioethics, "*Hastings Center Report* 19 (March/April 1989): 5–10.

"Theology and Bioethics: Christian Foundations," in *Theology and Bioethics*, edited by Earl Shelp (Dordrecht: Reidel, 1985): 95–114.

"Theology and Biomedical Ethics," *Église et théologie* 13 (1982): 311–332.

"Theology as a Dangerous Discipline," *Georgetown Graduate Review* 1 (1981): 2–3.

"The Theology of Revolution," *Catholic Mind* 67 (April 1969): 23–32.

"Therapy or Tempering? The Ethics of Reproductive Technology," *America* 153 (1985): 396–403.

"To Save or Let Die," *America* 130 (July 13, 1974): 6–10. Simultaneously published in *The Journal of the American Medical Association* 229 (July 1974): 172–176. [Reprinted in *Life or Death Who Controls?* edited by Nancy C. Ostheimer and John M. Ostheimer (New York: Springer Publishing Company, 1976): 254–265.

"To Save or Let Die: State of the Question," *America* 131 (October 5, 1974): 169–173).

"Toward a Dialogue," *Commonweal* 80 (June 5, 1964): 313–317.

"Toward a New Sexual Morality?" *The Catholic World* 202 (October 1965): 10–16.

"Transplantation of Organs: A Commentary on Paul Ramsey," *Theological Studies* 36 (September 1975): 503–509.

"Unanswered Questions on Test Tube Life," with Andre Hellegers, *America* 139 (August 12–19, 1978): 74–78.

"The Vatican Document on Bioethics," *America* 156 (1987): 24–28.

"The Vatican Document on Bioethics: A Response," *America* 156 (1987): 247–248.

"Von Umgang mit dem Lebensraum," Theologie der Gegenwart 14, no. 4 (1971): 209–216.

McCormick, Richard A., S.J., et al. "A C & C Symposium: Paying for Abortion: Is the Court Wrong?" *Christianity and Crisis* 37 (September 19, 1977): 202–207.

——, and CTSA Study Committee, "The Problem of Second Marriages: An Interim Pastoral Statement by the Study Committee Commissioned by the Board of Directors of CTSA–Report of August 1972," *CTSA Proceedings* 27 (September 1–4, 1972): 234–240. [Reprinted in *America* 127 (October 7, 1972): 258–260.

——, and Andre E. Hellegers, "Legislation and the Living Will," *America* 136 (March 12, 1977): 210–213.

——, George W. MacRae, and Ladislas Orsy, "Brussels Hosts the Theologians," *America* 123 (October 3, 1970): 232, 234.

——, and Leroy Walters, "Fetal Research and Public Policy," *America* 132 (June 21, 1975): 473–476.

C. *BOOK REVIEWS*

Bier, William C., ed., *Personality and Sexual Problems, America* 110 (May 23, 1964) 738.

Callahan, Daniel, ed., *The Catholic Case for Contraception, America* 120 (May 24, 1969): 627-628.

Callan, Charles J., and John A. McHugh, revised and enlarged by Edward P. Farrell, *Moral Theology, The Priest* 15 (April 1959): 342-344.

Chafetz, Morris E., *Alcoholism and Society, America* 107 (June 9, 1962): 386-387.

Contraception and Holiness, introduction by Archbishop Thomas D. Roberts, *America* 111 (November 14, 1964): 626-628.

Curran, Charles E., *Catholic Moral Theology in Dialogue, America* 127 (July 22, 1972): 44-45.

——, *Contemporary Problems in Moral Theology, America* 122 (May 16, 1970): 527.

de Lestapsis, Stanislas, *Family Planning and Modern Problems*, trans. Trevett, Reginald F., *America* 106 (December 9, 1961): 370.

Dupre, Louis, *Contraception and Catholics, America* 111 (November 14, 1964): 628-629.

Ford, John C., and Gerald Kelly, *Marriage Question: Contemporary Moral Theology, Vol. II, America* 110 (January 18, 1964): 112.

Gassert, Robert G., *Psychiatry and Religious Faith, America* 111 (September 19, 1964): 312-313.

Gibbons, William J., ed., *Population, Resources and the Future, The Catholic World* 194 (October 1961): 56-59.

Gilbert, Henri, *Love in Marriage, America* 111 (June 27, 1964): 870.

Gilleman, Gerard, *The Primacy of Charity on Moral Theology*, trans. William F. Ryan and Andre Vachon, *The Priest* 16 (July 1960): 346-347.

Grisez, Germain G., *Abortion: The Myths, the Realities, and the Arguments, America* 124 (April 17, 1971): 412-413.

——, *Contraception and the Natural Law, The American Ecclesiastical Review* 153 (August 1965): 119-125.

Gustafson, James, *Christian Ethics and the Community, America* 126 (February 26, 1972): 214-215.

Hagmaier, George, *Counselling the Catholic, Review for Religious* 19 (1960): 391.

Häring, Bernard, *Christian Maturity, America* 116 (April 8, 1967): 538.

——, *Christian Renewal in a Changing World, America* 112 (March 27, 1965): 433.

——, *Morality Is for Persons, America* 125 (September 11, 1971): 155-158.

——, *Road to Relevance, America* 122 (May 16, 1970): 527.

——, *The Time of Salvation, America* 114 (June 18, 1966): 859-860.

Kelly, George A., *Birth Control and Catholics, America* 109 (October 19, 1963): 465-466.

Lepp, Ignace, *The Authentic Morality*, *America* 112 (March 27, 1965): 433–434.
Monden, Louis, *Sin, Liberty, and Law*, *America* 113 (November 13, 1965): 602–604.
Oraison, Marc, *The Celibate Condition and Sex*, *Homiletic and Pastoral Review* 68 (February 1968): 446–448.
——, *The Human Mystery of Sexuality*, *Homiletic and Pastoral Review* 67 (May 1967): 707–708.
Osborn, Fairfield, ed., *Our Crowded Planet*, *America* 107 (November 3, 1962): 110–115.
Vaux, Kenneth, *Who Shall Live?*, *America* 122 (April 18, 1970): 424–425.

SECONDARY SOURCES

Aristotle. *Nichomechean Ethincs*. Translated by Martin Oswald. New York and Indianapolis: Bobbs-Merrill Co., 1962.
Aubert, Roger. "Modernism." In *Encyclopedia of Theology: The Precise Sacramentum Mundi*, edited by Karl Rahner, 969–974 New York: Crossroad, 1986.
Baum, Gregory. "The Christian Adventure – Risk and Renewal." *Critic* 23 (1965): 41–53.
Bernadin, Joseph Cardinal. *Consistent Ethic of Life*. Kansas City, Mo.: Sheed and Ward, 1988.
Bromiley, Geoffrey W. "Casuistry." In *Baker's Dictionary of Christian Ethics*. Grand Rapids, Mich.: Baker Book House, 1967.
Boyle, John P. "The American Experience in Moral Theology." *CTSA Proceedings* 41 (1986): 23–46.
Brody, Baruch. "The Problem of Exceptions in Medical Ethics." In *Doing Evil To Achieve Good*, edited by Paul Ramsey and Richard A. Mc-Cormick, 54–68.
Burghardt, Walter J. "The Role of the Scholar in the Catholic Church." In *Moral Theology: Challenges for the Future*, edited by Charles Curran, 15–31.
Cahill, Lisa Sowle. "Human Sexuality." In *Moral Theology: Challenges for the Future*, edited by Charles Curran, 193–212.
——. "On Richard McCormick: Reason and Faith and Ethics in Post-Vatican II Catholic Ethics." *Second Opinion* 9 (November 1988): 108–130.
——. "Teleology, Utilitarianism, and Christian Ethics." *Theological Studies* 42 (1981): 601–629.

——. "Within Shouting Distance: Paul Ramsey and Richard McCormick on Method." *Journal of Medicine and Philosophy* 4.4 (1979): 398–417.

Carney, Fredrick S. "On McCormick and Teleological Morality." *Journal of Religious Ethics* 6 (1978): 81–105.

Chenu, M.-D. "The Plan of St. Thomas' Summa Theologiae." *Cross Currents* 2 (1952): 67–79.

Childress, James. "Reproductive Interventions: Theology, Ethics, and Public Policy." In *Moral Theology: Challenges for the Future*, edited by Charles Curran, 285–312.

Chirico, Peter. "Tension, Morality and Birth Control." *Theological Studies* 28 (1967): 258–285.

Congregation for the Doctrine of the Faith. *Instruction on Respect for Human Life in Its Origin and on the Dignity of Procreation.* Vatican Polyglot Press, 1987.

——. "Instruction on the Ecclesial Vocation of the Theologian." *Origins* 28 (July 5, 1990): 119–126.

Connell, F. J. "Systems of Morality." In *New Catholic Encyclopedia*, vol. 9: 1131–1134. San Francisco, Toronto, London, Sydney: Catholic University Press, 1967.

Connery, John. "Catholic Ethics: Has the Norm for Rule-Making Changed?" *Theological Studies* 42 (1981): 232–250.

——. "Morality of Consequences: A Critical Appraisal." In *Readings in Moral Theology No. 1*, edited by Charles E. Curran and Richard A. McCormick: 244–266.

——. "Quality of Life." *Linacre Quarterly* (February 1986): 27–32.

——. "The Teleology of Proportionate Reason." *Theological Studies* 44 (1983): 489–496.

Crotty, Nicholas. "Conscience and Conflict." *Theological Studies* 32 (1971): 208–232.

Curran, Charles E. "Introduction." In *Moral Theology: Challenges for the Future: Essays in Honor of Richard A. McCormick, S.J.*, edited by Charles E. Curran, 1–11. New York: Paulist Press, 1990.

——. "The Teaching Function of the Church in Morality." In *Moral Theology: Challenges for the Future*, edited by Charles E. Curran, 155–179.

——. "Theology and Genetics: A Multi-faceted Dialogue." *Journal of Ecumenical Studies* 7 (1970): 61–89.

——, ed. *Moral Theology: Challenges for the Future: Essays in Honor of Richard A. McCormick. S. J.* New York: Paulist Press, 1990.

Daly, Robert J., et al. *Christian Biblical Ethics: From Biblical Revelation to Contemporary Christian Praxis: Method and Content.* New York: Paulist Press, 1984.

Davis, Henry. *Moral and Pastoral Theology* (4 vols.). London: Sheed and Ward, 1945.

Dolan, Jay P. *The American Catholic Experience: A History from Colonial Times to the Present*. Garden City, N.Y.: Image Books, 1986. Reprinted; Notre Dame: University of Notre Dame Press, 1992.

Dulles, Avery. "Authority and Conscience." In *Readings in Moral Theology No. 6*, edited by Charles E. Curran and Richard A. McCormick (1988): 97–111.

——. "The Magisterium in History: A Theological Reflection." *Chicago Studies* 17 (1978): 270–290.

——. "What Is Magisterium?" *Origins* 6 (1976): 81–87.

Finnis, John. *Moral Absolutes: Tradition, Revision and Truth*. Washington, D.C.: Catholic University Press, 1991.

——. *Fundamentals of Ethics*. Washington: Georgetown University Press, 1983.

Flannery, Austin, ed. *Vatican Council II: The Conciliar and Post Conciliar Documents*. Northport, N.Y.: Costello Publishing Co., 1984.

Flectcher, Joseph. "Ethical Aspects of Genetic Controls." *New England Journal of Medicine* 285 (1971): 779.

——. "Four Indicators of Personhood–the Enquiry Matures." In *On Moral Medicine: Theological Perspectives in Medical Ethics*, edited by Stephen E. Lammers and Allen Verhey, 275–278. Grand Rapids, Mich.: William B. Eerdmans, 1987.

Fogarty, Gerald P. *The Vatican and the American Catholic Hierarchy from 1870 to 1965*. Wilmington, Del.: Michael Glazier, 1985.

Ford, John, and Germain Grisez. "Contraception and the Infallibility of the Ordinary Magisterium." *Theological Studies* 39 (1978).

Ford, John, and Gerald, Kelly. *Contemporary Moral Theology*, vol 1: *Questions in Fundamental Moral Theology*. Westminster, Md.: Newman Press, 1960.

Ford, John C., and John J. Lynch. "Contraception: A Matter of Practical Doubt?" *Homiletic and Pastoral Review* 68 (1968): 563–574.

Frankena, William. "McCormick and the Traditional Distinction." In *Doing Evil to Achieve Good*, edited by Richard A. McCormick and Paul Ramsey, 145–164.

Fuchs, Joseph. "The Absoluteness of Moral Terms." In *Readings in Moral Theology, vol. 1*, edited by Richard A. McCormick and Charles E. Curran (1979): 94–137.

——. *Christian Ethics in a Secular Arena*. Dublin: Gill and Macmillan; Washington: Georgetown University Press, 1984.

——. *Christian Morality: The Word Becomes Flesh*. Dublin: Gill and Macmillan; Washington: Georgetown University Press, 1987.

——. "Conscience and Conscientious Fidelity." In *Moral Theology: Challenges for the Future*, edited by Charles E. Curran.

——. "Is There a Specifically Christian Morality?" In *Readings in Moral Theology No. 2*, edited by Charles E. Curran and Richard A. McCormick (1980): 3–19.

——. "An Ongoing Discussion in Christian Ethics: Intrinsically Evil Acts?" In *Christian Ethics in a Secular Arena*, 71–90. Washington, D.C.: Georgetown University Press; Dublin: Gill and Macmillan, 1984.

——. "Teaching Morality: The Tension between Bishops and Theologians within the Church." In *Readings in Moral Theology No. 6*, edited by Charles E. Curran and Richard A. McCormick (1988): 330–353.

Gallagher, John A. *Time Past, Time Future: An Historical Study of Catholic Moral Theology*. New York: Paulist Press, 1990.

George, William P. "Moral Statement and Pastoral Adaptation: A Problematic Distinction in McCormick's Theological Ethics." *Annual of Society of Christian Ethics* (1992): 135–156.

Grisez, Germain. *Abortion: The Myths, the Realities, and the Arguments*. New York: Corpus Books, 1970.

——. "The First Principle of Practical Reason: A Commentary on the *Summa Theologiae* 1-2, Question 94, Article 2." *Natural Law Forum* 10 (1965): 168–201.

——. "Infallibility and Specific Moral Norms: A Review Discussion." In *Readings in Moral Theology No. 6*, edited by Charles E. Curran and Richard A. McCormick (1988): 58–96.

——. *The Way of the Lord Jesus*, vol 1: *A Summary of Catholic Moral Theology*. Chicago: Franciscan Herald Press, 1983.

Grisez, Germain, and Russell Shaw. *Beyond the New Morality*, 2d ed. Notre Dame, Ind.: University of Notre Dame Press, 1980.

Gula, Richard M. *Reason Informed by Faith: Foundations of Catholic Morality*. New York: Paulist Press, 1989.

——. *What Are They Saying about Moral Norms?* New York: Paulist Press, 1982.

Gustafson, James M. "Basic Ethical Issues in the Bio-medical Fields." *Soundings* 53 (1970): 151–180.

——. *Christ and the Moral Life*. Chicago: University of Chicago Press, 1968.

——. "The Focus and Its Limitations: Reflections on Catholic Moral Theology." In *Moral Theology: Challenges for the Future*, edited by Charles E. Curran (1990): 179–190.

——. "Roman Catholic and Protestant Interaction in Ethics: An Interpretation." *Theological Studies* 50 (1989): 44–69.

Halsey, William M. *The Survival of Innocence: Catholicism in an Era of Disillusionment, 1920-1940*. Notre Dame, Ind.: University of Notre Dame Press, 1980.

Hamel, E. "Casuistry." In *New Catholic Encyclopedia*, vol. 3. San Francisco, Toronto, London, Sydney: Catholic University Press, 1965.

Hamilton, Michael. "New Life for Old: Genetic Decisions." *Christian Century* 86 (1969): 741–744.

Häring, Bernard. "Moral Systems." In *Encyclopedia of Theology: The Concise Sacramentum Mundi*, edited by Karl Rahner, 996–1000. New York: Crossroad, 1986.

——. "Moral Theology: Catholic." In *Encyclopedia of Theology: The Concise Sacramentum Mundi*, edited by Karl Rahner, 987–993. New York: Crossroad, 1986.

Hauerwas, Stanley. "Nature, Reason, and the Task of Theological Ethics." In *Readings in Moral Theology No. 7*, edited by Charles E. Curran and Richard A. McCormick (1991): 43–71.

Hennesey, James. *American Catholics: A History of the Roman Catholic Community in the United States*. Oxford, New York, Toronto: Oxford University Press, 1981.

——. "Leo XIII's Thomistic Revival: A Political Philosophical Event." *Journal of Religion* 58 (1978 Supplement): S185–S197.

Hill, John. "The Debate Between McCormick and Frankena." *Irish Theological Quarterly* 49 (1982): 121–133.

Himes, Kenneth R. "The Contribution of Theology to Catholic Moral Theology." In *Moral Theology: Challenges for the Future*, edited by Charles E. Curran (1990): 48–73.

Hollenbach, David. "Fundamental Theology and the Christian Moral Life." In *Faithful Witness: Foundations of Theology for Today's Church*, edited by Leo J. O'Donovan and T. Holland Shanks, 167–184. New York: Crossroad, 1989.

Hoose, Bernard. *Proportionalism: The American Debate and Its European Roots*. Washington, D.C.: Georgetown University Press, 1987.

Janssens, Louis. "Artificial Insemination: Ethical Reflections." *Louvain Studies* 8 (1980): 3–29.

——. "Morale Conjugale et Progestogènes." *Ephemerides Theologicae Lovanienses* 39 (1963): 787–826.

——. "Norms and Priorities in a Love Ethic." *Louvain Studies* 6 (September 1977): 207–238.

——. "Ontic Evil and Moral Evil." In *Readings in Moral Theology No. 1*, edited by Richard A. McCormick and Charles E. Curran (1978): 40–93.

Janssens, Louis, and Jacques Ferin. "Progestogènes et Morale Conjugale." In *Bibliotheca Ephemeridum Theologicarum Lovaniensium* 22: 9–48. Louvain: Publications Universitaires; Gembloux: Duculot, 1963.

Johnstone, Brian V. "From Physicalism to Personalism." *Studia Moralia* 30 (1992): 71–96.

——. "The Meaning of Proportionate Reason in Contemporary Moral Theology." *The Thomist* 49 (1985): 223-247.

Jonsen, R. Albert, and Stephen Toulmin. *The Abuse of Casuistry: A History of Moral Reasoning.* Berkeley: University of California Press, 1988.

Kaiser, Robert Blair. *The Politics of Sex and Religion.* Kansas City: Leaven, 1985.

Kiely, Bartholomew M. "The Impracticality of Proportionalism." *Gregorianum* 66 (1985): 655-686.

Kirk, Kenneth E. *Conscience and Its Problems: An Introduction to Casuistry.* London, New York, Toronto: Longmans Green and Co., 1927.

Knauer, Peter. "A Good End Does Not Justify an Evil Means–Even in a Teleological Ethics." In *Personalist Morals,* edited by Joseph Selling (1988): 71-85.

——. "The Hermeneutic Function of the Principle of Double Effect." In *Readings in Moral Theology No. 1,* edited by Charles E. Curran and Richard A. McCormick (1979): 1-39.

Langan, John. "Catholic Moral Rationalism and the Philosophical Basis of Moral Theology." *Theological Studies* 50 (1989): 25-43.

——. "Direct and Indirect–Some Recent Exchanges between Paul Ramsey and Richard McCormick." *Religious Studies Review* 5 (1979): 95-101.

Leo XIII, Pope. *Aeterni Patris.* In *The Great Encyclical Letters of Pope Leo XIII.* New York, Cincinnati, Chicago: Benzinger Brothers, 1903.

——. "True and False Americanism in Religion." In *The Great Encyclical Letters of Pope Leo XIII.*

Levy, Sanford S. "Richard McCormick and Proportionate Reason." *Journal of Religious Ethics* 13 (1985): 258-278.

Lindbeck, George, A. *The Nature of Doctrine: Religion and Theology in a Postliberal Age.* Philadelphia: Westminster Press, 1984.

Lonergan, Bernard J. F. *Method in Theology.* Minneapolis, Minn.: Seabury Press, 1972.

——. "Theology in Its New Context." In *A Second Collection; Papers by Bernard J.F. Lonergan, S.J.,* edited by William F. J. Ryan, S.J., and Bernard J. Tyrell, S.J., 55-86 London: Darton, Longman and Todd, 1970.

Long, Edward Leroy, Jr. *Conscience and Compromise: An Approach to Protestant Casuistry.* Philadelphia: Westminster Press, 1954.

MacIntyre, Alasdair. *After Virtue: A Study in Moral Theory,* 2d ed. Notre Dame, Ind: University of Notre Dame Press, 1987.

——. "Epistemological Crises, Narrative, and Philosophy of Science." In *Why Narrative?: Readings in Narrative Theology,* edited by Stanley

Hauerwas and L. Gregory Jones, 138-157. Grand Rapids, Mich.: William B. Eerdmans, 1989.

——. *Three Rival Versions of Moral Enquiry: Encyclopaedia, Genealogy, and Tradition.* Notre Dame, Ind.: University of Notre Dame Press, 1990.

——. *Whose Justice? Which Rationality?* Notre Dame, Ind.: University of Notre Dame Press, 1988.

MacNamara, Vincent. *Faith and Ethics: Recent Roman Catholicism.* Dublin: Gill & Macmillan; Washington: Georgetown University Press, 1985.

——. "Religion and Morality." *The Irish Theological Quarterly* 44 (1977): 105-116; 175-191.

Maguire, Daniel C. "Moral Absolutes and the Magisterium." In *Moral Absolutes in Moral Theology?* edited by Charles E. Curran. Washington, D.C.: Corpus Books, 1968.

——. "Review of *Doing Evil to Achieve Good.*" *Journal of Religion* 61 (1981): 115-117.

——. "Review of Notes on Moral Theology." *Theological Studies* 43 (1982).

Maguire, Majorie Reiley. "Personhood, Covenant, and Abortion." In *Abortion and Catholicism: The American Debate,* edited by Patricia beatie Jung and Thomas A. Shannon 100-121.

Mahoney, John. "McCormick on Medical Ethics." *The Month,* December 1981: 408-413.

——. *The Making of Moral Theology: A Study of The Roman Catholic Tradition.* Oxford: Clarendon Press, 1989.

Mangan, Joseph. "An Historical Analysis of the Principle of Double Effect." *Theological Studies* 10 (1949): 41-61.

McCarry, William J. "Recent Canon Law and Moral Theology: Some Important Items." *Theological Studies* 1 (1940): 412-443.

McCool, Gerald. *Catholic Theology in the Nineteenth Century.* New York: Seabury Press, 1987.

——. "Twentieth Century Scholasticism." *Journal of Religion* 58 (1978 Supplement): S198-S220.

McDonagh, Enda. *The Making of Disciples: Tasks of Moral Theology.* Wilmington, Del.: Michael Glazier, 1982.

——. "Teaching Moral Theology Today." *Irish Theological Quarterly* 32 1966: 195-207.

Meehan, Mary. "Defending the Vulnerable." *Second Opinion* 10 (1989): 60-65.

Mortimer, R. C. "Equiprobabilism." In *Baker's Dictionary of Christian Ethics.* Grand Rapids, Mich.: Baker Book House, 1967.

Murphy, F. X. "History of Moral Theology." In *New Catholic Encyclopedia,* vol. 9: 1117-1119. San Francisco, Toronto, London, Sydney: Catholic University Press, 1967.

Ngindu, M., ed. *Combats pour un christianisme africain: Mélanges en l'honneur du Professeur V. Mulago.* Kinshasa: Faculté de Théologie Catholique, 1981.

Noldin, H., A. Schmitt, and G. Heinzel. *Summa Theologiae Moralis,* 2 vols., 33rd ed. Innsbrück: Felizian Rauch, 1960.

Odozor, Paulinus I. "Richard A. McCormick and Casuistry: Moral Decision-Making in Conflict Situations." Unpublished Th.M. thesis. Regis College, University of Toronto, 1989.

Pius XI, Pope. *Casti Connubii.* In *Seven Great Encyclicals.* Glen Rock, N.J.: Paulist Press, 1939.

Pius XII, Pope. "Apostolate of the Midwife: An Address by His Holiness to the Italian Catholic Union of Midwives, October 29, 1951." *Catholic Mind* 50 (1952).

——. "The Prolongation of Life." An Address to an International Congress of Anesthesiologists, 24 November 1957, *The Pope Speaks* 4 (1957).

Poole, Stafford. *Seminary in Crisis.* New York: Herder and Herder, 1965.

Pope, Stephen. "Book Discussion: Richard McCormick's *The Critical Calling.*" *CTSA Proceedings* (1991): 118–120.

Porter, Jean. "Moral Rules and Moral Actions: A Comparison of Aquinas and Modern Moral Theology." *Journal of Religious Ethics* (1989): 123–149.

——. *The Recovery of Virtue: The Relevance of Aquinas for Christian Ethics.* Louisville, Ky.: Westminster/John Knox Press, 1990.

Rahner, Karl. "Anonymous and Explicit Faith." In *Theological Investigations,* Vol. 16. London: Darton, Longman and Todd, 1979.

——. "Anonymous Christians." In *Theological Investigations,* Vol. 6. London: Darton, Longman and Todd, 1969.

——. "History of the World and Salvation History." In *Theological Investigations,* Vol. 5. London: Darton, Longman and Todd, 1966.

Ramirez, J. M. "Moral Theology." In *New Catholic Encyclopedia,* Vol. 9. San Francisco, Toronto, London, Sydney: Catholic University Press, 1967.

Ramsey, Paul. "The Case of the Curious Exception." In *Norm and Context in Christian Ethics,* edited by Gene H. Outka and Paul Ramsey, 74–93. New York: Charles Scribner's Sons, 1968.

——. *Fabricated Man.* New Haven: Yale University Press, 1970.

——. "Incommensurability and Indeterminacy in Moral Choice." In *Doing Evil to Achieve Good,* edited by Paul Ramsey and Richard A. McCormick, 69–144.

——. "Two-Step Fantastic: The Continuing Case of Brother Fox." *Theological Studies* 42 (1981): 122–134.

Ratzinger, Joseph. "Dissent and Proportionalism in Moral Theology." *Origins* (March 1984): 666–669.

———. *The Ratzinger Report: An Exclusive Interview on the State of the Church.* San Francisco: Ignatius Press, 1985.

Rautenberg, Joseph F. "Abortion: Questions of Value and Procedure." In *Moral Theology: Challenges for the Future*, edited by Charles Curran (1990): 240–263.

Rigali, Norbert J. "Dialogue with Richard McCormick." *Chicago Studies* 16 (1977): 299–308.

———. "On Christian Ethics." *Chicago Studies* 10 (1971): 227–247.

———. "The Unity of Moral and Pastoral Truth." *Chicago Studies* 25 (1986): 224–232.

Schillebeeckx, Edward. *Christ: The Experience of Jesus as Lord.* New York: Crossroad, 1986.

Schüller, Bruno. "Christianity and the New Man: The Moral Dimension–Specificity of Christian Ethics." In *Theology and Discovery: Essays in Honor of Karl Rahner, S.J.*, edited by William Kelly, S.J. 199–208 and 227. Milwaukee: Marquette University Press, 1978.

———. "The Debate on the Specific Character of Christian Ethics: Some Remarks." In *Readings in Moral Theology No. 2*, edited by Charles E. Curran and Richard A. McCormick (1980): 207–233.

———. "Direct Killing, Indirect Killing." In *Readings in Moral Theology No. 1: Moral Norms and Catholic Tradition*, 1979: 138–157.

———. "The Double Effect in Catholic Thought–A Reevaluation." In *Doing Evil to Achieve Good*, edited by Richard A. McCormick and Paul Ramsey: 138–157.

———. "Various Types of Grounding for Ethical Norms." In *Readings in Moral Theology No. 1: Moral Norms and Catholic Tradition*, edited by Charles E. Curran and Richard A. McCormick (1979): 184–198.

———. "What Ethical Principles Are Universally Valid?" *Theology Digest* 19 (1971): 23–28.

Selling, Joseph. "The Development of Proportionalist Thinking." *Chicago Studies* 25 (1986): 165–175.

———. *Personalist Morals: Essays in Honor of Professor Louis Janssens.* Leuven: Leuven University Press, 1988.

———. "The Problem of Reinterpreting the Principle of Double Effect." *Louvain Studies* 8 (1980): 47–62.

Shannon, Thomas A. "Ethical Implications of Developments in Genetics." *Linacre Quarterly* November 1980.

Slater, Thomas. *A Manual of Moral Theology*, 2 vols. New York, Cincinnati: Benzinger Brothers, 1931.

Smith, William B. "The Revision of Moral Theology in Richard A. McCormick." *Homiletic and Pastoral Review* (March 1981): 8–27

Spohn, William C. "Richard A. McCormick: Tradition in Transition." *Religious Studies Review* 13 (January 1987): 39–42.

——. *What Are They Saying about Scripture and Ethics?* New York: Paulist Press, 1983.

Stark, Werner. "Casuistry." In *Dictionary of the History of Ideas*, vol. 1 New York: Charles Scribner's Sons, 1922.

Sullivan, Francis A. *Magisterium: Teaching Authority in the Catholic Church.* Mahwah, N.J.: Paulist Press, 1983.

——. "The Authority of the Magisterium on Questions of Natural Moral Law." In *Readings in Moral Theology No. 6.* edited by Charles E. Curran and Richard A. McCormick (1988): 42–57.

Tanner, Norman P., ed. *Decrees of the Ecumenical Councils*, 2 vols. London: Sheed and Ward; Washington, D.C.: Georgetown University Press, 1990.

Tauer, Carol. "The Tradition of Probabilism and the Moral Status of the Early Embryo." In *Abortion and Catholicism: The American Debate*, edited by Patricia Beattie Jung and Thomas A. Shannon, 54–84. New York: Crossroad, 1988.

Tettamanzi, Dionigi. "Is There a Christian Ethics?" In *Readings in Moral Theology No. 2*, edited by Charles E. Curran and Richard A. McCormick (1980): 20–59.

Thiselton, Anthony. "Knowledge, Myth and Corporate Memory." In *Believing in the Church: The Corporate Nature of Faith*, 45–78. Wilton, Conn.: Morehouse-Barlow; Toronto: Anglican Book Centre, 1982.

Tracy, David. *The Analogical Imagination: Christian Theology and the Culture of Pluralism.* New York: Crossroad, 1989.

Vacek, Edward. "Proportionalism: One View of the Debate." *Theological Studies* 46 (1985): 287–314.

Van Der Marck, William. *Toward a Christian Ethic: A Renewal of Moral Theology.* Westminster: Newman Press, 1967.

Van der Poel, Cornelius. "The Principle of Double Effect." In *Absolutes in Moral Theology?* edited by Charles E. Curran, 186–210. Washington, D.C.: Corpus Books, 1968.

Veatch, Robert M. "Defining Death at the Beginning of Life." *Second Opinion* 10 (1989): 51–59.

Vereecke, L. "History of Moral Theology: 700 to Vatican I." In *New Catholic Encyclopedia*, vol. 9: 1119–1122. San Francisco, Toronto, Sydney, London: Catholic University Press, 1967.

Vermeersch, Arthur. *Theologia Moralis*, 2 vols. Bruges, 1922.

Wall, James, and David Heim, eds. *How My Mind Has Changed*. Grand Rapids, Mich.: William B. Eerdmans, 1991.

Walter, James J. "The Foundation and Formulation of Norms." In *Moral Theology: Challenges for the Future*, edited by Charles Curran (1990): 125-154.

——. "Proportionate Reason and Its Three Levels of Inquiry: Structuring the Ongoing Debate." *Louvain Studies* 10.1 (Spring 1984): 31-40.

Weisheipl, J. A. "Scholastic Method." In *New Catholic Encyclopedia*, vol. 12: 1145-1146. New York, San Francisco, Toronto, Sydney: Catholic University Press, 1967.

Wenley, R. M. "Casuistry." In *Encyclopedia of Religion and Ethics*, vol. 3, edited by James Hastings. New York: Charles Scribner's Sons, 1922.

INDEX

A number in parentheses following a note number indicates the text page where a quotation from the given author may be found.

247

248 Index